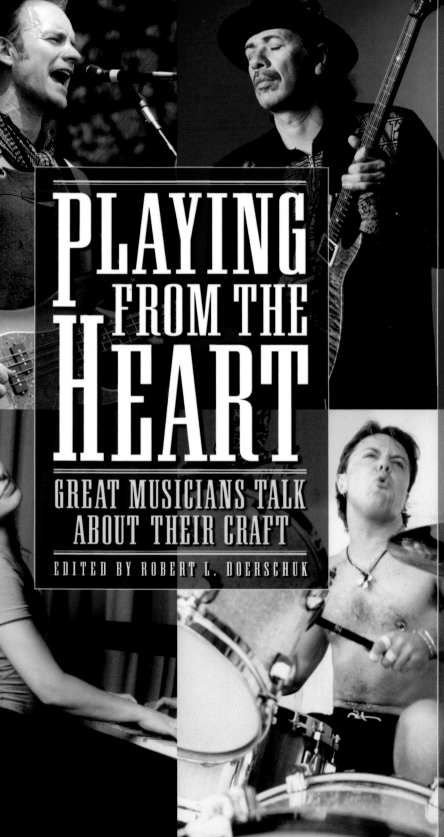

PLAYING FROM THE HEART

GREAT MUSICIANS TALK ABOUT THEIR CRAFT

EDITED BY ROBERT L. DOERSCHUK

PLAYING FROM THE HEART

PLAYING
FROM THE
HEART

Great Musicians Talk About Their Craft

Edited by Robert L. Doerschuk

Backbeat
Books
San Francisco

Published by Backbeat Books
600 Harrison Street, San Francisco, CA 94105
An imprint of the Music Player Network
United Entertainment Media
www.backbeatbooks.com
books@musicplayer.com

Distributed to the book trade in the US and Canada by
Publishers Group West, 1700 Fourth Street, Berkeley, CA 94710

Distributed to the music trade in the US and Canada by
Hal Leonard Publishing, P.O. Box 13819, Milwaukee, WI 53213

Cover Design by Richard Leeds
Text Design and Composition by Leigh McLellan
Front Cover Photos by Jay Blakesberg

Library of Congress Cataloging-in-Publication Data

Playing from the heart : great musicians talk about their craft /
edited by Robert L. Doerschuk
    p . cm.
  ISBN 0-87930-704-8
  1. Musicians—Interviews. 2. Popular music—History and criticism. I. Doerschuk, Bob.

  ML394.P58 2002
  784.164'092'2—dc21   2002022953

Printed in the United States of America

02 03 04 05 06   5 4 3 2 1

CONTENTS

Foreword   vii

Introduction   ix

The Interviews

1 GUITAR PLAYER *1*

2 KEYBOARD *83*

FOREWORD

Writers can babble all they want about their craft, but such speeches are merely self-important blather if their printed words don't seduce readers. This is especially true in the magazine world, where editors are typically at the mercy of a niche audience that demands to be excited, educated, and entertained each and every month. Just try convincing your circle of friends to pony up $4.99 every time you offer them the sheer joy of your presence, and you'll quickly understand exactly how wonderful you are!

Obviously, being a dedicated servant to one's audience is a daunting and never-ending task. Our mission at *Bass Player*, *Keyboard*, and *Guitar Player* has always been to teach readers how artists construct their music, make their sounds, and channel their creative muses. And we've been lucky enough to be blessed with excellent staffs and groovy readers that have kept *BP* rocking for twelve years, *KB* for 27 years, and *GP* for 35 years. (If you're one of these people—thanks a bazillion for your support!)

But we haven't always talked to our communities the same way. *Playing from the Heart* editor Robert L. Doerschuk has done a brilliant job of combining and clarifying the different voices, styles, and vibes of our interviews. In the "good old days" of the late '60s/early '70s, for example, discussions with artists tended to be homey and rambling. The writer/editor typically documented the happening as if the artist was speaking directly to the reader. During the *Rolling Stone*–influenced "me generation" of music journalism, writers started imposing themselves into the stories—often elevating themselves to a near-peership role with the artist. And today's Web-savvy, short-attention-span audience usually demands concise, extremely focused information.

However, throughout all the stylistic permutations and music-industry evolutions/revolutions, one thing *has* remained constant in the pages of our magazines: Our major interviews have been penned by musicians who are journalists, rather than journalists who don't play an instrument. That's a critical differentiation, as fellow musicians can zero in on the emotional and technical details of making music with more empathy and insight than non-players.

And that's why the interviews in this book—as well as the articles that appear in our magazines each month—are the real deal. If you want to curl up in the artistic neural net of your fave musician, our writers and editors are absolutely your best tour guides into the often messy wonderland of his or her creativity. We intuitively get where they're coming from, we're motivated to dig deep into their process, and we *adore* what they do—which is making people happy, sad, or thoughtful through music.

It's no surprise, then, that this book is a love-fest of ideas, attitudes, fears, inspiration, perspiration, insanity, brilliance, dumb luck, and everything else that can drop-kick a creative muse into overdrive. It's also a peek into emotional worlds that many of us fear to tread. But the next time you hear a great song on the radio, you'll have a better understanding of how that montage of sound, melody, and passion came to be. And if that's so, you'll not only be honoring the creativity of some transcendent artists, you'll also be paying tribute to 35 years of our writers and editors striving to unveil the clang and chug of an invisible machine.

—Michael Molenda
Editor in Chief, Guitar Player
Editorial Director, Music Player Group

INTRODUCTION

We live in an era of interviews.

At any time of day or night, you can find somebody interviewing someone else on television or on the radio. Pick up almost any magazine, and you'll find some writer grilling some expert, self-styled or otherwise, about some issue. We even go through interviews ourselves: serious interrogations when we're looking for a job, annoying *faux* interviews when a telephone solicitor is after our business.

The motives behind interviews are infinitely varied. Most often, it's about selling some kind of product: an actress fielding softball questions about her latest movie, or some buff stud explaining how his exercise contraption can turn us all into muscle sculptures.

The main thing we learn from these scripted encounters is that they mirror a cynical era. We learn as well that the person answering questions is somehow seen as valuable. Journalists chase after them, trying to pry loose some bits of wisdom. It's a process that glamorizes celebrity, often for no reason other than to make someone a lot of money, while inferentially degrading the public as it waits for enlightenment.

If that were all there were to interviews, I'd have unplugged my tape recorder, sold my computer, and gotten a real job years ago. But I'm lucky: I've had the privilege of learning what it means to do a *real* interview, one that's based on respect both for the subject and the public, in which relevant information is gleaned and the readers come away with something that stimulates their own creativity.

I learned how to do this on the job, beginning in 1976, when I began freelancing for *Keyboard* magazine. In my first two assignments I learned the difference between interviewing an expressive, almost excessively voluble person (the classical organist Virgil Fox) and an amiable but barely communicative one (rock organist Billy Preston). Fox was a torrent of anecdotes and opinions; Preston a trickle of yes, no, and uh-huh.

Of course, I learned far more from the Preston experience. When *Keyboard* brought me onboard as an assistant editor the following year, the education began in earnest. Quickly I came to understand that almost everybody *wants* to have something to say, especially when talking to a publication as respected in its field as *Keyboard* or the other magazines in what was then the GPI family: *Guitar Player, Bass Player, Frets,* and *Drums & Drumming.* It's the interviewer's job to help that person discover his or her own knowledge, sometimes through gentle prompting and occasionally through confrontation and disagreement.

Over the years I've done hundreds of artist interviews, ranging from a thirty-second quickie with Waylon Jennings to all-day marathons with Tori Amos. I've had David Bryan of Bon Jovi threaten to "smack" me; I've listened to Billy Joel snarl hair-raising obscenities about the music business. I've waited patiently while Bruce Springsteen slowly awakened and Stevie Wonder fell asleep as my tape was rolling. I've been scolded by Lucinda Williams for having "no faith in human nature." Christine McVie spent more than a year arguing with me that she didn't have anything to say—before allowing me into her home and sharing plenty of useful stuff culled from her career with Fleetwood Mac. I've been told by Prince that I had to jam with his band in Paisley Park before he'd consent to speak with me, and I've still got a drawing that Miles Davis created and signed while we were talking about Bill Evans at his Malibu home.

What matters most about all these encounters is that I came away from each with something that my readers could use to make their own music. I've learned how to find something in the character of each artist that could open the door to discussion. And I never forgot that it was my job to connect the artist with the reader, nothing more.

In other words, I was your typical GPI interviewer. Everyone who has ever worked on staff at *Guitar Player, Keyboard, Bass Player,* and the other magazines has gone through the same kind of enlightenment. All of us have felt the same obligation to our readers, and the same responsibility to keep our standards high. This was true during my seventeen years at *Keyboard,* and it remains true today for those same publications, now within the Music Player Network of the United Entertainment Media family.

This book examines the GPI/MPN tradition of the artist interview. The range of artists profiled here is vast. The techniques of each journalist/editor vary as well. But the results are consistent, as writer and performer work together to uncover the mysteries and methods of music. Yes, the artist derives publicity from the experience, and the journalist feels a sense of accomplishment. But unlike the more disposable interviews that define the babble of our time, these pieces go further, to the point that you, the reader, are the ultimate beneficiary.

Whether you play guitar, bass, keys, or drums, or whether you simply want to listen as your favorite players discuss their work, *Playing from the Heart* will open your eyes and ears. Read, enjoy—and listen.

—*Robert L. Doerschuk*

1

GUITAR PLAYER

Guitar Player was founded in 1967 by Bud Eastman, an amiable soul with no background in publishing but loads of experience in studying and teaching music, rehearsing, gigging, shopping for gear, and all the other activities still associated with music as practiced by professionals and serious amateurs. This accounted for some of the magazine's quirks but also its essential premise: *Guitar Player* would act as a forum not for writers or editors but musicians; a magazine "for musicians, by musicians" was the way they put it in the early days. Even when the staff was gradually replaced with experienced authors and just-the-facts editorial was supplemented with opinionated commentary, the respect for interviewees' viewpoints remained a cornerstone of the magazine's personality and success.

You'll find a good mix among the interviews excerpted here. Some of the players had gained iconic status long before the articles appeared. On the other hand, Eric Johnson and Vernon Reid were practically unknown outside their hometowns; despite the commercial magazine risks, we felt their artistry and promise merited cover stories. All of the writers were steeped in *Guitar Player*'s commitment to avoiding the witless "it's so cool to be hanging out with you" junk so common in pop-culture "journalism." We worked hard to provide the kinds of insights into techniques, gear, and musical concepts that were unavailable elsewhere.

Not that we didn't have a blast. Among my favorite memories at *Guitar Player* are the post-interview gabfests where we would hear the writer's firsthand observations of the artist's quirks. Are the accounts of Chuck Berry's distrust of writers accurate? How many guitars in Keith Richards' hotel suite? In the published stories, we tried to let the interviewees' personalities shine through—along with our own enthusiasm. After all, they're our heroes too.

—Tom Wheeler
Editor, Guitar Player, *1981–1991*

CHUCK BERRY

Just a Lucky Guy

Interviewed by Tom Wheeler,
Guitar Player, March 1988

C huck **Berry should have** shown up to the gig in a flaming chariot drawn by winged steeds, but screeching up to the loading dock out behind San Francisco's Circle Star Theater in a rented Cadillac was close enough. I knew he was suspicious of writers, and his assistant had suggested that if I said the wrong thing or pissed him off in any way the interview wouldn't happen. But I guess he decided I was okay, because we spent the next two hours gabbing about guitars, rhythms, and rock & roll. By the end of the interview he was enthusiastic, slamming his palm on the table while expressing his admiration for Harry James's horn section and grabbing a napkin so he could draw me a picture of his first amp, a little slant-top Epiphone. It was the journalistic highlight of my fourteen years at the magazine—not because he co-invented rock & roll, and not because none of the million bar-band players he inspired ever did it as well as the master himself, but simply because his ringin'-a-bell tone, slippery lines, and jolting syncopations changed my life. Chuck Berry is the reason I play guitar.

—Tom Wheeler

• • •

Mystery surrounds the roots of your style. When developing it, did you first hear a melody and then locate it on the fingerboard, or did you think visually, moving through the patterns?

I didn't know anything about style when I started. I mean, I knew what a style was, but I wasn't aware of having one myself. That sort of thinking was far too technical for me at that time. But putting a song together? Now, that did come in anticipation of a melody that I heard in my head, or it could be by jamming with someone, or hearing something someone else was doing and maybe thinking I might like it to go a little differently. But you say *my* style? See, I still do not recognize any style of my own.

In the film Hail! Hail! Rock 'n' Roll *you apply the phrase "nothing new under the sun" to your own playing.*

That's right. What I do is just a portion of all that I've heard before me: Carl Hogan with Louis Jordan and His Tympany Five [in the forties and fifties], blues players like T-Bone Walker. Illinois Jacquet too—big influence.

His guitar player?

No, Illinois himself! Tenor sax player. His choice of notes, his melodies. You'll hear it in my music, if you know how to listen. Charlie Christian too: "Solo Flight." It's so great, man; it's a son-of-a-bitch! I got the first sixteen bars down, took me thirty years [*laughs*].

Still, don't you recognize the Chuck Berry style when you hear someone else do it?

I know what you mean, but if someone can play everything I can play, and that's the way he plays, then maybe it's his style now. That's how I look at it.

You downplay your accomplishments, but if you take away your influences, there's a lot of pure, concentrated Chuck left over in your work.

> "There's no such thing as black and white music."

Well, that's a good way to look at it. In between the various things I was doing with the Muddy Waters things and Illinois Jacquet and Carl Hogan—my leftovers in between—that's maybe where my own creation comes in [*Berry holds two fingertips close together, suggesting a wee bit*], trying to link those things. But it's still just a portion of what I knew. No one can reproduce another person's mind exactly like him, and that difference in there is what's all new, what one would call my style. That's all I can say.

What was it in Carl Hogan's playing that attracted you?

Simplicity. He stuck to the I–IV–V, played mainly quarters and eighths, and played right *on* the beat.

Did you really borrow the "Johnny B. Goode" intro lick from him, as you've hinted?

I can't really say exactly, but he did something that influenced the way I do "Johnny." Something similar.

Your fans might be surprised that your early goal was to play big-band jazz, backed up by horn sections.

But that's what I wanted! I really did. Wanted to comp chords behind a big band and play swing tunes.

Why, then, did you wind up playing rock & roll?

At the time I was in need of a house and a wife, and looking forward to raising a family. Even my friend Ira Harris, who could really play, he couldn't find a job playing jazz, if you see what I mean.

If the money and opportunities had been there in blues or the big bands, would you have played different music all these years?

Come on, man—don't make me answer that [*laughs*]! Maybe if the money was good, I'd have even had a few hairdressing salons—big chain of 'em.

What did you learn from your friend Ira Harris?

He was into jazz, and the way he could manipulate the sound [*Berry scat-sings a jazzy major-scale riff*], I knew I had to do that. He played a bit like Christian, and a lot of what he showed me is a part of what I do.

You studied Nick Manoloff's Guitar Book of Chords.

Yes, that book had it down so plain. Many of the fingerings I couldn't do at first, because I couldn't double up on the strings for those six-string chords. But I struggled with it, then took music at Ludwig's Music in St. Louis, studying theory and harmony.

Many of your tunes have similar tempos, progressions, or keys. How do you keep them separate and give them distinct personalities?

My approach doesn't matter from a musical, theoretical way of looking at it. I'd like to remember just what I did back on the record, but it's not always that way, unless it's really distinct, like "Brown Eyed Handsome Man."

So you don't really have separate approaches to songs with similar structures?

No. In fact, sometimes I have to catch myself and go back to the record to check on something. There may be a lawsuit coming up about someone using one of my guitar things on TV. My lawyer called and said, "Is this 'Roll Over' or 'Johnny'?" I had to go play them and listen to them myself to see [*laughs*].

Muddy Waters was your greatest career inspiration. Was he also a specific influence on guitar?

Yes. I couldn't really get that inspiration without trying to play some of his things, and I still do, or try to, on my own blues. Definitely Muddy. His sound! That's what I played before "Maybelline"—before I turned pro, I guess you call it. And Muddy, with that slide [*Berry mimics a slow, grinding blues turnaround and sings*]: "Mercy, mercy, baby!" Now, *that's* blues.

Chuch Berry, 1995: If not for rock & roll, he might have been a carpenter.

Did other blues artists influence your guitar playing?

Oh, yes. Elmore James, T-Bone Walker—especially those two.

Do you remember your very first guitar?

I remember my first electric. I got it from Joe Sherman, who played *The Sacred Heart Club*, a religious program on WEW in St. Louis. He'd got a new one, so he let me have his old one for thirty dollars. I was making ten dollars a week, and he let me take it after I'd paid a ten-dollar installment. I really started to play a lot after that— it looked so good, you know, and it was easier to play than the other ones I'd had.

Do you see two distinct sides to your music: rock and blues?

Well, things like "Johnny B. Goode" and "Carol," those were for the mass market. "Wee Wee Hours," that was for the *neighborhood*. But this isn't a black/white thing. That irks me. There's no such thing as black and white music. And do you know what? I wish there was just some way I could bring Muddy's blues to the white populace. I mean, not even all the black people know. Like I said, it's not a black-and-white thing. I've seen some of the white brothers—yes, *sir!* Tonight we gonna play some Muddy! And they've got heart. Lord, they're close to him; they're right on his ass! And I look up, and I know Muddy looks down and just loves it so much.

Roy Orbison had an impression of you as a black country singer. Was country music an influence?

Oh, yes. When I was growing up, the country people played fiddles and all that, but then there were these pianos, and these saxophones, and I liked it all—very much into it. I did it every night back in St. Louis before we recorded. It was called country, or hillbilly, or honky-tonk. We were doing "Mountain Dew," "Jambalaya" …

This was your first band, with Johnnie Johnson on piano?

Yes. He had asked me to join his little group [Sir John's Trio] for a gig on December 31, 1952. We had Ebby Hardy on drums.

Who were your rivals around St. Louis at the time?

Ike Turner, over at the Manhattan Club. I'd have gone to see him more often, but we were always working the same hours. Me and Johnnie were at the Cosmopolitan Club, a big place that's been changed over from a market, and we became quite popular, mainly with things by Nat King Cole and Muddy Waters.

How'd your hillbilly music go over?

That's a good question, with a very important answer. There's a great span in music, and variety I *cherish*. When you go to hear jazz, very often that's *all* you hear. Same thing with other types. But if you like *all* music, then variety adds to the performance. We'd do "Day-O" ["Banana Boat Song"] by Harry Belafonte, "Jamaica Farewell," then jump back with some Muddy, then some *sweet* Nat. No spirituals, though. I always say, when you sin, go ahead and sin. When you ask forgiveness [*laughs*], you know—keep it separate!

> "I do not recognize any style of my own."

Is it possible to draw a line between fifties country and early rock & roll, or between fifties boogie and early rock & roll?

No, you can't draw *any* lines like that. You can't draw a line between science and religion, man! Even the edge of a razor blade is round if you get up close to it. It's like a shadow on the wall—no sharp edges. These people like Linda Ronstadt, coming out of rock and then doing country—you see what I mean? No lines.

When you started recording for Leonard Chess, was he looking for something in particular from you?

He just wanted to capture the sound I'd had on the tape I made at home on my little $79 quarter-inch machine. He thought it was hilarious, in a way, and he knew how to market it as a product.

You did 36 takes of "Maybelline." Was that typical of those early sessions?

No, the next one was six takes. See, sessions were supposed to be six hours, and if you went overtime you kicked it up to a higher rate, so they kept track. But we were just glad to be there. We also did "Thirty Days," "Wee Wee Hours," and "You Can't Catch Me." We had the trio: Johnnie on piano and Ebby Hardy on drums. [*Other sources name Jasper Thomas as the drummer on "Maybelline" and "Thirty Days," and Otis Spann as the pianist on "You Can't Catch Me."*]

Whose idea was it to add Willie Dixon on acoustic bass for those first sessions?

Leonard Chess.

What did you think of the added bass sound?

Well, in the first place, I didn't see myself as having any authority to kick about it. I was glad for it to be there, anyway. It was a professional sound, a fuller sound.

> "I didn't give a shit about fame. The only thing I cared about was being able to walk into a restaurant and get served—and I should have had that anyway."

But you didn't take a bass on the road.

No, me and Johnnie were so compatible, and the way I play, when I go down into the lower area of the guitar, I want it to sound real boomy already. I liked bass, and it would've sounded better, but it would've meant paying the extra airfare. I liked the way the piano could solo, and even the drums, but when you give a bass player a solo, he feels like he's got to do something *jazzy*, you know. And a bass doesn't really have an appetizing tone for takeoff; it's a backup instrument.

In Hail! Hail! Rock 'n' Roll, *when Keith Richards observes that some of your songs are in "piano" keys, he seems to be getting at Johnnie's influence on you.*

I don't know what he's talking about. First, Johnnie does not have a style; he has an *ability* to fill in over a progression, to play a solo. He and I discovered a harmony together, where I could be playing, then lay off for just two beats, and he'd pick it up, fill it out. I could just look back at him, and we had such a complete sense of each other that no other communication was necessary.

But how important was Johnnie to your style? Would you have played differently if you'd teamed up with another piano player?

No, I would have just had to play *more*, that's all.

Your early records have a unique atmosphere. Did you imagine a specific sound and experiment until you got it, or was it unpredictable?

Sometimes planned. Like, when we were recording "Wee Wee Hours" [1955], it was inspired by Big Joe Turner. Then "Wee Hour Blues" [1965] was inspired by a particular *song* of Big Joe Turner's, "Wee Baby Blues." When I recorded I was trying to re-create the mood of that song.

In May 1955 you were doing some carpentry and studying cosmetology. Three months later your first record was No. 5 in the Hot 100 and No. 1 on the R&B chart. How did that almost literal overnight success change your life?

The only thing it changed was my determination to follow through as long as it could go. My lifestyle did not change one bit. I had been saving eighty percent of my income as a carpenter, and I saved eighty percent of my income as a musician.

Was fame what you had expected?

No, because I didn't expect it! I was making $21 a week at the Cosmo, and it went to $800 a week after "Maybelline." I didn't give a *shit* about the fame, and you can print that. Still don't. The only thing I cared about was being able to walk into a restaurant and get served, and that was something I should have had anyway, *without* all the fame. See, this was 1955, and all the [civil rights] marching and things were about to start. I liked the idea that I could buy something on credit and the salesman knew I could really pay for it. I could call a hotel, and they wouldn't automatically offer me the economy rooms after hearing how my voice sounded. *That* I admired.

Do you remember your first big white audience?

The Paramount in Brooklyn, shortly after "Maybelline" in '55. Damn near totally white. Tony Bennett on top of the bill.

What were your feelings about going out on that stage?

Just that it wouldn't happen again. That was only our fifth engagement, and we really thought the whole thing would last for just a few months.

What did you think when the Stones, the Beatles, and other bands started reworking your songs? Did you like the newer versions?

Did I like it? That doesn't come under my scrutiny. It struck me that my material was becoming marketable, a recognizable product, and if these guys could do such a good job as to get a hit, well, fantastic. I'm just glad it was my song.

How do you feel about "Johnny B. Goode" being sent into space aboard Voyager?

There are many, many records that I thought equaled it, and I don't mind being chosen. Other than that, I guess I'm just a lucky guy.

Your fans never tire of hearing that song. Do you ever get tired of playing it?

No, *because* of the former, *because* they never get tired of hearing it.

KEITH RICHARDS
Learning to Listen

Interviewed by Tom Wheeler,
Guitar Player, April 1983, December 1989

As a musician, fan, and connoisseur, Keith Richards is the real deal. He really does seem to have tracked down every rock and blues record to have made it into the U.K. during his adolescence, devouring not only the music but the liner notes, memorizing who played what, figuring out how it all worked, pretty much wiring the whole thing. He can talk at length about the history of rock guitar, and has many insights to offer. Supposedly fierce and intimidating, he struck me as powerful, to be sure, but also smart and in his own way genteel, the perfect host. Most of all, he remains as enthusiastic about his heroes as we are about him. I remember him kneeling on the floor in the hotel suite amid a pile of cassettes. The boom box is blasting one of my favorite Everly Brothers tunes. A hip guitar lick goes by. Keith looks up and with the glee of a teenager calls across the room, "Chet Atkins!"

—*Tom Wheeler*

• • •

Chuck Berry was a major influence on your guitar style.
    That's quite a left hand he's got there [*laughs*].

Was there a time when you thought you'd have to get away from the Chuck Berry style if you were ever going to have your own voice?
    Oh, sure. Chuck's style is to me one of the loosest and most exciting to play. I was playing acoustic before, and Chuck and Scotty Moore were the ones that turned me

on to saying, "Oh, yeah, I've really got to get my hands on an electric." Of course, you can fall into a rut of getting someone's licks down so well that you are never gonna find yourself. After suddenly becoming a pop star, we worked three or four years and had maybe two weeks off in four years. Then a break came in, I think, '66. When we took time off, that's when I became aware that there was nowhere else for me to go like that. With all the years of not hearing myself onstage, I hadn't really progressed much as a player. I'd learned how to make records and how to write songs, but there was no real opportunity to grow as a player.

Your decision to adopt open tuning seems to have been a watershed.

Open tuning was something that had intrigued me for quite a while before I took it up, but I'd never had the opportunity or time to get to it, and it takes time; it's almost like picking up a brand-new instrument. Brian Jones used to use certain forms of open tuning: tuning the third string down, or sometimes an open-*D*. I thought, "I can't go any further in concert tuning," so I sat down with open tuning, and it stretched out. Again, it wasn't really a conscious thing, but a necessary one, maybe. Sometimes the subconscious bits come up front and say, "In order to save you, we're taking over for a bit." [*Laughs.*] So that sort of shoots the idea forward. I listened to some of the old-time blues and read about it, especially on the back of album jackets. I got more and more intrigued about reading charts of different tunings—of *suspected* tunings, you know, the one we *think* he's using. Working with Ry Cooder, that was also a great spur to it.

That was around 1970, when Let It Bleed *was released.*

Right, because I had already been working a lot with open-*E* and open-*D* tuning for *Beggars Banquet* [released in December 1968], working from what I'd learned during that year off the year before.

> "Listening to the music is an art; it can keep your sanity."

*Weren't you using the open-*G *at that time?*

No, not at that time, except I played around with it for slide, but I very rarely play slide on records. There's always a better slide player in the band than me. I did use slide on things, mostly on acoustic stuff like "You've Got to Move" and "Prodigal Son," stuff like that—open-*D* or open-*E*.

Your open-string parts are always in tune, but in standard tuning the pitches of your guitar are often kind of ragged—appealingly funky, out of tune a bit.

That's usually the way I finger, usually my thumb. I push the bass string just off of key a little. I don't know if it's because I'm sloppy or because I like the sound of it going slightly out of whack. Or maybe just because in a lot of the blues stuff, they would deliberately pull it off of key, especially on the bass notes. It's not so much on the top notes, usually, but when you hit the thing, you kind of compress the bass string. Sometimes I do it too much, though not as much as I used to.

Does anyone ever try to tell you that your guitar is out of tune and you should tune it up?

Many times, but tell that to a Japanese, tell that to an Arab. I mean, there's plenty of times when maybe it's not "supposed" to have been out of tune when I cut it, but then when I hear it back I say it'd be *lost* without it. We're talking about a certain tension that's created by jarring the nerve just a little. As a professional musician, you cringe, and it's not perfect, and there is always that tendency to go for the perfect tuning. But that's kind of an illusion anyway. If you're a musician, it's very hard to stay a dispassionate listener, but try to preserve a bit of the enjoyment of listening without dissecting, without confusing it with work. Once you are a musician it's easy to listen to it with a professional ear instead of what I call the real art of music: just listening to it and what it does. Listening to music is maybe the greatest art. Playing is not—maybe sometimes it is—but listening to the music is an art. It can keep your sanity.

Let's talk about rhythm.

A hard subject to put into words.

In Chuck Berry songs such as "Sweet Little Rock and Roller," the hybrid rhythm mixes straight 4/4 and shuffle. You also like to explore that in-between-the-beats territory.

It's always fascinated me, man, yeah. Mainly because I realized after quite a few years that the thing that really intrigued me, that turned me on to playing, was precisely that: *suggested* rhythms going on, or a certain tension. Especially in early rock & roll, there's a tension between the 4/4 beat and the eighths going on with the guitars. That was probably because the rhythm section was still playing pretty much like a swing band. There was still a regular jazz beat, 4/4 to the bar, a swing/shuffle, which is a lovely light rhythm—very African, with a lovely bounce to it. It suddenly changed in '58, '59, '60, until it was all over by the early sixties. The drummers were starting to play eight to the bar, and I thought at first maybe they were just going for more power. Then I realized that, no, it was because of the *bass*—the advent of the reliable electric bass guitar. The traditional double bass went bye-bye, this thing that's taller than most guys that play the goddamn thing [*laughs*]. The guitar players were being relegated to bass.

> **"You can fall into a rut of getting someone's licks down so well that you are never gonna find yourself."**

If you didn't even have a bass, you could tune down a guitar and play four strings; once you had an actual bass, it was much louder than an acoustic pumping eight to the bar. And the natural inclination of the drummer is then to pick up on what the new bass is doing, because that's what you've got to follow.

Rock seems to have turned its back on that kind of rhythmic ambiguity.

Well, most music has, in actual fact, because there's not that much of an opportunity to actually hear it these days. You don't get a lot of shuffles or swings, but I think it's something that's innate in me. I grew up on that beat, even before they added the eighths. That swing/shuffle gives it quite a little lift. To me, the eighths are the rock, and that lift is the roll. But again, there's very few drummers that can really play eight to the bar and also make it take off with that lift. Your lift is very appealing but so hard to do properly, especially these days, when most records are made on a typewriter anyway.

Your music is similarly ambiguous in the way it scrambles conventional roles of rhythm and lead guitar, sometimes mixing them at the same volume. Most people don't make records like that.

They have a fixed idea that rhythm is supposed to just do *this*, and the lead is supposed to be really loud. But I've been very fortunate: The guys that I've always worked with, they've all gotten off in the same way as I have. Rather than going for the *separation* of the guitars, we get them to start to sound to the point where it doesn't *matter* which guitar is doing what. They leap and weave through each other, so it becomes unimportant whether you're listening to rhythm or lead, because in actual effect, as a guitar player, you're in the other player's head and he's in yours, and you two are on this little mental plane where no one else is, trying to predict and guide and follow, all at the same time. You're in front and you're at the back, and this is a fascinating thing, and on a larger scale that's what a good band is. See, a lot of guys are scared to do that. They don't *want* you to know what they're thinking [*laughs*], or they're out for personal glory, so with a lot of players, you can't do that.

Certainly that defines the way that you and Ron Wood have of working together within the Stones.

Well, Ron's getting better [*laughs*]. I think that's due to the fact that Ron and I have been working together now since '75, and the more we play together the tighter we get it.

It sounds as if you and he are two sides of the same coin, like you could almost change places.

We do [*laughs*]. If he drops a cigarette, I'll play his bit, and we'll realize later that I've covered for him or he's covered for me. And you think at the time, "Oh, my God, what a gap," but when you listen to the tape you find that it's been fixed right there at the moment, in a very un-thought-about way. We pick it up and cover each other so that sometimes you can't really tell who's playing.

When Ron joined in 1975, did the band have to change to accommodate him?

No, that was the beauty of it. He was already so familiar with our stuff. After Mick Taylor left, we rehearsed for about six months with a lot of good guitar players from

Keith Richards, 1988: Bending rules and strings.

all over the world. And we could work with them, you know; they could work with us. But when Ronnie became available and suddenly walked in, that was it; there was no doubt. It was easy.

With Mick Taylor's style so well defined as a lead guitarist, there seemed to be a clear distinction between the two of you.

It was much harder to get a Rolling Stones sound with Mick Taylor. It was much more *lead* and *rhythm,* one way or the other. As fabulous as he is as a lead guitarist, he wasn't as great as a rhythm player, so we ended up taking roles. But also with Ron, the basic way we play is much more similar. This isn't in any way to knock Mick; I mean, he's a fantastic guitar player. And even if he couldn't play shit, I'd love the guy. But *chemically* we didn't have that flexibility in the band. It was, "You do this, and I'll do that, and never the twain shall meet." With Ron, if he drops his pick, then I can play his lick until he picks it up, and you can't even tell the difference.

You've used very different types of guitars, and yet a listener can tell right away that it's you playing—not just from stylistic clues, but also from the sound.

I use a whole load of different guitars, that's true, but they're not all that dissimilar in type. I mean, ninety percent are probably [Fender] Telecasters, old ones. But more than that, you can't really separate style and sound, you see. People do separate them when they're talking about music, but all of that often misses the whole point.

You're suggesting that the style is the sound?

Yes, part of it, more than any particular tone setting or pickup or anything like that. I'll just adjust to the sound of the track as we go—the sound of the bass drum and especially Ronnie's guitar. The style is adjusting along with the sound. There's never a conscious effort to get that "Honky Tonk Woman" tone or anything like that. You may get it or you may not. But that's not what you're thinking about. You're thinking about the track.

Which explains why your mixes have always emphasized a single overall sound, even if that meant burying the vocals a bit into the instrumental bed.

It was just what sounded right to use, and also because we were brought up in the era where a four-track was a rarity. We started recording at a point when the best sound you got was all *air*, and all the room sound and everything was leakage and jammed together, and the vocal fought its battle with the rest of the instruments. We tried it the usual way, but whenever we brought the vocals up we'd never like the mix as much. I always thought about those other records where the voice was too far forward, so you never really got a sound; you just got a vocalist with some accompaniment.

And that's not what you were after.

Not for us, but you see, you've got to treat each type of music in the appropriate fashion. I mean, if you're mixing the Everly Brothers, then you've got those fantastic goddamn voices and you put them out front as much as you can. But even those guys *never* sacrificed the sound of the *record* for the sound of their voices. They had it all there, quite a light sound, but always very powerful as well, never wimpy.

Those early Everly Brothers records have huge acoustic guitar sounds. Were any of them influential?

Yeah, *all* of their records. Also there's the fact that the first major tour we ever did was supporting the Everly Brothers, Little Richard, and Bo Diddley—plenty to learn in a real short time, following those guys around. The Everlys came on with just their trio and themselves, and it was great. On their recordings there is a certain power in the steel-string. It's a different instrument from electric—not that different in the way you play it, but in terms of the sound. There are times when an acoustic guitar will *make* a track. You'll be despairing, nothing working, hashing away. Take 43 on electric guitar, and somebody will say, "Why don't you try it on acoustic?" You try it one time, and you've got it.

Some people were amazed to read in your first Guitar Player *cover story that on "Street Fighting Man" there are no electric guitars.*

Two acoustics, one of them put through the first Philips cassette player they made. It was overloaded, recorded on that, and then hooked up through a little extension speaker, and then onto the studio tape through a microphone.

You've paid a lot of attention to finding a place for acoustic guitars in rock settings.

Well, I started on acoustic guitar, and you have to recognize what it's got to offer. But also you can't say it's an acoustic guitar sound, actually, because with the cassette player and then a microphone and then a tape, really it's just a different process of electrifying it. You see, I couldn't have done that song or that record in that way with a straight electric, or the sustain would have been too much. It would have flooded too much. The reason I did that one like that was because I already had the sound right there on the guitar before we recorded. I just loved it, and when I wrote the thing I thought, "I'm not going to get a better sound than this." "Jumpin' Jack Flash" is the same too; that's acoustic guitar.

> **"That's one of the great things about rock & roll: Every night there's a different world's greatest band."**

People have been calling the Stones the world's greatest rock & roll band for a long time.

It's embarrassing.

Are there any drawbacks to getting that kind of respect?

Yeah, you've gotta keep *being* it [*laughs*]! I've decided that every night there's another world's greatest rock & roll band, because one night somebody has an off gig, and some other shit band has a *great* gig. That's one of the great things about rock & roll: Every night there's a different world's greatest band. We've been maybe a little more consistent, for whatever reason, mainly when we're going on a tour and also because we've managed to stick together. The chemistry—that's got nothing to do with musicianship. It's got to do with personality and characters and being able to live with each other for twenty years.

What's the secret to that kind of longevity?

The secret is, there *is* no secret. It's finding people that not only play well with you, but that you can get along with. There's no constant battle about who's Mister Big, none of those problems. When I see Charlie and Bill—I ain't seen 'em for a few weeks—it's like a pleasure. Ron says we're his closest friends. I guess that's the only secret.

Is that what it means to play in a band?

Most people don't know what a band is. People have heroes, and they copy them. I mean, we copied things very carefully when we started. But you don't get this picture and then do everything to fit in. You do what you do. The musicians are there to contribute to the band sound. The band isn't there for showing off solos or egos. A lick on a record, it doesn't matter who played it. All that matters is how it fits. The chemistry to work together like that has to be there. You have to work on it, always—figure out what to do with it. But it's not an intellectual thing you can think up and just put there. It has to *be* there. You have to find it.

B.B. KING &
JOHN LEE HOOKER

There's Nothing Like the Real Thing

Interviewed by Jas Obrecht,
Guitar Player, September 1993

Thee two aging titans of postwar blues had been friends for many years, and in 1993 they collaborated on their first duo recording. But they had never done an interview together. So when B.B. King announced he was playing San Francisco's Circle Star Theater near John Lee Hooker's home in Redwood City, California, it was too good an opportunity to pass up. A flurry of calls set the stage for the interview, but there was one catch: We had only 35 minutes for the backstage interview and the photo shoot with Bill Reitzel. I shouldn't have worried about a thing. B.B. King and John Lee Hooker greeted each other warmly and immediately launched into an unforgettable conversation on the state of the blues. This was a true meeting of the masters. One item that didn't make it into the published interview was a joke B.B. shared with John Lee during the photo shoot: "This old bull and a young bull are standing on a hillside one evening, watching cows going into the barn. The young bull says, 'Hey, old-timer, why don't we run down there and make love to one of those cows?' The old bull looked over his spectacles and replied, 'Why don't we *walk* down there and make love to all of them?'" Hooker, ever the ladies' man, laughed knowingly.

—*Jas Obrecht,* Guitar Player, *1978–1998*

• • •

The two of you have probably made more blues recordings than any other pair of artists in history.

King: I would think so. I think John has made many more than I.

Hooker: Oh, yeah, I have. I did a lot more before he did.

18

King: See, John was playin' when I was plowin'. I was still in Indianola—just come to Memphis, and John was makin' music then.

Hooker: You know who I met you through? [Promoter] B.B. Beaman.

King: B.B. Beaman, Atlanta, Georgia.

Hooker: He was thin [*points to King*]—weighed about 125, 130 pounds.

King: Yeah.

Do you hear traces of the Delta in John Lee Hooker's music?

King: I don't think of John as a lot of people do. I think of John Lee Hooker as John Lee Hooker. And he plays the blues like I heard 'em when I first started to play. And he still plays 'em. He plays the blues like John Lee Hooker does. It was two or three people that I knew before—in other words, that was older than John—and that was Lonnie Johnson, Robert Johnson, and Blind Lemon. I didn't know them all personally, but I did get a chance to meet Lonnie before he died. But these people, the way they played, they were so themselves. Well, in the modern times—and what I call modern times is the time I started to play—John Lee Hooker was one like that. Lightnin' Hopkins was like that.

Hooker: Oh, yeah.

King: You know who they were the minute you hear 'em play. When John Lee Hooker plays, it's like writing his name: "I'm John Lee Hooker." So I don't necessarily think of it as Delta or city or any other type. The only thing I take issue with a little bit is when people say, "Oh, that's a city blues, that's Delta blues, that's Mississippi, that's Chicago," and so on. Muddy Waters, for example, is to me the first of the so-called Chicago blues.

> "There's nothing wrong with trying to play like someone— in the beginning. But then as you learn, you start to think that there's already one of those, so you try to play as you play."
> —B.B. King

Hooker: That's right.

King: Muddy left Mississippi, went to Chicago. John left and went to Detroit. I left and went to Memphis. We was still migrating, and wherever we went our identity was pretty strong, like Muddy's was and the people surrounding him. So you had a lot of the new guys to be born and started to play later. But to add to that, to me, blues is that label again. For instance, when John Lee made "Boogie Chillen," that wasn't blues. That was get up and get it!

Hooker: Get up and go! That was the first rock!

King: That's right.

Hooker: You get rock & roll from that.

King: So when people say blues and you say "Boogie Chillen," how in the heck could he be blue? He's havin' a ball! He's havin' a good time. If I sing "I got a sweet little angel," I'm not blue at all.

What can someone gain by listening to B.B. King play guitar?

Hooker: Well, I'll tell you what he just told you about me. There only one B.B. There's a lot of imitations—lot of people pick up the guitar and follow this man, many of 'em. Used to be everybody that pick up a guitar try to sound like B.B. King. But you can tell when the main person, the main man, hit it. You know it's B.B. There was a boy in Chicago called Little B.B.

> "[The record industry] just didn't push the blues like they should. They just used to push it under the cover."
> —**John Lee Hooker**

Andrew Odom?

Hooker: I think so. Tried to sound just like B.B., but I know it wasn't B.B. He be playin' with my cousin a lot, Earl Hooker.

King: Yeah! That's a bad man. Ain't been but one other person play slide like Earl Hooker. You know who that is, for me?

Hooker: What, Bonnie Raitt?

King: Bonnie Raitt. She is the best that is today, in my opinion.

Hooker: Yeah. So let me finish. So you can tell in a minute if you hear B.B. from an imitation—I can. What they don't know, maybe—and I think you know this, B.B., you know it [*points to interviewer*], and I know it: Anybody can sound like John Lee Hooker, but it ain't the real John Lee Hooker. He make it real good, but I can come along and just hit it, and they gone. They'd rather see me. Like King: Lot of B.B.'s out, but it ain't like the real one. You can tell it's B.B. King.

It's interesting that you both play Gibson's B.B. King guitar.

Hooker: Yeah, I went and bought one.

King: John has played so many different guitars through the years, though. So many different ones, and they all sound like John.

Hooker: I got my identity. I got my style. I got nothin' to regret. I got nothin' to try again. I got nothin' to try to change. I wouldn't change for all the tea in China and all the money in the world. Who else you gonna sound like?

King: It's just like one piano that sits over in the corner. If John go and play it, he gonna sound like himself, 'cause that's the way he play. If I go play it, I'm gonna sound like myself, 'cause that's the way I play. Now, if you don't believe it, you can hear Ray Charles play it, or Pinetop [Perkins], or Elton John: They gonna sound like themselves. That's just one of the things that we're lucky we were blessed to be able to do—to be ourselves and do our own style. Like, when I heard John, I know it was John. If I hear Jimmy Reed, I know it's Jimmy Reed. My cousin Booker White, know it's him. Even in jazz and rock & roll, certain guys—not all—have that identity. Like an architect or some of the Old Masters painters—da Vinci and all these guys that was doin' whatever they did. You knew the way that they did it. Same with the classical musicians: Some of 'em you knew. Well, that's what I think of John. John couldn't change if he wanted to.

Hooker: I'm like in the old way. I couldn't change if I wanted to. But like B.B. said, if I did it, it wouldn't be me.

King: It's just like a way of talkin'.

Is it a waste of time for someone to try to play like you?

Hooker: I would think so.

King: Well, not really, John. Think about it, 'cause when we first started—I know I did—when you first started, you heard somebody you liked.

Hooker: Oh, all the time. I did, I did.

King: So I liked somebody when I first started. We had our idols then, just like kids do today. So there's nothing wrong, I don't think, with listening to or trying to play like someone—in the beginning. But then as you learn, you start to think that there's already one of those, so you try to play as you play.

Hooker: Don't play like Jimi Hendrix or B.B. King or somebody else. Play …

King: … as you feel yourself. Put you in it. We all like somebody. Everybody did. John, who was your idol? Who did you like when you first started to play?

Hooker: Well, when I first started to playin', T-Bone Walker was my idol.

King: Me too. [*Both laugh.*]

Hooker: Boy, I used to follow him like a little puppy followin' his mama.

King: Yeah, me too. I tell ya somebody else I liked: I was crazy about Lowell Fulson.

Hooker: *Whoo-weee!* "Everyday I Have the Blues," and then "Blue Shadows Fallin'."

King: Yeah. You know, a lot of people don't know it, but after Memphis Slim wrote it and recorded it, Lowell Fulson was the first one that ever made a hit on it, 'cause I don't think Memphis Slim called it "Everyday I Have the Blues." He called it something else, but it had the same lyrics.

Hooker: It was the same. Same thing.

King: Even before that—Lonnie Johnson.

Hooker: Oh, man!

King: I was crazy 'bout him. Lonnie Johnson and Blind Lemon. Those were my people, along with T-Bone Walker.

Hooker: Lonnie Johnson, he sing, but it didn't sound like deep blues. What would you call that?

King: I don't know. He was so versatile, he did some of all of it. Lonnie Johnson. Now, most of the kids today are crazy about Robert Johnson. Now, I think Robert was great. I think he was really great, but he wasn't my idol.

Hooker: No, he wasn't mine either.

King: Johnny Winter swears on him [*laughs*]. He says he's the greatest thing ever happened—that's what he told me. And a lot of the kids are crazy about it because they say it's authentic.

Hooker: It's authentic. Let's put it like this: The man has been out of existence so long that they really built him up a lot just talkin' and writin' about it. Then when they did put it out, everybody went for it. He get so much publicity.

King: There you go. You just hit it.

It's all about publicity?

King: Of course!

Hooker: So much publicity.

King: Here's what happens in a lot of cases. We'll take John as an example: John has been great since I first heard him. He was doin' great things all the time, but he couldn't get the publicity until he got this manager he have today and Bonnie Raitt.

Hooker: This man right there. [*Hooker points outside the room to Mike Kappus of San Francisco's Rosebud Agency.*]

King: So that was the same thing with me. My manager's name is Sid Seidenberg. So when Sid and I got together, that's when things started to change. Gosh, as great as Bonnie Raitt is—I've known her all her career—and as great as Robert Cray and Roy Rogers and a lot of the people we hear today are, John has been like that since before they were born.

Hooker: It's true.

King: You understand? But thanks to John's manager and other people that know how to package it, the people that knew Robert, that knew Roy, that knew Bonnie now can hear John. Like a guy told me not long ago: He said he heard his son came home and says, "Daddy, you got to hear this guy I just heard!" And his father say, "Who is it, son?" He said, "Oh, you wouldn't know him. You wouldn't know anything about him."

> **"A lot of the youngsters that come around can play rings around me."**
>
> — B.B. King

Said, "Well who is it, son?" He says, "You got to hear B.B. King! You just got to hear it [*laughs*]!" So his father said, "Son, long before you was thought of, I was listening to him." He said, "Yeah, but Dad, you don't know about things like that! This is new!" So it's the same thing. John and myself and a lot of us that's been playing for a long time just never got the break.

Hooker: Never got the breaks, and then they just didn't push the blues like they should. They still don't, like they really should right now. But they pushin' more than they used to. They just used to push it under the cover.

Does recording with rock stars make a difference?

King: Oh, yeah. Of course, of course! That's why I mentioned Bonnie Raitt. It's like U2 and myself: Had it not been for U2, a lot of people wouldn't know. But thanks to Sid, we were able to have this happen. Now, don't misunderstand me: Nobody gave Bonnie nothin'. Nobody gave Robert Cray anything. They earned it. But today they are superstars. What I'm trying to say is that had people known John in the beginning as they have known him now, he would have been a superstar years ago. Even today, if I wasn't on the record with U2, nobody would have played B.B. King.

I don't know about that.

King: Can you take my word for it?

Hooker: Gettin' back to Bonnie Raitt, she was on about twenty years that nobody ever knowed her. Remember that?

King: Yeah. Used to be an opening act for me.

Hooker: Me and her used to party together. She used to drink liquor like water.

King: One of the nicest people I ever met, though. One of the nicest.

Hooker: Oh, she's nice. *Whooo-wee!*

King: She's a great person. Nobody gave her anything. She earned it. I was so happy to see it.

Hooker: She earned it, like this man here—nobody give him nothin'. Nobody give me nothin'. But they just beginning to play us now, but not like they should.

> **"If I wasn't on the record with U2, nobody would have played B.B. King."**
> —B.B. King

Does playing the guitar bring you as much joy and satisfaction as it did when you were younger?

King: Yes. I think it brings even more today …

Hooker: It do.

King: … because I'm more concerned about what I'm trying to do. Then, I was just havin' fun.

Hooker: Havin' fun, drinkin', stayin' out.

King: [*Laughs.*] As you said, stayin' out all night long. But now today I'm concerned about it, because if I get out there now and I hit something that don't sound right, I know that there are a lot of people that are listening to me.

Hooker: Critics.

King: Well, not only that, but a lot of the kids that are listening to me. Reminds me of a story I heard once: There was a trumpet teacher teachin' trumpet to his class. And one little boy, the teacher was tryin' to teach him to play non-pressure, where his jaws wouldn't balloon out. So the teacher was talkin'. So there's one little smart egg in the class [*laughs*], and the teacher say, "Why are you playin' like that? I keep tryin' to tell you that when your jaws pop out like that, that's not good." So the little smart egg, he said, "Well, Dizzy Gillespie plays like that!" So the teacher thought about it for a moment, and he says, "Yeah, but there's only one Dizzy Gillespie." So I think about it a lot of times now when I'm playin', that the kids out there idolize me. And not just kids, but people that are starting to play or the people that's already playin' and maybe came out to admire what I do or be critical of what I do. And if I make them wrong notes or put them in the wrong way or hit something I don't intend to hit …

Hooker: B., I have never heard nobody as true as you, man. Nobody.

King: Well, thank you. But I make mistakes, though. So when I make 'em now …

Hooker: Everybody do.

King: Yeah. To answer your question, when I make a mistake now, it hurts [*thumps chest*]. Oh, yes. It hurts.

Hooker: You're right.

King: Because, see, I'm supposed to be professional. That's what I think to myself. I'm supposed to entertain. I'm supposed to rehearse, practice enough to not do that.

Hooker: But some people, when you look out into the audience, they don't even notice what you did, they so excited about lookin' at him. But he know it [*points to B.B.*]. They may not know it, but you know you made that mistake. And you lookin' back at the fellows, and some of them look like they kind of smile, you know, because they know I did.

King: But when you're able to run it into something else …

Hooker: To cover up.

King: Yeah, like you and I, say we talkin', and we got a male conversation goin' on, and all of a sudden a lady walked in—you gotta change it into something else [*laughs*]! That's the way it is with playin'. Here's another thing: When guys start gettin' to be our age, John, they're not quite as fast as they used to be.

Hooker: I know.

King: And as you get a little older, you think more about it. Remember when you was young and somebody said "Come here"—you get up and start running? Now you think about it: Do I really want to run, or will I just walk on over there?

Hooker: Yeah, walk to the car!

King: And a lot of the youngsters that come around can play rings around me. This is not false modesty, but what they do, they think of what I did that gave them a chance to think beyond that. I was able to go and see one of my idols, Lonnie Johnson, and I was able to shake his hand and thank him because he was one of the people that made me want to play. I don't know. Here I am, still doin' somethin' with it.

Hooker: Well, B., time for me to go.

Is this the first interview you've done together?

King: Yes, the very first.

Hooker: I've done it with a lot of people, but this is the first I ever did with B.B. And I couldn't wait for tonight to come!

CARLOS SANTANA

The Art of Not Breathing

Interviewed by James Rotondi,
Guitar Player, January 1993;
Andy Ellis, August 1999

When I taped my interview with Carlos Santana in the summer of 1999, his album *Supernatural* hadn't been completed, much less released. Still, he spoke with utter confidence about how his new music would reach a worldwide audience and the impact his six-string would have on young listeners. He spoke factually, as if recalling events that had already transpired. It was a bit spooky. I knew his comments were crucial to the story, and I was determined to let them stand even though there was a distinct possibility, in my mind at least, that the album wouldn't achieve the success he described. In a time when hip-hop, boy bands, and electronica dominated pop music, how could a sixties rock guitarist hope to shake things up? But Santana was right: In a matter of weeks, *Supernatural* soared to the top of the charts. Ultimately it won eight Grammy Awards, including Album of the Year.

—*Andy Ellis, Senior Editor,* Guitar Player

• • •

Supernatural *was a remarkably collaborative album. How did this come about?*

Through meditations and dreams, I received these instructions: "We want you to hook up with people at junior high schools, high schools, and universities. We're going to get you back into radio airplay." I said okay, because a lot of young people are not happy unless they are miserable. You can tell by what's happening at the schools. The vibrations of this music and the resonance of the lyrics will present these people with new options. I don't want them to feel like me or think like me—we're all individuals, and we're all unique. But with our music, we're presenting a new octave, a new menu. This menu says, "We are multi-dimensional spirits dwelling in the flesh, solely for the purpose of evolution." You see, if you take the time to crystallize your intentions, motives, and purpose, and direct them for the highest good of life and people on the planet—behold, you get synchronicity.

Give me an example of how that works.

Working with [Arista label head] Clive Davis, we got hooked up with Lauryn Hill. She said, "Oh, man, I love your music. Since I was a child, I listened to 'Samba Pa Ti.' I even wanted to put lyrics to it." So Lauryn invited me to play with her at the Grammy Awards. Playing with her was my first time there.

And she won five Grammys that night.

Yes, she cleaned up. Eric Clapton was in the audience, and he saw us perform. After the show he called and said, "Look, man, I heard that people at Arista were trying to contact me to play on your new record. I've been going through some serious changes in my life, and I was at a really critical point, but things are better now. Do you still hear me on your album? Is there room for me?" To hear Eric say that! I grew up listening to him, Peter Green, and Michael Bloomfield.

So what happened?

Well, my spirits are Miles Davis and [impresario] Bill Graham. Even though they've left the physical world, they still come in my dreams and give me instructions. So when Eric asked if there was room for him on the record, I could hear Bill saying, "*No*, you schmuck! You're too late!" So I'm on the phone, having a conversation with Bill and Eric at the same time. To Bill I said, "Wait. Maybe *you* can talk to him like that, but I can't." And to Eric I said, "Yeah, but you know what? I wouldn't think of dipping you into something that has already been recorded. Why don't you come over? We'll write something from scratch." And that's how we started. We went through a couple of things and settled on something I had written but never recorded. It has a Prince bass groove, but it's very swampy—you could hear John Lee Hooker or the Staple Singers playing it.

> "From Miles [Davis] you get the alchemy of making 50,000 notes into five. But with those five, you shake the world."

You also co-wrote a song with Dave Matthews for Supernatural.

There's a story behind that one. When my father passed away two or three years ago, I didn't listen to music for four days. That's a long time for me. I was picking up my son from school, and I thought, "Okay, time to listen to some radio." I turned on a classical station, and the first thing I heard was this melody. [*Santana sings a slow, six-note theme.*] The melody just stayed with me. They didn't say who the composer was, but I thought it was Strauss. I wanted to find out who this was, so I went to the classical music section at Tower Records and said, "All I have is this melody." I sang it, and the guy goes, "Oh, yeah. Brahms Concerto No. 2." They get me the CD, and that's the song! I said, "Damn, you guys are good!" So I brought this melody to Dave Matthews in New York. I said, "I hear this with a 1999 bass. I also recited these lines: "You're the love of my life./You're the breath of my prayers./Take my hand, lead me there./With you is where I want to be." Dave sat down and—*bam*—wrote the song lyrics right there on the spot, and we recorded it.

Your guitar melody swings a bit more than the Brahms theme.

If Brahms were alive today, he would swing it too, because that's what's happening. Listen to Dave's phrasing: He sang it like Billie Holiday or Frank Sinatra, *way* behind the beat. It's that human thing. Only squares sing in the middle.

> "You make the best music when you're not conscious of doing it."

As always, your guitar sound is very vocal.

When you listen to vocalists like Aretha Franklin and Dionne Warwick, you learn to phrase differently. For a long time I wouldn't listen to guitar players—Joe Pass, Pat Martino, Jim Hall—because I felt that was another generation's music. I felt *my* music was blues and rock. But now I'm discovering all this music by Jim Hall, Kenny Burrell, and Wes Montgomery, and it's like, "Oh, this guy is burning just as hard, but with a different fire." I'm able to check out all the guitar players, take what I need, and still make those notes like Miles—you know, when you hit that note, you don't want to breathe until you finish with it. You go [*exhales*]. Miles, Peter Green—there are very few people who make you hold your breath until that note is *ended*. You literally feel like you've got a colic in your stomach. You get goose bumps. I love musicians who make you want to cry and laugh at the same time. When they go back for it, you go with them, and you don't come back until they come back [*laughs*]. There are not that many players who can consistently do that. Potentially, we *all* should be doing it.

Were you listening to any particular musicians while working on this album?

I was listening to Peter Green, John Coltrane, and Miles Davis.

What were you listening for?

Peter Green for his legato tones. I mean, the first four or five years of Peter Green, because lately he plays more like Pat Martino. Staccato notes—John Coltrane. And from Miles you get the alchemy of making 50,000 notes into five. But with those five, you shake the world. That was Miles's supreme gift. He could play two or three notes and, man or woman, you'd just go, "Oh, my God." Listen to *Sketches of Spain*. Play your guitar and try to keep up with the notes, the way he holds them, the breath of it. That's the voice of angels, man.

What's the key to achieving that level of performance?

You see, great music comes not from thinking, but from pure emotion. As the Grateful Dead people say, it's when the music plays *you*. You make the best music when you're not conscious of doing it. I've been saying these things since the beginning. I remember getting in trouble with Frank Zappa; I'm pretty sure he coined the phrase "shut up and play your guitar" for people like me, because we talk a lot! But I am passionate about turning on massive amounts of kids and pulling them out of that miserable state. I want to turn them over. You don't have to be Jimi Hendrix or Charlie Parker; you can get it done in your own way. God made the world round so we can all have center stage. Everybody is important, as long as you're doing it from your heart. Frustration and depression lead to homicide and genocide, but inspiration and vision lead to a spiritual orgasm. That's the goal: to lose yourself to the point that Miles used to call "a two-hour orgasm," a spiritual orgasm onstage. That's what he'd wake up every morning for. That's a great goal in itself.

Can you describe this?

It's where you're constantly happy, and you don't have to feel weird when people say, "Man, what are you laughing about?" I'm laughing because I know the secret of life. And the secret of life is that I have *validated* my existence. I know that I am worth more than my house, my bank account, or any physical thing. When I hit that note, if I hit it correctly, I'm just as important as Jimi Hendrix, Eric Clapton, or anybody. Because when I hit that note, I hit the umbilical cord of anybody who is listening. Once you learn to validate your existence, you have the wind in your sails and you can never commit suicide. I would say that as great as Danny Gatton was, he never took the time to validate his existence. When you feel that the world is not appreciating your genius, you're already setting yourself up to be a victim. There are a lot of musicians like that: "My manager ripped me off. My record company ripped me off. I'm going to eat beans, but I'm *not* going to play what you want me to play."

Which albums inspire you?

Tell everybody to hear *Spellbinder* by Gabor Szabo. That is a *must* for anybody who plays guitar. He's the person who I credit with pulling me out of B.B. King. B.B. had us in a headlock. Michael Bloomfield, Peter Green, we were all under his spell. Gabor played like a gypsy, but different from Paco de Lucia. Also, "The Supernatural" by Peter Green, Bola Sete's *At the Monterey Jazz Festival,* and Wes Montgomery's *Goin' Out of My Head.* Unplug the phone, sit down with these, and you're in for a real surprise.

What do all of these albums and musicians have in common?

The musicians I love, like Coltrane, Miles, Jimi, and Bob Marley, they didn't have a Ph.D. in anything except life. If you told them they were legends, they'd probably look at you like you were stupid. The most important thing is to live life and tell the truth in a language of the heart. Bill Graham was the one who told me, "Your music is a perfect balance of spirituality and sensuality, whether you accept it or not." I'm not trying to exploit it, but I am trying to explore it.

Beyond spirit and sensuality, what role does technique play in your music?

I very rarely think of what chords or what notes or where I put my finger. You should have learned all the technical and physical aspects of the guitar in junior high school, as far as I'm concerned. I don't think musicians who can really play think of music like that. When I'm playing a solo now, most of the time I'm thinking of combing my daughter's hair before she goes to bed, and I have to do it in a special way so I don't make her cry by pulling her hair. Believe me, that's what I'm thinking lately, man! I don't know if it's like domestic or midlife or whatever, but I think of things about my family, because when I'm playing it's automatic now—unless I'm playing with Wayne Shorter. Wayne has an incredible way of writing everything. Those are the few times that I'm a musician with a short leash. If you read music, you've got to turn it down and get to the paper and get to what Wayne is trying to say. There are rules you need to learn when you play with Wayne Shorter or Joe Zawinul. You have to learn really quickly what they're trying to get across and then make it your own. But to make it your own requires street learning. You cannot learn that in Harvard or Berklee—that you have to learn from the streets, and that's my approach to music. The street university is very important, man.

> **"When I hit that note, if I hit it correctly, I'm just as important as Jimi Hendrix, Eric Clapton, or anybody."**

If someone were searching for the essential Santana, which of your records would you recommend?

For pure songs, *Abraxas*. For pure guitar, I would say *Caravanserai*. Neal Schon and I played really well on that album. At the time, the Allman Brothers had two guitar players. I remember Miles was really upset with me because I had another guitarist, but I told him, "I think Neal is a great guitar player, and that's what I hear right now." I believe it worked. Later Neal went to do his thing with Journey, and because I still craved to play with another guitarist I played with John McLaughlin. Once I got that craving out of the way, I wanted to learn why I was so fascinated with Coltrane and that sky-church music, as Jimi called it. So I got together with [pianist and harpist] Alice Coltrane, and I found out why she writes, and how she writes those celestial strings. It's important for guitarists to listen to her and [tenor saxophonist] Pharoah Sanders.

Any other advice for your fellow guitarists?

The last thing I want to say is that whether you play blues, bluegrass, or jazz, whatever, realize that when you get older you either get senile or become gracious.

There's no in-between. You become senile when you think the world shortchanged you, or everybody wakes up to screw you. You become gracious when you realize that you have something the world needs, and people are happy to see you when you come into the room. Your wrinkles either show that you're nasty, cranky, and senile, or that you're always smiling. That's why I hang around with Wayne Shorter, John Lee Hooker, Herbie Hancock—people who have passion. I've never seen them bored. I'm like a kid—I'm 51 years old, but I still feel like seventeen. Whether you've got a green Mohawk or a suit and a tie, it's still the same: Are you saying something valid? Are you contributing, bringing new flowers that we haven't seen in the garden?

What about your own personal goals?

What I'd like to do before I die is bring people closer to the same reality that John Coltrane and Bob Marley were trying to bring people to: no borders, one race, just one body, and we all take responsibility so nobody starves to death tomorrow morning. If you could do that with music, that's more important than becoming Jimi Hendrix or Beethoven, because you cause-and-affect the whole wheel of life in such a way that even though you are one person you make a difference, like Martin Luther King or Mahatma Gandhi. Then songs become like windows for people to look inside or look outside. That's why we love Jimi Hendrix—because they're beautiful windows; when we look into them, we like what we see.

DAVID BOWIE
& REEVES GABRELS

Remembering to Forget

Interview by Joe Gore,
Guitar Player, June 1997

Hang out a little with Reeves Gabrels and you'll understand why he's David Bowie's friend as well as his guitarist of choice for the past fifteen years. Like Bowie, Gabrels is a well-spoken gentleman with a restless intellect and a tendency to draw musical inspiration from the other arts. His thinking, like his playing, doesn't stick to the conventional channels. Example: My wife and I took Reeves and David on a tour of our native San Francisco. But instead of gaping at the dramatic bay vistas like other tourists, the pair stopped to discuss the geometric patterns formed by the power lines crisscrossing a busy intersection. But the day's highlight was taking the guys to a hardcore piercing parlor to get their ears done. It was all the hipper-than-thou piercing technicians could do to not run down Market Street screaming, "Oh, my God! It's David Bowie!" I felt precisely the same.

—*Joe Gore, Consulting Editor,* Guitar Player

• • •

You've said you were drawn to Reeves for his ability to let go of his musicianship. Does a player need to have to let it go?

Bowie: Yes. There's a certain self-security factor involved. Musicians who are involved with their instrument to the extent that there are no thought processes involved in their playing have far less of a problem reducing down and deconstructing what they're doing, making technique sound ugly and rubbing it up the wrong way. Guitar players who are less confident of their abilities are more likely to regard it as just sounding like noise if you ask them to do something that's not "musicianly."

31

Guys who are really into it can let it go more easily. [Robert] Fripp is like that. Reeves is much the same. You can give him a mental trip and he will benefit from it and enjoy it, whereas a lesser guitarist is more likely to be worried by it. The most obvious example on *Earthling* is the solo from "Watching the Satellites." I told him I only wanted him to play on one string at a time. He had to stay on the low *E* string until the chord changed, then he could go up to the *A*. When he changed again he could go to the *D*. He was hemmed in by the chord until it changed, and that made his run-up most unorthodox. Anyone else would say, "Let me practice it a few times."

Gabrels: When I got to the section where I was supposed to stop, I just thought, "Fuck this!" and broke out of the rule, playing through the chorus. And David said, "That's great." Because of the restriction that David put on me, it has a nice developmental curve, even though I'm overplaying. It has a nice orgasmic release.

> "If it's a cheap guitar, I can do what I want with it. If you give me a real guitar that real musicians play, I'm suddenly very insecure."
>
> —David Bowie

That ambivalence about "overplaying" is one of your defining traits.

Gabrels: I want to have the chops to play what I hear, but I don't want technique to lead me by the nose. I suppose the ambivalence came with time, since by the time you acquire a skill, you might have outgrown the reason you wanted it in the first place. But there is also a competitive side to my personality—not like I have to have what another person has, but in the late eighties I needed to be able to do the Vai/Satriani/Yngwie thing because of my desire to be able to play whatever I wanted to play.

You both tend to describe music in visual terms.

Bowie: Ever since I was very young I've seen music in visual terms. I see the textures that I'm hearing, and I equate certain sounds with the relative roughness and smoothness or density and transparency of color. I really see it in painters' terms. The idea of, say, Rimsky-Korsakov developing a "color organ"—a primitive thing with colored glass and candles—always made perfect sense to me. It always made perfect sense that you could go to, say, *E* minor, and it would have a particular hue.

The guitar neck is also very graphic.

Bowie: I see the guitar neck as a landscape. I see length and barrenness. I see each note or cluster of notes as objects within a landscape: a tree, a fence. I describe instrumental parts in visual terms: "The first part should be like a moor with a light fog. As we approach the chorus, it shouldn't emerge as a clear figure, but as an approaching object in a darker gray than the gray of the fog. It takes on recognizable features by the time it gets close to you." And then I'll make a hand gesture to indicate the sort of shape it should gradually take on. I just happen to be lucky to be working with people who understand what the fuck I'm saying! That's what I do as a producer: Give me five knobs and I'll hit the wrong two ones, but I *am* good at knowing exactly what the album looks like. I'm also good at opening musicians to areas of their own technique or creativity that they might not have looked at before.

There's an aspect to your own playing that's a throwback to the coffeehouse/ garage roots of rock guitar, when technique was less scientific than it is now.

Bowie: Completely! My guitar playing hasn't moved with the times at all. I use the same chords as always. But I do know a lot of them, and I'm able to put them together in interesting juxtapositions. Any time I did spend being disciplined was learning how chords work together. I spent a lot of time taking rock songs apart. I have no technique, but I have very good timing. The guitar was my orchestra when I would play solo shows in the sixties. I'd set up two Selmer P.A. columns on top of my little bubble-shaped Fiat 400. I'd drive up and down the M1, doing shows with just twelve-string guitar. But I was never interested in becoming a "guitar player." I have no lead guitar abilities. I can't play anything at a party. I don't know one of my songs unless I'm learning for a tour. But Reeves can play anything. I expect he can play the entire Elton John songbook.

Gabrels: Yeah. "Daniel," "Rocket Man" …

Bowie: "Daniel Rocket Man"? Sounds interesting!

Gabrels: Sort of a Charles Ives thing.

As much as you disparage your own playing, Diamond Dogs *was a great guitar album. A lot of people assume it was a Mick Ronson record, but it was all David.*

Bowie: During that period when I left the Spiders, I knew that the guitar playing had to be more than okay. That couple of months I spent putting that album together before I went into the studio was probably the only time in my life where I really buckled down to learn the stuff I needed to have on the album. I'd actually practice two hours a day. I knew the sound in my head, and at that time I didn't know musicians who could carry it off.

> "I want to have the chops to play what I hear, but I don't want technique to lead me by the nose."
> — Reeves Gabrels

How has the cut-and-paste nature of digital recording affected your perspective on guitar sound and arrangement?

Gabrels: I remember on a Tin Machine track like "Shopping for Girls," where I'd put down track after track of guitar noise. I was always looking for the *event*, that shard of sound that would hit and then be gone. I was deeply into Nine Inch Nails' *Pretty Hate Machine* at that time, and I was looking for that industrial edge. So the ability to cut things up and move them where I wanted onscreen is what I wished I could have done then.

Has the digital medium more fundamentally changed the way you see the instrument?

Gabrels: Well, any improvisation is a series of ideas that you link together, and that's still true in a cut-and-paste situation. But you can be more economical, jumping from good idea to good idea without having to go through the less interesting series of notes that originally connected them. You don't see me going through my pockets musically, looking for change. It's not, "I need a quarter. Let's see, here's a penny, here's a dime." It's more like, "I need a quarter—here's one." At that point guitar is merely a sound source for me. It's not about how well I play; it's just sound and its attendant emotion. And this time [on *Earthling*] my goal was to get the guitar into techno, jungle, and trip-hop in a way that doesn't have the cock-rock baggage of electric lead guitar. I think we did it.

Bowie: We're going in a different way from what everyone else is doing with drum-n-bass music. We're trying to give it a sort of complexity. There's this incredible dynamic sense, like it's just coming out of them *now*. It was as aggressive as any punk thing. That spontaneous combustive atmosphere is terribly important to what we're doing.

Jungle beats have super-fast snare patterns over a lumbering, half-time bottom end. Do you feel them at the slower tempo or in double-time?

Gabrels: Well, I'm a pretty slow-moving character, so I always feel it in half-time. It's a lumbering beat with a lot of 32nd-note fills—just like heavy rock! I'm actually getting tired of drum-n-bass, and I'm interested in the current shift towards darker flavors. David and I feel differently at times about where we wanted this record to go. I leaned a bit towards the American industrial side, and he inclined towards a more Euro sound. Just like some people prefer the Beatles to the Stones, or Oasis to Blur, David is a Prodigy fan, while I'm more a fan of Underworld. Ironically, Carl from Underworld is using almost the same setup as me. [*At the time Gabrels was playing a custom Parker Nitefly guitar through a Roland VG-8 digital-modeling system and a GR-09 synthesizer module.*]

David, on the other hand, played all his guitar parts on Earthling *with a little travel guitar through a built-in amp and speaker.*

Bowie: It's all I need. It's all Reeves would give me! It's a self-esteem thing: I actually don't think I'm worth a better guitar. Why give me a nice Gibson? Give me something I don't feel so precious about. If it's a real cheap guitar, I can do what I want with it, fuck it up, make it do silly things. If you give me a real guitar that real musicians play, I'm suddenly very insecure. I much prefer a cheap Parker.

Gabrels: There's no such thing as a cheap Parker.

Bowie: In my case, there are. They give them to me. Or did I pay for that one?

Gabrels: That one's mine. It doesn't get much cheaper than that, does it, David?

So a little stamped-out guitar is relatively free of psychological baggage. Does it ever work in reverse? Do you ever seek out a guitar that's rife with associations?

Bowie: Maybe something like a Rickenbacker twelve-string, a guitar that almost has a manifesto attached to it.

Gabrels: Or your one-string Flying V. One string, Floyd Rose, tuned to *D*.

Bowie: That one *is* beautiful. It's context, always context. For example, I have one of Marc Bolan's old guitars. If we have that in the studio, all the luggage of the guitar comes with it, and it definitely changes the attitude of what we're doing. I can't pick up a guitar and play just anything on it. Whatever guitar I'm given contextualizes the thought. I'm sorry to keep using the word "context," but it's a governing principle. Context is almost everything. This is something too pretentious for words, but there's another attitude that's very much a part of what I do as a musician and performer. Brecht … [*dissolves into laughter*]. Can you believe I said that?

Gabrels: I believe it.

Bowie: Bertolt Brecht [an early-twentieth-century German playwright and theorist] believed that it was impossible for an actor to express real emotion in a natural form every night. Instead, you portray the emotion symbolically. You don't try to draw the audience into the emotional content of what you're doing, but give them something to create their own dialog about what you're portraying. You play anger or love through stylistic gesture. The voice doesn't rise and fall, and the face doesn't go through all the gambits you would portray as a naturalistic actor.

> "I see the guitar neck as a landscape. I see each note or cluster of notes as objects within a landscape: a tree, a fence."
> —David Bowie

I've done that an awful lot throughout my career. A lot of what is perceived as mannered performance or writing is a distancing from the subject matter to allow an audience to have their own association with what I'm writing about. That comes straight from Brecht, who was a major influence on me as a whippersnapper. It applies to any art form. It's a question of creating a space between your subject matter and yourself as an artist. I sing notes that stand in for emotion. I honestly couldn't care less about what the subject matter of *Earthling* is. I need lyrics; I write some lyrics. I guess a lot of subconscious things come through, and that probably says something about me. But it's almost like lyrics standing in for lyrics: [*sings*] "Some words go here, and here's some more words." That's enough. It's almost like when you do an undersketch for a painting. You sketch out what it looks like—a sun here, a house here. That's fine. The enthusiasm fleshes things out.

Gabrels: That works instrumentally as well. The undersketch is one of the things you can retain because of recording to hard disk. You can see the pencil line of the house that ended up getting painted. You don't have to lose it. You can make a glorious mistake, and then edit off the mistake, so all you have is the glory.

Bowie: Then you have the intrusion of the musician's abilities. However principled and idealistic your vision, you can't help the intrusions of others. Intentions and expectations are very different for the artist. An artist may have an intention, but by the time he's applied himself to his work, that intention might have gotten lost. Certainly, an audience's expectations of the work are a million miles away from what the artist's intention was. It's the space in the middle that's actually the art—the mysterious, almost magical place in the middle where the receptions and intentions become something else.

To my advantage, I haven't got a clue where we're going to take it. It may be the dilettante side of me, but when I know where things are going, I lose interest real fast. That's probably the root of the majority of the critical hostility against me. They don't like the fact that, one, I'm not a rock & roll person and I don't care to be considered one, and two, I treat most of what I do as an exercise in moving textures around. It's not my lifeblood or anything. The idea that I'm not honest because of that makes me seem offensive, and that's kind of cool because I don't know anyone else like that. But not knowing where you're going is what makes it exciting for me. It leaves a permanently open landscape.

BONNIE RAITT

Sweet Inspiration

Interviewed by Michael Molenda
Guitar Player, July 1998

Unfortunately, it's risky business putting a woman on the cover of a
guitar magazine. Predominantly male readerships often make it difficult
to sell issues that don't trumpet the testosterone factor. But the most recent Bonnie Raitt issue, released to cover her album *Fundamental,* did very well for
us. After all, who could have a huff with a kick-ass blues player who has lived the life
and tells the tale with searing slide riffs? She's also absolutely fearless. Raitt was in
Hawaii rehearsing for a performance at a charity festival when I spoke to her over the
telephone. Although she maintained a no-nonsense attitude throughout the interview, she was not guarded or evasive. If you get anything from the interview, I hope
it's the fact that, after decades in the biz, Raitt still lives for holding a guitar in her
hands and playing a great song. This is a musician with one hell of a heart.

—*Michael Molenda, Editor in Chief,* Guitar Player

• • •

After all these years, what still inspires you about playing the guitar?

How little I *know* inspires me tremendously! I'm a huge fan of other people's
playing. I don't have the drive to learn how to play like Jimi Hendrix or Stevie Ray
Vaughan, but that doesn't mean I don't get what they're doing. I can still incorporate the feel of what they play into one of my songs.

Also, there's this whole world of African guitar players that are very, very inspiring. My aim in the next few years is to learn the difference between a lot of the guitar styles I hear on African radio shows. I'll be driving my car, trying to hear what the

deejay is saying about an artist, but it's usually impossible to decipher the syllables and write everything down without getting into a wreck.

How do outside cultural influences seep into your playing? You can study the forms, of course, but it's harder to assimilate the emotional context of music from other countries.

That's what I had to do when I first picked up the guitar. I may not have *really* known what John Hammond was doing when I was fourteen and I heard *Blues at Newport '63* on Vanguard. But I figured it out. I made enough of a stab at it in my room to be able to play the song and feel the way that record made me feel.

That was my first inspiration for playing the guitar. It wasn't enough to hear it on a record; I had to be able to play it in my room. Now, I'm not judging whether I play the song as well as the record. I'm not trying to duplicate it. I just want to have the internal experience—the feeling that, when I'm doing a John Lee Hooker song, I'm nailing the emotion of how his singing and playing makes me feel.

If you're trying to sound like John Lee Hooker, you're obviously not him, so some kind of creative empathy is critical to capturing the feel, if not the stylistic veracity.

Right. That's what true inspiration is. That's why I don't like people saying somebody doesn't have the *right* to play a certain type of music because they don't have the capacity. In my case, putting my style of guitar over other styles and feels is totally thrilling to me. I wake up hearing bagpipes and slide guitar and Cajun fiddle all together with this South African beat. I know that would be a great combination. There are the same scales in Celtic a cappella singing as there are in blues field hollers. That's the thing that really blows my mind—that so many cultures have those quarter-tones and can produce that mournful kind of sound, or play sevenths off majors just like Bob Marley and the Wailers did.

> "To actually have to get reviewed and judged on my playing is frightening."

That's the place that knocks me out: taking majors and minors and exploring what those sounds mean musically and *emotionally*. That's the place that inspires me. And of course, some reviewer will say, "Oh, she's trying to mix Scottish music with the blues," or whatever, as if I sit around and deliberately plan what would be the cool move for my next record so that somebody will give me a good review. It has nothing to do with that. It's totally innocent. It comes purely from being a fan of music.

Do you ever reassess your own playing?

I don't listen back to my records very much, but I know when I've managed to absorb or digest something that knocks me out. On "Spit of Love" [from *Fundamental*], for instance, it doesn't really matter that I'm not the greatest guitar player in the

Bonnie Raitt, 1995: "The best that is," said B. B. King.

world; it just matters that playing the solo got the feeling out of me. That's all I ever go for, and to actually have to get reviewed and judged on my playing is frightening. If you're reviewing a record and telling your readers not to buy it because the person is lame, that's your job. But the person who made the record probably did the best they could, you know?

How did you go about developing the new direction we notice in your approach throughout Fundamental?

Mitchell [Froom, co-producer] said he wanted to hear what I would do in a situation that was totally unfamiliar. He wanted to hear how I would react, how my guitar playing and singing would change, to reflect a new environment. But what happened was that the other musicians' playing was also affected by *me*. So we all got closer to the essence of ourselves by playing together. That's the best you can hope for—that you become even more yourself by playing with other people. To me, I sound more like myself on *Fundamental* than on any record I've ever made.

It would be a weird vibe if everyone were actively working to make a "different" Bonnie Raitt album.

Nobody thought about it. You put those people in the room and that's what they come up with. I think most of making great music is being sure that you have the right people in the room in the first place, and then you just let them do what they do. The stuff they came up with was just mind-blowing, but nothing was really thought out. Each person just did what they did naturally. Every song on the record was pretty much one or two takes, and everybody played what they thought was going to be cool. None of us knew whether something was going to work or not. The sessions were totally unpredictable.

Did Tchad Blake, who shared production duties with you and Mitchell, bring in any outlines for how to approach each song?

Tchad never even *heard* any of the songs before we recorded them. Take the vocal sound on "Round & Round," for example: When we started to play, he just happened to pick a certain mic for my voice that sounded a certain way. A lot of the sound of this record is the choice of mics because Tchad tends to make these records that are just totally the sound of being in the room. He has a whole arsenal of mics and things that make his art great, but he comes to every song totally fresh—he doesn't have any preconceived notion of what he's going to do until the day he hears what's going on. It's like they say in Zen: He uses his "beginner's mind."

It sounds like inspiration was running rampant all over the studio.

Oh, yeah! It was definitely "go for what you feel." It's really fun for me to just naturally jam on something. I don't plan it out. I don't sit there and go, "I'm going to put a reggae part on top of an African part, and lay down an accordion track." It's just what sounds good at the time.

For example?

"One Belief Away" is based on a record by a Zimbabwean artist [Oliver Mutukudzi], and it was a total cross-cultural collaboration. But I woke up at six one morning, like on the last day of recording, with that drunken mariachi horn arrangement in my head, so we tracked it. It happened in the blink of an eye. It probably *wouldn't* have happened if I was sitting in the studio with the horn players waiting for me to come up with something. I mean, it might have been too much input to all those people in the room.

Did you end up taking the best bits of inspiration and editing them together through Pro Tools?

No, no, no! It was all done completely live. No rehearsal, no preparation, and all the mistakes were left in. That's the record. The whole album was recorded and mixed in 29 days.

It's pretty nervy for an established artist—a hitmaker—to trust in the process so much.

True. You don't know whether it's going to work out or not. But the worst thing that could have happened is that after the first few days it didn't work out. Then I'd have to find somebody else to work with. It's not like you get shot. And it's a very innocent thing to love Sheryl Crow and Los Lobos and say, "God, I'd love to make records that sounded like that." What's more pure than going where your ears lead you?

In putting songs together for Fundamental, *did you look for songs that, as a whole, tell a story, or did you select the best individual songs?*

I'm always at the mercy of the best songs. The hardest part of what I do is finding good songs. It's beyond daunting. It gets to the point where it's a week before I'm going into the studio and I still only have nine songs. Now sometimes it's two or three years between albums, and I'm listening for songs the whole time! So I really do record the best ten, eleven, or twelve songs around at the time. I've never had a record where there was more than one or two extras—and even then it's *very* clear that the songs I've picked for the record are markedly better.

What usually kills a song for you?

Right off the bat, if the lyrics are lame, I can't do it. If somebody writes lyrics that lame, they're usually not hip enough to write good music either. Everybody who writes a song puts their heart and soul in it—I'd like to think they do, anyway—but some lyrics are just so obvious and so silly. You know, they tell a silly little story, or they're full of puns. If you listen to my records, have you ever heard me do a song like that? Why would you send me stuff like that? Sometimes you wonder whether people in the music publishing business put two and two together. They should listen to my records, listen to the five songs on the tape they're sending me, and then ask themselves, "What's the picture here? Is there a difference in songwriting quality? Yes. Well, maybe I shouldn't send these five songs to her!" On the other hand, maybe ninety percent of the stuff on radio sounds like that, so I'm not putting myself above anybody. It's just a difference of taste.

> "Making great music is being sure you have the right people in the room, and then you let them do what they do."

How do you find the gems?

Something about the lyrics and the music has to get me in a way that makes me want to sing it. Songwriting is a mysterious gift. You want to stay out of its way and not analyze it too much. It's like you're on autopilot: There's somebody driving who is the same person who came up with the inspiration for a really great song. And that same part of your soul is also the one that picks the songs that other people write.

Can we talk about your own songwriting process?

I just sit and jam around on some stuff. When it's time to start planning the next record, I'll take walks or ride my bike and start thinking about the things I feel like singing about. What in my life is really bugging me? What situations do I see around me that might lend themselves to a good song? But I don't write enough songs to be good at it. Right up to the minute it's time to record, I'm still thinking that I'm not going to be able to say what I really feel because it's too personal, or somebody else has already said it better. There's just a lot of anxiety about whether you have what it takes to write a song as good as something you've done before.

Do you listen to the work of other songwriters for inspiration?

I try not to do a lot of listening, because that can be intimidating. I have a certain amount of innocence regarding the musical part of songwriting, because my tastes sometimes exceed my grasp. I wish I could immediately play everything I hear in my head, but I can't.

Does your commercial success insinuate itself into your writing or song selection? Does a devilish little voice go, "Hit song, hit song, hit song"?

I'm not sales-driven in my choice of songs. I mean, I'm not stupid enough to release a whole album of stuff that nobody is going to like, but I've always felt that if I like a song, someone else will like it too.

> **"I wish I could immediately play everything I hear in my head, but I can't."**

What's the biggest drag about being a rock star?

Well, when you "go mainstream," which is what the successes of *Nick of Time* and *Luck of the Draw* did for me, and you're at that point where you start hearing your music played in supermarkets, you have to expect that some people are going to try to knock you down. I think it's so unfair to be judged, for someone to try to assume what my motivation was when I made a record. They don't know. That's partly why I do interviews: to straighten people out so they don't sit around and think I do market surveys on what might be the cool thing to do next.

That should be obvious to everyone who listens to your music.

I have the luxury to take risks because I've already proven myself over and over again. I also have the financial freedom to try and fail, and the record company can't tell me when to put a record out. So, let's face it, experimenting is easier if you can say to the record company, "You can't tell me who to work with, and you can't tell me when to be finished." I was able to do that in 1971. Very few artists have that freedom anymore. If you're a young band and you have no money in the bank, everything is riding on your record. You're probably not going to get into a room with a bunch of musicians you don't know and wing it. You'd be committing career suicide.

What advice can you pass along to musicians who are trying to put together a successful first album?

Hopefully, when you make a record, you won't use an engineer that will make it sound like a James Ingram record. You pick an engineer that's appropriate for your music. You have to be conscious enough to tell your record company, even if you don't have as much clout as me, that you need to work with a producer that's going to get *this* sound. If you want to sound like Shawn Colvin, don't let someone try and force you to sound like Celine Dion. There's no need for people to be uneducated and unaware of the subtleties of engineering differences in this day and age. It's really true that a Michelle Shocked record sounds different from a LeAnn Rimes album for a reason. Learn what the reason is, and don't let your music get put in a suit that you don't want it to wear.

But even for an established artist, it still takes guts to do what she wants when everyone in the biz is probably expecting a slick hit-fest.

Yeah, except every record I've made has been like that. You have to realize that radio only decided to play me when my age group got old enough to own stations [*laughs*]. I never try to make hit records. Whether somebody decides that I have a hit or not is completely up to the whims of what's going on in radio. My style is to just *play*. I mean, I'm basically an R&B artist. The more *live* you capture your music, the more *un*-thought-out, the more magical it is.

ERIC JOHNSON

Skimming over Water

Interviewed by Jas Obrecht,
Guitar Player, December 1982,
May 1986, March 1990, January 1993

D uring the early eighties *Guitar Player* editors often got tips about
extraordinary new talent. What set apart Eric Johnson, then virtually
unknown outside of Austin, Texas, was *who* was singing his praises:
Johnny Winter, Billy Gibbons, Steve Morse, and especially Jeff Baxter, who claimed,
"If Jimi Hendrix had gone on to study with Howard Roberts for about eight years,
you'd have what this kid strikes me as." With endorsements such as these, Johnson
was impossible to ignore, and in December 1982, long before his debut solo album,
his first lengthy feature ran in *Guitar Player*. Among the many hundreds of guitarists I interviewed during twenty years at *Guitar Player*, Eric Johnson is doubtlessly
my favorite: warm, soft-spoken, spiritual yet down to earth, and utterly devoted to
playing his best. As Stevie Ray Vaughan expressed it, "I've never known anybody
who tries harder than Eric Johnson."

—*Jas Obrecht*

• • •

How did you first get interested in playing guitar?
Ever since I was young, I have been so in love with the way a guitar sounds. I
remember when I was three years old, the very first time I ever heard a guitar. It was
like, that was it. This friend of the family was doing some construction work around
the house, and he had this guitar that he'd plug in. We'd have a little party outside,
and he'd play these great blues—Elmore James and stuff. It was great! I just went,
"God, what is this?"

44

Did you eventually take lessons?

Jimmy Schade taught me the first things I ever learned on guitar; he was a really fine player around these areas in the mid sixties. We would sit around and jam. I learned chords and leads at the same time. I was more of an imitator then, although I would be a little innovative. I took guitar lessons for a few months and learned "Walk, Don't Run" and stuff like that. I started hearing the Ventures really early, and that was a real big influence. And then the Stones, the Kinks … I just got real enamored of rock at that time. I spent as much time with the guitar as I could as a teenager, at least four or five hours a day.

Who else inspired you as you continued to learn?

I listened to a lot of records. Several of Wes Montgomery's solos are landmarks to me, [and] a lot of the Jimi Hendrix and Django Reinhardt solos. John McLaughlin has been really inspirational to me. I have the utmost respect for him because he always goes in a path with music that inspires him to pioneer and explore, and he doesn't let business aspects be too much of a deterrent to him. When I was real young I liked Brian Jones of the Rolling Stones. When I was thirteen or fourteen I used to sneak into the Vulcan Gas Company and hear Johnny Winter play for fifty cents. He would play a [Fender] Mustang through two or three [Fender] Twins. It was really neat.

What about the Vaughan brothers, Jimmie and Stevie Ray? You knew both of them for a long time in Austin.

I haven't ever really sat down with Jimmie, but I have with Stevie—very casually. We've talked and jammed, and we've played onstage at each other's shows. Stevie had a certain power and fieriness that so few players have. It's so reminiscent of Hendrix. Stevie was one of a kind, and I learned a lot from him. Sometimes you don't realize how much you've learned until you stop and give it some true thoughts.

What kind of things did he teach you?

The kind of tone he'd get with rhythm, the power, the fluid voicings that he would use when he was playing that neck-pickup tone. Hendrix did a lot of that, and Stevie kept the ball rolling. Hendrix—he made the guitar sound like it was from outer space. It really knocked down doors, changed the definition of what the guitar was. That was so exciting; it was almost the energy behind the guitar playing more than the actual playing that made it so incredible. There's a certain energy people have that could be in whatever they do—a universal energy that others can feel. With Hendrix it happened to be voiced through the guitar, and that made it more special to me because I love guitar.

Does his music still inspire you?

Oh, absolutely. Every few months I still sit down and learn a new Hendrix tune, just to study it. Some of them are real difficult. You can learn the notes, but it's tough to learn his inflections, attitudes, and the informal spontaneity he had when he recorded the stuff. His playing was almost like a beautiful dance; it was so free, and there's such a wealth of information to learn. It's not only his notes, but where he puts the glissandos and slides. He mutes the strings and then comes in on the three-and-a-half [*second eighth-note of the third beat*] of a measure and plays a certain chord and hangs it over. I don't think he was so much thinking of his guitar playing sometimes; he was just attuned to that energy within himself that gave this incredible spontaneity to his music. It's like all the notes are there in their regimen, but it's all just chance and happenstance. I learned a lot from studying that, because I have a tendency to be more regimented. I wish I wasn't that way so much, that I could allow myself to relax and really expand the barriers.

Your guitar style has changed enormously since your early years. How would you describe the difference between how you played then and what you're doing now?

I'm trying for a more universal approach now, using chords and rhythms in leads. I'm trying to take from other nationalities of music. I love koto [Japanese lute] music, and there's a way you can play the guitar so it sounds like this. It's kind of like Lenny Breau and Ted Greene's really nice technique of playing chromatic harmonics, but you actually fret the harmonic. You use your index finger of your right hand to fret a note, and you pick it with your thumb behind it. Then that note can be the same note or a second or third from the note you are playing with your left hand, and you move real fast. You can use this technique and employ a fast vibrato. It's neat-sounding, kind of like the Yardbirds—[Jeff] Beck's playing in particular. Sometimes Beck intentionally plays a little out of key, so it sounds Eastern and Mecca-approved, like some kind of strange Asian instrument. It's a hip effect, and I think there's a whole world there.

How do you psych yourself up for a performance?

I try to be concentrated. I try to remind myself that I'm free to feel great instead of feeling reserved or insecure, that if I want I can attach myself to a very enlightening feeling. The more I try to do that, the more it promotes it. I try to get in tune with what I'd want to do if I had my choice, which really I do. When I'm feeling that way, I'll take chances onstage. If I make a bunch of mistakes, it doesn't matter. It's almost like you're the instrument; it's flowing through you like electricity. Then it doesn't matter what you do. Errors become unimportant.

Is that sort of feeling more important in your playing than technique?

I like to achieve both perfection and emotion, but the emotion is much more important. Sometimes I'll sacrifice technique to get emotion. When I record now, I think maybe I should go for the first take that gets that feeling. I have a habit sometimes of wanting to do it three hundred times so that the notes are just right. I don't know if that's good.

Do you often play at the outside edge of your ability?

I do when I'm playing my best. It seems that when I play from a mental standpoint of what I think I can and cannot do, I create a corral that limits me to the way it was in the past. I play my best when I can turn everything off and just go to that edge.

How can you encourage that state of mind?

I've wondered about that for years. Sometimes I think maybe it's what you don't do. I've often thought, "God, what do I have to do?" And then I buy a new amp or get another-color guitar and think, "Now it'll work." It seems better if you don't put too much exterior energy into all the incidental things that are really just preoccupying distractions. If you quit trying with the rational mind to develop a blueprint for that tapping of your inherent unlimited musical ability, then you have to work more from the other hemisphere of the brain—the creative side. It's hard for the rational mind to even think about that because then you're transferring it into words.

Do you ever get frustrated while you play?

Aw, absolutely. Sometimes I get into a rut of playing patterns. And when you do that, you're basically practicing what you know, rather than trying to create an opening to something new. You're uncomfortable with yourself because you realize you're just going over the same stuff again. If you face that discipline of doing something unfamiliar, you create a situation that can take you out of the rut. It's kind of hard to do that; there's a bit of hurt and pain involved. It's like moving into a new house, and the floor's cold.

What do you expect from an Eric Johnson solo?

I want it to have a good tone, whether it's rhythmy or distorted. Once I have that certain tone, I like to pull the licks off right to where they kind of have a skimming-across-the-water sound. As far as theme or content go, I hope it's something that can move me when I hear it back. It should say something and have some lyricism.

> "I wish I wasn't so regimented, that I could allow myself to relax and really expand the barriers."

Some classic solos are very simple.

Yeah. I might have played something a little faster or crazier, and it was okay, but could you listen to it fifty times? Sometimes the more lyrical things with just the right tone and inflection are really a better statement in more of a longevity-type way.

In many of your solos, you seem to make long intervallic skips.

I skip strings. I go from maybe the B string to the A string. Every string has its own tightness of sound; some are more relaxed than others. You can play a D, say, on all the different strings, and every string has a different-sounding D. When you want a certain sound on a passage, you might have to play on certain strings. Sometimes it's worth jumping all the way down to a D note, rather than just hitting it on a lower string up high where you might be.

Do you change pickup selection as you move higher up the neck?

Not unless I want to change the tone. Typically, I don't.

You sometimes strum way up the neck, near your fretting hand.

Yeah, because it has a different sound. Close-voiced chords sound a little tighter when you strum them above the frets. As you strum further away from your fretting hand, the strings move more and the notes have a tendency to intermodulate more. As you go up the neck, they are a little cleaner and the voices ring out better. It's a give-and-take, though, because you don't quite get the richness.

Does your vibrato come more from the wrist or elbow?

More from the wrist. It's an up-and-down motion, like bending a string. I usually use either the first or third finger for this.

> **"I like to achieve both perfection and emotion, but the emotion is much more important."**

What's the best way to speed-pick?

It's important to develop down-and-up strokes. As you're picking down, instead of going from top to bottom, try to pick at an angle so that you go diagonally from the left horn of the guitar down to the control knobs. On the way back up, do the opposite diagonal. If you were to look at someone doing that real fast, it would be a circular technique. This way, you don't hit the strings dead-on, therefore minimizing the amount of extra noise and friction. You are more like skimming over the string. I hold the pick with my thumb and first finger, and I don't use the pointy end as much as the side of the pick to brush the note. As you pick diagonally, you also pick from the guitar's body up into the air, up and down, perpendicular to the string. You have to have a bounce in your wrist. It's hard to do, and it almost works against playing fast sometimes, but that bounce gives you all the tone of the fretted note without getting all of the extraneous noise.

Do you ever use a pick and your other right-hand fingers at the same time?

Yeah. Sometimes I palm the pick with my index finger and hold it up out of the way, if I want to do some Chet Atkins–type stuff. But most of the time when I play with a pick, I also use my third and fourth fingers.

Does your visualization of the fingerboard change when you go from acoustic guitar to electric?

No, but I play them a little differently. I usually play acoustic with my fingers. I'm just as comfortable on each instrument, but I sometimes have a different style when I play acoustic. I like to do more double-note stuff.

What would you most like to improve about your playing?

I'd like to learn more about classical and jazz music—their chord progressions and harmonic majesty—and use that in a rock context. I'd like to refine and add a special class to the tone of the guitar. I'd like to learn more about scales—not to particularly play them, but to be able to draw upon them freely from feeling. I want to become freer to where I can play whatever I feel or hear. I'd like to write music that is a little more universally reaching and, hopefully, healing to people. Rather than just writing music that's cute and interesting, I'd like to actually touch someone deeply.

If you could go back in time and jam with any musician, who would it be?

I'd so much love to jam with Wes Montgomery! I'd love to jam with Jimi Hendrix and talk with him. I'd just like to be with him and experience his whole aura, which I think was so beautiful and special.

How about people you could play with today?

I'd love to sit in with B.B. King! Have you ever seen that commercial where some guy is trying to buy a car in a lot across the street from Toyota, and the salesman grabs onto his ankles and is pulling him across the floor, like, "Don't leave me! Don't leave me!"? That's the way I feel around B.B. King: "Oh, please, let me jam with you!" [*Laughs.*] I always love to play with [Steve] Morse. I'd love to play with Pat Metheny; he's one of my favorite players. He's so fluid and graceful. He can really tear the guitar up, but he opts for playing within the song, rather than just, "Wow, look what I can do!" If anybody is carrying a torch from where Wes Montgomery left off, I think it's Pat.

When you're dealing with stress and recording deadlines, what keeps you centered?

Not thinking about the music helps. But meditation is real necessary for me. I'm very thankful that I'm allowed to have the desire to put some time away for that. There are a lot of different exercises and techniques that people can use to try to center their selves, if for no other reason than to try to address the continual battle in everybody's life. We try to center ourselves with dignity, poise, serenity, and peacefulness. The more we can get into that flow, the more we do whatever we do better. It helps me in every way for playing and living.

> "It's good to stop and become aware of how we're manipulated by what we want."

Does music ever come to you while you're meditating?

Boy, I wish! I'd love that. Someday, hopefully. That would be great. That's what I'm working toward. The fundamental stage is to be able to concentrate and let everything go, which is really hard to do. We get so much in the whirlwind of life that we think we do this, we do that, but in actually *that* is doing *us*, *this* is doing *us*. It's good to sit in a room by ourselves, stop, and become aware of how we're manipulated by what we want, what we have or don't have, what we can get rid of, or what's not going right. We have to try to disassociate the manipulation that these consequences have over us in life. The only thing that allows us to get a little bit of mastery over it is our ability to deal with it by gaining a better detached insight. I'm still trying to do that.

EDDIE VAN HALEN

Inspiration/Imitation

Interviewed by Jas Obrecht,
Guitar Player, April 1980, December 1982

Eddie Van Halen redefined rock guitar with the release of his band's debut album in 1978. With its fire-breathing tones and unprecedented fingertapping techniques, *Van Halen* rapidly became the most influential guitar record since Jimi Hendrix's *Are You Experienced?* Soon after the album's release, the band played its first show in northern California, at one of Bill Graham's Day on the Green extravaganzas. I was there to interview Pat Travers, who blew off our interview to party with groupies. To stem my anger, I began shooting basketball backstage. A sweaty, wiry young man soon joined me on the court and after a few shots asked what band I was in. When I told him who I was and what had happened, his response was, "Travers blew you off?! Why don't you interview me? Nobody ever wants to interview me." "Who are you?" I asked. "Eddie Van Halen." I pulled out my tape recorder, we sat at the edge of the court, and Eddie Van Halen gave his first-ever interview to a national magazine. He was so pleased with the published story that he began calling me from the road, just to talk guitars and music with someone he trusted. It was the beginning of a friendship that led to several cover stories and feature articles. To this day, that first Van Halen album remains an unsurpassed milestone in rock guitar history.

—Jas Obrecht

• • •

How did you get into music?

Me and Al [Alex Van Halen] were born in Holland. My father used to be a professional musician there, played saxophone and clarinet. He used to play for radio shows, because back then they used to have live radio shows instead of records. So he got us into music real early. We both started playing piano at the age of six or seven.

Did you take lessons?

Sure.

Learn to read music?

Oh, yeah! Definitely. I slightly know how to read for the guitar, because I know notes. But if I see an *A* or an *E*, I don't know which one it is in relation to the piano. But piano, yeah, I played for a long time. Got all my musical theory and stuff like that from playing piano. We used to have this old Russian teacher that was a super concert pianist, and that's what our parents wanted us to be: concert pianists. Started working, had a paper route. I bought myself a drum set.

Was this in Holland?

No, this was here. We moved over in '67, '68—right around the Cream days. Rock & roll, man, I wasn't into it at all back then. Wasn't much of a scene going on. When we came here, and I saw Hendrix and Cream around '68, I said, "Fuck the piano! I don't want to sit down. I want to stand up and be crazy!" But before then, when we first came here, I started playing drums, and my brother was taking guitar lessons—flamenco, you know, and nylon strings, stuff like that. While I was out doing my paper route so I could keep paying the payments for my drum set, he'd be playing my drums, and eventually he got better. I mean, he could play "Wipe Out" and I couldn't [*laughs*]. So I said, "Keep the drums. I'll play a guitar." From there on, we've always played together. I've never played with another drummer.

> "People like Joe Perry or Ritchie Blackmore, who all hate my guts anyway, they wouldn't go out of their way to help anybody, because they would feel threatened."

What kind of guitar did you start on?

Teisco Del Rey. Four pickups in a row. Cost seventy, eighty bucks.

Did you take lessons?

No, not for guitar. I've always been around music all my life, so I've kind of got an ear for it. I pick up things pretty easy.

What guitar players most influenced you?

That's a toughie, really. But I'd say the main one, believe it or not, was Eric Clapton. I mean, I know I don't sound like him....

You sound more like Hendrix or Ritchie Blackmore.

Yeah, I know. I don't know why, because Hendrix I like, but I was never into him like I was Clapton. Clapton, man, I know every fuckin' solo he ever played, note-for-note, still to this day. The live stuff, like "Spoonful," "I'm So Glad" live, all that stuff.

You've certainly inspired a legion of imitators yourself.

> "I ain't no extrovert. I'm a quiet person. That's probably why I do all these weird things on guitar."

Yeah, that's a trip. You know, it's funny. The things I do, like "Eruption" and "Spanish Fly"—I hate to say it, and it's not hard to do, but I came up with us. Like, Rick Derringer opened for us last year, and he did my exact solo. After the show, we're sitting in the bar, and I said, "Hey, Rick. I grew up on your ass. How can you do this? I don't care if you use the technique—don't play the melody." And he's going, "Yeah, yeah, yeah." The next night he does my solo again, and he ends the set with "You Really Got Me," which is exactly what we do. So I hate to say it, but I just told him, "Hey, if you're going to continue doing that, you ain't opening for us." So I kicked him off. But it's fucked, you know, because I've seen him plenty of times. I've even copied his chops way back when—you know, [Johnny Winter's] *Still Alive and Well*, stuff like that. And here's a guy copping my stuff. It's pretty weird. Tom Scholz from Boston too: We played right before them—I forget where—and I do my solo. Then all of a sudden he does my solo. It was real weird, because it was a daytime thing, and I was standing onstage and the whole crowd was looking at me like, "What's this guy doing?" I was drunk, and I got pissed. He never comes around, he doesn't say, "Hi." He doesn't do anything. He just kind of hides out, runs onstage and plays, and disappears afterwards. So I started talking to the other guitar player, and I told him, "Hey, tell him I think he's fucked!"

Which players do you admire now?

There's two types of guitarists. Like, [Ritchie] Blackmore, I used to hate, because I met him once at the Rainbow with [Led Zeppelin drummer John] Bonham when we were just playing gigs. You know, I grew up on him too, and I ran over and said hello, and they both just looked at me and said, "Who are you? Fuck off." And it pissed me off. To this day I remember that.

Do you run into guitarists who resent you out of jealousy?

Fuck yeah! The one thing that's bothered me so much in the very beginning, in '78, our first tour, is how some guitarists would just give me the shaft with their eyes—you know, wouldn't say hello, wouldn't be nice, nothing. I'm not that way. I don't give a fuck if I'm playing a Holiday Inn lounge; I enjoy playing. But I just think people like Joe Perry or Ritchie Blackmore, who all hate my guts anyway, they wouldn't go out of their way to help anybody, because they would feel threatened. The more they hate you, the better you are. I mean, no other guitarist is gonna hate you if you're no good—you're no threat. But I don't really think about that, because everybody can do their own thing. Hey, the way I look at it, I wish there were more people that were innovative, so I would have somebody to cop licks from. It might sound a little egoed-out, but there are very few guitarists that make me turn my head and go, "Whoa! How did he do that?" Allan Holdsworth is about the only one.

Where did you first hear Holdsworth play?

U.K. opened for us for a few shows. I never heard of the band U.K. Here we are in an arena, I'm sitting here tuning up, and all of a sudden [*in a reverent voice*] … "Is that Bill Bruford? Whoa!" I got the chills. I was freakin' out. Then Allan Holdsworth walks in. I'm going, "My God! These guys are opening for us? These guys are better; they've been through it." They played before us—and they bombed! People hated 'em, but I'm standing here with tears in my eyes, just getting off, trippin'. It was so good. But they're artists: "I'm playing my art, and I don't care if you like it or not," that type of thing, which I think is a real bad attitude. Music is for people. It's not for yourself—or if it is, sit in your room and play it. But if you're gonna play it for people, you better play something that they're gonna want to hear, instead of walking up there and pretending you're so good and beyond your audience. That's what they were doing, playing all this offbeat stuff, which to an average person sounds like mistakes.

But you were getting off on what he was playing.

I love Allan Holdsworth, and I can play like that, but it doesn't fit the music that we're playing. He's got feeling. He's got an ear that's unbelievable. I mean, he can play any chord change you want, and he can improvise over it. But at times he does get a little monotonous, because he never stops.

Did you know Randy Rhoads? [The metal guitar virtuoso died at age 26 in an airplane crash on March 19, 1982, while touring with Ozzy Osbourne in Florida.]

Yeah. Poor guy. He was one guitarist who was honest, anyway, because I read some interviews that he did, and he said that everything he did he learned from me. And he was good. I mean, goddamn, what a fuckin' way to go—jerkin' around with the airplane. It was an accident, but somebody had to have been fucked up. You don't fly that low and smash into a crew bus and then hit the house. That's just plain stupidity. I feel sorry for him. Hey, you never know, man. He might be up there jammin' with Bonham and everyone else who kicked the bucket.

He was the first guitarist to come after you and inspire in a similar way.

Yeah. Oh, sure. But I don't really think he did anything that I haven't done. What do you think?

He was different, but you could hear a lot of your playing in his.

That's what I mean. Just like anyone who does the things I do, obviously it's gonna sound a little different, but I can tell when someone's coppin' my technique. But there's

Eddie Van Halen, 1978: "I want to stand up and be crazy!"

nothing wrong with that. I mean, I learned from other people too. I copied some other people's licks, you know.

What's your strategy for playing guitar with this band?

I do whatever I want. I don't really think about it too much. I'd say that's the beauty of being in this band—that everyone pretty much does what they want. It's not that strict. They throw out ideas, and whatever happens, happens.

Do you leave room for experimentation onstage?

Oh, yeah, definitely. Half the time I forget the solos I played on the record. Everything is pretty spontaneous. It's not so set. We used to have a keyboard player, and I hated it, because you have to play everything exactly the same all the time with the guy. You couldn't noodle, like in between vocal lines, because he'd be doing something to fill it up. I didn't dig it, because I played too much. I don't want someone else filling where I want to fill it. I've always liked to play three-piece, because I just play too much, I guess. That's why when we did our first album I said, "Hey, Ted [Templeman, producer], I've never done overdubs. Can I just play live?" You know, go for what you know. So I did, and Ted freaked out. He's going, "Whoa! It doesn't even need another guitar."

You didn't need to overdub any of your parts?

We never thought much about recording or overdubbing. Actually, everything we do is the reverse of other people, because what we did was apply our live performance to plastic, whereas people like Boston and Foreigner do it the opposite way: They work it out in the studio, and then when they have to go out on tour, they have to rehearse to make it happen live, and it's obvious. With us there's more mania and more feel and more excitement live, because that's where it's based. I mean, that's the bottom line. That's the only thing that sells us: the live show. It's not hype.

What's the downside of being famous?

The fucked thing is that the kids only know me through what they read, because interviews always fuck me over. They always write things that twist and bend what I say. I did an interview once with *Circus* magazine, and they asked me, "Who are your main influences?" I said, "Well, Clapton, you know." And they said, "Oh, not Jimi Hendrix?" I go, "No, actually I didn't like Jimi Hendrix at all. He was too flash for me. I get off on the bluesy feeling that Clapton projected, even though I don't sound like him at all"—which doesn't sound egoed-out, because I *don't* sound like him. But when I read it back, they made it seem like, "I don't play like Clapton—I'm *better* than all of 'em." That's the way it read in print. So I called the guy up, and I just go, "Hey, fuck you, man! That's the last time I'm doing an interview with you." I feel like going door to door and saying, "Hey, this is bullshit. Don't believe it." But the kids do. I ain't no extrovert. I'm a quiet person. That's probably why I do all these weird things on guitar.

> "There are very few guitarists that make me turn my head and go, 'Whoa! How did he do that?' Allan Holdsworth is about the only one."

Jimi Hendrix was like that too.

Yeah. There's a lot of people who don't know me but they hate me, because they think I'm some egoed-out motherfucker. That's just one thing that I never expected. Doing interviews … God! It's like, I'm not an entertainer with my mouth, but everyone expects you to be.

How do you deal with that?

Don't talk to 'em. But then they really think I'm egoed-out. They don't understand; it's just that I got nothing to say. Then if I don't talk to them, they get pissed and they hate me. I just feel like saying, "Everything I got to say is in the notes." It really is. I project more feeling out of playing than I can with my mouth. I feel like I can never explain myself right. No one really understands what I'm trying to say, and then they just use their own imagination to figure out what I'm trying to say, which is usually wrong.

Are you happy with your career?

Oh, yeah. It's the same as it's always been. We do everything ourselves. We got rid of our first manager because he had a heavy ego problem. He wanted to be the big manager, in control of everything. We'd say, "Hey, don't do that. For better or worse, we want it our way," and he couldn't handle it. We went through a big lawsuit. It's just fucked; this is all stuff I never imagined I'd get into. I just figured, hey, I can make my music, period. But I'm handling it. I've learned things you can't learn in any book or any school.

What are your plans for the future?

Plans for the future, man, is to keep fuckin' rockin' out! Playing the guitar.

What advice would you have for a young guitarist who wants to follow the route you've gone?

You just have to enjoy what you're doing. I mean, you can't pick up a guitar and say, "I want to be like him," just because you want to be a rock star, you know? You have to enjoy playing guitar. If you don't enjoy playing guitar, then it's useless. I know a lot of people who really want to be famous or whatever, but they don't really practice guitar. They think all you do is grow your hair long and look freaky and jump around, and they neglect the actual musical end, which is tough. To tell you the truth, I'm not into the star bullshit at all.

Gets old fast, doesn't it?

Yeah. I mean, a lot of people get off on it. They let their hair grow, buy a Les Paul and a Marshall, and wanna be a rock & roll star. I don't even consider myself a rock star. I enjoy playing guitar, period.

VERNON REID

A Deeper Responsibility

Interviewed by Joe Gore,
Guitar Player, October 1988

A fter fifteen years of nonstop rock/hip-hop juxtaposition, it may be
difficult to remember how radical Living Colour's debut album seemed
in 1988. Rock radio was even more segregated than it is today, and an
all-black hard rock act was a rare thing, despite such crucial antecedents as Bad Brains
and Hendrix's Band of Gypsies. Even more unprecedented was the way guitarist Vernon Reid used his background in free jazz to create a harmonically subversive solo
style full of jagged leaps and jarring dissonance. No dissonance in the interview, however—Vernon is a gentle, modest man with a wide-open mind and a great sense of
humor. We had a long, leisurely poolside chat while Living Colour vocalist Corey
Glover ran around shouting and cavorting like, well, a lead vocalist. Chances are Vernon was as surprised as anyone when the band's "Cult of Personality" single sneaked
to the top of the charts shortly after our story ran.

—Joe Gore

* * *

You've said that you don't consider yourself a "natural."

I'm not. I had an inclination towards music because I loved it, but I wasn't a
prodigy. I wish I was. I've met really young players who had it all together. Martin
Aubert, who was the guitar player in the first Defunkt band, was *killing* me when he
was thirteen or fourteen years old. I came to playing late, when I was fifteen. Playing
the guitar is something I really had to work at. Things had to happen to really push
me; I had to be embarrassed. When I was with the Decoding Society I sometimes

57

found myself sitting in a hotel room, thinking, "Maybe I have no talent." Ronald Shannon Jackson was very demanding: You had to throw yourself into the music and not be distanced from it. A lot of people approach music in that way—"Yeah, I can *kind* of play"—but don't immerse themselves headlong in the feeling of it. I *had* to because he demanded that. At the same time, I never left any of the other things that I loved behind. I never left my love for Santana or Hendrix or whoever.

> "If you've got a lot of chops, you can play by rote. [But] you've got to really work to connect."

Even though Living Colour sounds very different from the more experimental work you previously did with the Decoding Society, you don't seem to have compromised your approach in an attempt to "go rock."

It's funny. Rock was the music I felt I had the clearest voice in. I was always struggling with jazz, even though I loved it. I loved Dolphy, Coltrane, and Ornette so much that I tried to integrate the two things.

How do you respond to people who accuse you of going commercial?

In all seriousness, look at the statistical averages of black rock & roll bands that are killing on the charts and really making it. You'll see that there's a definite amount of risk. It's not something that's happening in a mass, across-the-board sort of way—not since Hendrix. This is just as challenging as being in the Decoding Society, but it's challenging on another level because you're dealing with a whole social milieu, a whole way of thinking about rock & roll that's been locked in place since the middle seventies.

You're very outspoken on the issue of the black guitarist's position in rock music.

It's a curious thing. We constantly ask ourselves, "Where do we fit in?" I remember how, years ago, the rock guitar poll in *Guitar Player* never included Ernie Isley, who was in the Isley Brothers, one of the few successful black rock bands after Hendrix. That always bothered me. It was like there was an alternate history; there was the history of everything you knew about, and there was this other thing happening off to the side. At least half the guitarists who really influenced me are not known. There are horrendously under-recorded players, like Ray Muton from New Orleans; he played with [drummer] Billy Cobham's band for a couple of tours and one record. Charlie Singleton was also in that band; he went on to play with Cameo. He was an astounding, well-rounded player. I thought, "This guy is going to be a star," but since then? Never heard from him. Arthur Rhames, from Brooklyn, had a fusion band called Eternity, a trio based around the Mahavishnu Orchestra. I've never heard a better guitar player. He also played piano and saxophone; he was frightening. Blackbird McKnight—he played with Parliament, the Brides of Funkenstein, and Herbie Hancock. Kelvyn Bell, from the original Defunkt band … there are so many.

Your concern is that these artists don't get their share of respect, compared with the reputations of better-known white guitarists.

Being disconnected from the roots and dealing only with the branches is odd. You have to hold onto the past. It's important to see things in perspective and see how one thing influences another. Eddie Van Halen says, "I never listened to Hendrix; I listened to Clapton," but Clapton … well, Robert Johnson was the one who influenced *him*. If you make a family tree or a timeline, you'll see that we're all influencing each other. To say Led Zeppelin influenced me is to say that Led Zeppelin got me into Muddy Waters and made me say, "Ah! *That's* where that was coming from."

In an interview with The New York Times *you said, "The existence of a 'black' music chart requires black artists to conform to what the industry considers rhythm and blues. That means you're not going to be able to sing about the illiteracy rate; you're going to have to sing about sex."*

There are certain expectations of black people, that they're into escapist entertainment, or that black people should provide escapist entertainment all the time. That's not cool, because you start to do what's expected of you—if that's your only option, that's what you do. After a while, you say, "Why bother practicing all this stuff if I'll never get a chance to play like that?" That's the kind of thing I'm afraid of. It's a human issue.

But pop artists in general tend to avoid addressing issues of real life in their music.

That's true; there's a conservatism all across the board. There are unique problems for black artists, but not all problems are unique to us. A lot of people are chafing under the strain of, "You gotta move those numbers. You gotta do silly love songs all the time." That can really frustrate and trap an artist. I hope we're entering into a time where there's going to be more creative music.

> "To say Led Zeppelin influenced me is to say that Led Zeppelin got me into Muddy Waters and made me say, 'Ah! *That's* where that was coming from.'"

You made a great statement to the Village Voice *years ago: "I don't separate Dolphy from Sly from Monk from Trane, because the common thing that links all these people together is the blues. The blues is what links Ornette to the Temptations or Hendrix to Trane."*

It's true. The blues is really more than a structure; it's a real feeling. Blues is a thread that links all these different experiences. It's a matter of expressing the blues in one's life, even getting past the point of, say, listening to Muddy Waters or Lonnie Johnson all the time, because when you do, you're listening to *their* lives. The only things you can draw from them are things that resonate in your own life. Other than that, everything will fall away, unless you're a total chameleon and you're trying to submerge your life. People either try to find resonances in their

Vernon Reid, 1989:
Finding his clearest
voice.

lives, or they try to obscure what their life is and take on another persona. It's like that Steely Dan song that says, "Any world that I'm welcome to is better than the one I come from." Some people will take on the persona of another player and say, "I want to be that, because I don't like my life." Is the music an expression of your state of being, or is it something you're just taking on?

So you consider yourself a blues player?

Yeah, I do. The blues is at the bottom of my playing. It's something that I constantly try to work with. I try to get to my center, to what I'm really feeling. Guitar playing is a sort of feeling analysis that tries to strip away all the crap.

Sometimes you play from a predominantly pentatonic vocabulary, and at other times you use more open, chromatic sounds. Do you shift gears conceptually when you move from one idiom to the other?

Part of it is a matter of separating myself from the tonal center. Partly, it's trying to connect with the rhythm. Sometimes I concentrate purely on what's happening with the drums and free it up that way. I also find myself working with dominant figures along with the pentatonic and chromatic things. I do find myself shifting gears, but I'm not sure whether it's a conscious thing. When I'm practicing I try to think of that stuff, but when I'm performing I try to just be in the moment.

Do you practice much these days?

It's tough on the road; I have to sneak in an hour here and there. I used to get up every morning and play whatever—it didn't matter what—just to have the guitar in my hands. I worked a lot on chords from Ted Greene's *Chord Chemistry* book. I try to do a little reading; I consider myself a struggling sight-reader.

You seem to have two different right-hand positions, with your right wrist curling when you start to play a really speedy passage.

When I started playing I had very thin arms, and I had to find a comfortable position to pick from. Some people pick straight up and down with their wrists locked, but my picking comes more from my wrist than my forearm. I used to hold my pick between my thumb, index, and forefingers, with my fingers extended. I could play very quickly, but my playing had no articulation, so I began to hold the pick between my thumb and the side of my curled index finger. I used to glue three heavy Gibson teardrop picks together and sharpen them to a point, but I gave that up when I discovered Jim Dunlop Jazz IIIs. They're a lot thinner, but they've got about the same density. When I first started playing, I used only downstrokes; I really had to work at alternate picking. I don't do much sweep picking.

You make very musical use of feedback. Do you have any special techniques for generating and controlling it?

Every guitar has its sweet spots. My main ESP, for example, is really good on the third string between the fifth and ninth frets. I usually try to find a good spot to stand onstage. I'll turn only part of the way towards the amp, and I'll hear it catch. I definitely got that from Santana. People say it's the neck, or the nut, or the body, or the pickups, or the bridge, or the amp, or the speakers, or the tubes, but everything is so interdependent that you've got to take a holistic view. I usually keep my volume and tone controls all the way up and use a volume pedal, although I sometimes pull back on the volume knob to reduce the feedback.

> "Guitar playing is a sort of feeling analysis that tries to strip away all the crap."

You're very knowledgeable about a wide range of musical styles. You must have a hell of a record collection.

A *hellish* record collection is more like it! I do try to listen to a lot of music to keep a perspective. If you don't, what you bring to your own playing will start to become real shallow.

If you could go back in time and play with any musicians who have ever lived, who would you choose?

There's so many! I would love to sit in a room with Eric Dolphy. I wouldn't even say anything, just sit. He wouldn't have to have a saxophone. To sit in a club and hear Charlie Christian when he was nineteen. To see the band that had Wes Montgomery,

Coltrane, and Dolphy that toured once and was never recorded. To meet Hendrix would have been fantastic. Charles Mingus, Tommy Bolin … if I could have said to Tommy, "Stop fucking with that shit!" Tommy was one of our great losses. If I could have just sat with Jimmy Nolen and said to him, "You're one of the greatest guitar players; you changed the music." Sonny Boy Williamson, just to have him curse me out: "Boy, what you doin' there? Get out of here!" Lonnie Johnson, Robert Johnson … Wait, I've got it: Reverend Gary Davis. A lesson with Reverend Gary Davis!

How about contemporary players?

I would love to sit with Carlos Santana. His attitude and the way he approaches music have been such an influence on me. Allan Holdsworth is fantastic because he's really searching. I never get a feeling from his playing that there's a heavy ego thing going on; it's just him trying to dig down. B.B. is truly great. People talk about "playing B.B. King style," but I don't know what they mean, because nobody plays like him. I really admire Steve Vai, because he's so knowledgeable. And Van Halen—he's so popular, but he's actually great. His playing is like breathing.

What about people you actually have played with?

One of the pleasures of working with Ronald Shannon Jackson was being able to play on stages with people like James Blood Ulmer and Sonny Sharrock. I was able to meet Fred Frith and Hans Reichel. The first time I heard Reichel, it took the top of my head off! It sounded like his guitar was made of rubber! And I had the real fortune of actually seeing Muddy Waters in Holland. Out of all the concerts I've seen, that was the greatest. I have a cheap tape of the concert that's one of my prized possessions. It was my first time out of the country, and I actually got to go backstage and shake Muddy Waters's hand.

Do you feel that you owe something to your audience, that you have a responsibility where they're concerned?

I have the responsibility to be honest and to do what it is in my power to do. That isn't to say that I should play a million notes every solo; it denotes a deeper responsibility. If you've got a lot of chops, you can play by rote. You've got to really work to connect.

What would you like to be able to do that you can't do now?

I've always been fascinated by ragtime guitar playing. I really want to do that; it's *killing* me. I want to have a richer chord vocabulary. I want to go back into jazz and really learn standards. I'd like to get to the point where I can smoothly integrate more intervallic skips in my playing. To keep learning stuff, to keep being fascinated, to keep loving it, to keep in touch with what makes guitar playing cool—that's how you keep yourself fresh.

BRIAN SETZER

Swing Shift

Interviewed by Chris Gill,
Guitar Player, June 1994;
Andy Ellis, November 1998;
Art Thompson, October 2001

ome 16 years after hitting the charts with the Stray Cats, Brian Setzer
was once again riding high. Propelled by the swing mania that swept
through pop music and culture in 1998, *The Dirty Boogie* was selling
briskly, and "Jump Jive an' Wail" was rocking the airwaves. In my interview, we discover
what really motivates Setzer—not the growing media frenzy or allure of stardom, but
the bare-knuckle challenge of leading a 16-piece big band with his rowdy guitar.

—Andy Ellis

• • •

You've recently returned to playing in a trio setting, with the '68 Comeback Special, after nine years of playing big-band music with the Brian Setzer Orchestra. How does that feel?

It's funny, because back in the eighties people used to ask me, "Don't you find it restrictive being in a three-piece rockabilly band?" Now they're saying, "Wow, it must feel really free to play in a three-piece rockabilly band again." This is more rock & roll. There's more space to fill, so I definitely play more.

You hit the big time as a rockabilly revivalist with the Stray Cats. How did you get into that style of music?

I was seventeen, and I was drawn by the power, the sheer magic, of rockabilly guitar. I don't know if those guys could read or write—I didn't care—but they sure could play. When I heard Cliff Gallup, *wow!* And have you heard "Rock n' Roll Ruby" by Warren Smith? That solo is genius!

Brian Setzer, 1998:
The power and magic
of rockabilly guitar.

So were those guys your inspiration?

My all-around guy was Eddie Cochran. I saw that album cover of his—the black-and-white one—and went, "Ah, that's me! I want to be like *that*. I want to play like him, sing like him, look like him." And then I started discovering the other guitar players. Cliff Gallup—I went, "Oh, my God, that's the guy." Then Scotty Moore! And so many players on those one-hit rockabilly records—I just fell in love with their sound.

Cliff Gallup had a pretty unorthodox way of picking with a flatpick and finger-picks. Did you try to incorporate his technique into your playing?

When I was learning, I wanted to flatpick. But I also wanted to play like Scotty Moore. I really couldn't do both, so I developed this way of tucking the pick into my palm so my thumb and fingers would be free. I knew those guys were using their thumbs and fingers, but I didn't know exactly how they did it. It was kind of like learning to ride a bicycle: One day I suddenly knew how to do it. I remember getting the melody going with my thumb; it was like, "Oh, man, I think I've got it!" I never gravitated to the really heavy rock that was popular at the time.

Was that because you found rockabilly more harmonically advanced?

Well, who did those rockabilly guys listen to? Back then, music was very regional, which probably explains why players picked up such different personalities—something that rarely happens today. Cliff Gallup came from Virginia, so what did he have?

Jazz coming down from New York on the radio, and country music coming up from the Deep South. He was right in the middle, so when he was growing up, he probably listened to Charlie Christian solos on Benny Goodman records and heard some Western swing, maybe Bob Wills and the Texas Playboys. Or cowboy jazz, like Jimmy Bryant—jeez!—or Billy Byrd. The rockabilly cats drew on everything.

What makes your playing unique?

I like to fingerpick jazz chords—nobody does that—and bring a rockabilly vibe into big-band voicings.

How did you develop your fondness for big-band jazz?

I've always loved big-band music. I grew up with that stuff. I'm from Long Island, and being from New York was great because I could cut class, go into the city, and hang around during the day with the models. When I was seventeen I started going into Manhattan with friends to see music—you know, the Ramones at CBGB's, that kind of thing. One Monday night we happened to stumble into the Village Vanguard with fake IDs. The Thad Jones/Mel Lewis orchestra was playing. I remember hearing them and going, "Wow, what a big, musical sound." It was as powerful to me as a guitar plugged into a big amplifier. I was blown away. So I made it a point to always go see Thad Jones/Mel Lewis on Monday nights. There would be twenty people in the audience—barely more than in the band. The musicians did it for the music. Those guys were playing for ten bucks or something, just because they love it.

When did you get the idea that you might be able to fit into that kind of a format and style?

My brother and I went to see Mel Lewis. I noticed that they didn't have any guitar player. I thought, "What a great idea if you could get a guitar player to *lead* a big band." The traditional big-band stuff is always with Freddie Green–style guitar. It's great, but it's at the back of the band. I realized that the electric guitar didn't make its mark until the fifties, which is when big band was dying out. So that sparked it. Getting from A to B was a whole other process.

> "I saw that Eddie Cochran album cover and went, 'Ah, that's me! I want to be like *that*."

How did you actually begin exploring the style yourself?

My neighbor, Michael Acosta, plays sax. He had a little jazz troupe. Some of his buddies recognized me and said, "Hey, come over and sit in with us"—kind of on the sly, not thinking I could keep up or read the charts. They had old Monk charts, Miles Davis—some pretty hard stuff that they were trying to get me with. I sat in with them, and they were like, "Gee, this guy's all right. He can play." So I became a regular in their quintet. [After a few months] I said to Michael, "What would you think about putting together a *rockin'* big band? We'll write brand-new charts." Michael said, "It'll never work. Working with seventeen guys is like trying to manage two baseball teams." I kept harpin' on him to the point where he gave in, sat down, and wrote a couple charts.

Where did you learn jazz voicings?

When I got my first guitar, I went through the Mel Bay book with a beautiful teacher, an old Italian gentleman named Mr. Scurti. He did amazing things for me. Like, I'd have a Little League game when I was supposed to be at a lesson. He would show up at the game in his Pontiac, and you know what? He'd wait for me. I'd get in his car and say, "I'm sorry, Mr. Scurti, I had a baseball game. I couldn't let the team down." And he wouldn't say anything; he'd just drive me home. Then he'd say, "*Now* you have lesson." Can you believe it? At that age, the fact that someone took the time to watch me, because he knew I had something, was more important than someone showing me how to play the most complicated chords. After Mr. Scurti took me through Mel Bay, I took jazz guitar lessons from another Long Island teacher, Ray Gogarty. He introduced me to all the chords I use today.

What's the key to being able to combine styles as diverse as rockabilly and jazz?

I can't say it enough: You have to learn how to read and write music. You don't even have to be fluent, but you'd be amazed at what learning all this stuff connects in your brain. Learning scales and chords and how to play jazz helps you connect the dots. Then you can start fingerpicking the jazz chords, or flatpicking some of the scales that are related to those chords.

How did shifting from the trio setting of the Stray Cats to a big-band setting affect your playing?

I've been forced to come up with some things that I definitely wouldn't normally do. Coming up with interesting solos against those chord charts was new stuff for me. There are no reference points for the guitar parts I create. I just had to take it as it comes. In the Stray Cats, when Lee Rocker played a *G* on his bass, I could play almost anything for a *G7*. Even a diminished run works fine. But in a big band, the horns are playing chords, so you have to be aware of each change as it flies by. There are some big, bad chords going on that I've got to play against, and if I play a line against the wrong chord, it's a wake-up call, believe me.

> "This is louder than any band I've ever been in."

Your guitar tone isn't that different from what you were doing with the Cats.

I basically kept my guitar sound the same; that's my tone.

Yet there's a vintage element to the sound too.

Here's the secret: At my urging, my drummer, Bernie Dresel, bought a 1940s Gretsch drum set with calfskin heads. When I heard them, I knew it was the sound I'd been looking for. Vintage drums don't go *tap-tap-tap*, like modern drums do—

they *thud*. But something was still bothering me. I told Bernie his cymbals didn't sound good, and he goes, "Well, they're new." So he found vintage cymbals, and it made all the difference in the world. I discovered that the sound of new drums interferes sonically with the slap bass, which has its own percussive click going on. Slap bass with old drums and a Gretsch guitar just smokes! For years I tried to get Slim Jim Phantom to use old drums in the Stray Cats, and he wouldn't do it. When I finally got Bernie to switch, it changed everything. Live, he uses new drums with calfskin heads.

What about your approach to playing in a big-band rhythm section?

The rhythm-section playing is my version of all that old rhythm-style playing—Django [Reinhardt] and Freddie Green stuff. We just turn it up a little louder than it should be in the mix.

How did you get such a high-energy sound on The Dirty Boogie?

I cut the rhythm section—guitar, slap bass, and drums—live. We went into the studio with all the horn charts written, so the three of us knew the arrangements. Everything had to be *now*—no overdubbed solos, none of that. If I ever second-guessed myself and thought, "Oh, I can do the solo better," and then tried to overdub it, it never sounded as good. There's something about the urgency of three guys rocking that you can't lose.

Did you sing too?

I would sing with the rhythm section to make sure the tempos were right and that everything fit. Later, we'd lose those vocal tracks, and I'd go back and re-sing my parts. We didn't waste time. Once we got the sounds we wanted, we would cut three or four tracks a day. We were done in five days.

Then you added the horns?

Right. After we finished the whole album as a three-piece, I sent the guys home and called in the horns. We moved the mics around—which, by the way, were vintage models—until we got a great big-band sound. It was like, "Ah, that's *it*."

Is it hard to be heard onstage over a wailing horn section?

This is louder than any band I've ever been in. It's *loud*. Those poor guitar players in the forties, trying to keep up with a big band on an acoustic guitar. Wow. There's no way you could ever solo. I've got to use two Fender Bassmans just to beat the band.

Vintage Bassmans?

They're the old, white, piggyback Bassmans from the early sixties. Billy Zoom, who used to play guitar in the band X, gets the heads running tip-top—totally stock, no hot-rodding. The original speakers are 15-watt Jensens, which just don't have enough power, so I replace them with Celestion Vintage 30s. However, I've got quite a few of the vintage Bassmans where I won't touch the speakers because the amps sound so nice.

Do you always use two Bassmans?

When I don't want to blast out the audience, one is loud enough. But in a big show, I'll use two.

In the studio too?

Yeah. I recorded *The Dirty Boogie* with two. I need the clarity. I don't want the chords to get too mushy. If you're cranked up too high, everything turns to mud.

Do you record with the Vintage 30s or the old Jensens?

Vintage 30s. With the horns, I need that power.

Tell me about your guitars.

I've been playing a Gretsch 6120—the Chet Atkins model—for years. It's got to be a '59—same year as me [*laughs*]. I tried a '58, and it sounded too solid, like a Gibson ES-335—nice, but not my sound. The '58s are too heavily braced; the top doesn't resonate enough. I looked inside, and there's tons of block bracing. In '59 Gretsch built the 6120 with just one block and two strips of wood. And it makes a *total* difference. Of course, nobody would notice that except a nut like me.

Do you have any special tricks or mods for your Gretsches?

We replace the bridge with a Gibson Tune-o-matic so you can adjust the intonation. And Rich Modica, my guitar tech, puts graphite in the nut and saddle slots. But you can use pencil lead; that's what I used to do. With a little lubrication, the Bigsby never goes out of tune.

> "Slap bass with old drums and a Gretsch guitar just smokes!"

Using the same gear, you get a wide range of tones on the CD, from fat and gnarly to clean and twangy. What's the secret?

That's down to just how hard I hit the strings—my attack. And I'm always making little adjustments on my amp. For something clean, like "Sleepwalk," I'll back the volume down to maybe 4½—just a touch, a quarter of a number. I'll never go past, say, 5½. That's as loud as I'll need to go. You know, guitarists always think it's about power—about being *loud*. That's where they make a mistake. It's not about volume; it's about what you do to get your tone. For instance, in the studio, I sometimes had two different echoes going at once, a different one through each amp, and it sounded *so* big. My guitar just filled up the whole room. Live, it's too complicated, but in the studio? *Wow.*

Now that you've gone back to trio playing, are you planning to retire the big band?

I'd like to continue doing both, if at all possible. A big band is expensive and a lot of work, but what a sound! I always dreamed about having a big band. Even with the Stray Cats, those horn parts were always in my head; I would just play them on guitar. That's why it's so hard to even think about giving up the big band.

You've had your big band since 1992. How do you feel now that swing bands are popping up all over and the world is finally coming around to your point of view?

When I first started, I was shaking people: "Listen to this! I know I'm not crazy; I know this is good. I don't know if it's going to sell a million records, but you've gotta appreciate that I can lead a big band with the guitar." I thought it was the coolest idea, but I just couldn't get people excited. This was a slow build—it took me six years— and I just kept our heads above water, but every gig got bigger and bigger. The trick, I suppose, is to keep the music going even after the trend passes and not become too retro with it. I'm not going to come out in a zoot suit, swingin' a chain and wearing a big hat. I want to keep it classy, yet still rockin'. Basically it's just good American music. We invented this stuff, and we have to be aware of it. It's so good musically that I can't see it going away.

THE EDGE

Battling the Guitar

Interviewed by Tom Nolan and Jas Obrecht,
Guitar Player, June 1985;
Darrin Fox, *Guitar Player,* January 2001

A ny time you talk to a guitarist who has influenced a generation of players, it's a big deal. Although I was a huge U2 fan and knew all the ins and outs of the Edge's technique and setup, the fact that he hadn't done any guitar press for nearly ten years made my interview an even bigger deal. Thankfully, the story turned out better than I could have ever hoped for, largely due to the fact that the Edge was one of the nicest, most knowledgeable and candid artists I've ever spoken with. He talked as openly about U2's first record as he did their latest one, and when he spoke of his famous Gibson Explorer (the same guitar he used on all early U2 recordings and recently brought out of hiding), you could hear the excitement in his voice. It's not always easy for artists to explain their creative process and what makes them tick. The Edge, however, has the ability to explain the source of his inspiration and, in the process, inspire others.

—*Darrin Fox, Associate Editor,* Guitar Player

• • •

How did you develop your style? It has so little relation to blues or jazz; it just …

… sort of exists [*laughs*]. I think it's that I've never really had any guitar heroes. All of the guitarists that I've liked have been total anti-hero stuff. I think of Neil Young: That guy gets so much feeling into his playing, but he's stumbling around a few notes. It means so much, but it's so simple and basic. Tom Verlaine was never an incredible virtuoso, yet he revolutionized guitar playing, as far as I was concerned. He suddenly said, "Look, you can do something different. You don't have to do the same thing. This

70

is nothing like anything you've heard before." There are bands to whom that is not an issue; it's not important for them to do anything new. But if you want to do something new, there is no reason why you shouldn't be able to. For us at our early stage, it was an important lesson. We've never as a group put up with anything that lacked that vitality, that originality. We've always dumped it if we felt it smacks of an era gone by or that it isn't musically relevant.

Is that why Achtung Baby, Zooropa, *and* Pop *are such departures for U2— because you were looking to keep your music fresh?*

Yeah. We were very inspired by what was happening in dance music and hip-hop. Technology has always been a very important dynamic in pushing music forward. You can point to almost every important development in music and see a technology that went with it—the fuzzbox launched rock & roll into the sixties. So for us, it seemed perfectly natural to be up to speed with the state-of-the-art technology happening in the dance culture. In that blend, we hoped we could hold on to the essence of what U2 is about. That's been, at times, a fine line you draw. We felt we crossed it during the making of the *Pop* record, and we had to bring things back a bit.

Did the more traditional band approach for the latest album, All That You Can't Leave Behind, *make you look at the guitar differently?*

Yes. It put a lot of emphasis back on the guitar—the parts and the sound. On the last few records I used the guitar principally to create textures that add light and shade. But on this album everything rested on the original band arrangement, so the guitar parts had to be in place *first.* I think the end result is our most "guitar" album since *Achtung Baby.*

But it also retains some of the electronic elements of Zooropa *and* Pop.

All That You Can't Leave Behind is not a roots record. We realized at a point during the *Pop* album that we were getting into musical areas that are not what we do best. As we delved more into the beat-driven sound, we had taken the sound of the *band* further and further away. The organic sound is what made us unique in the first place.

What dance influences carried over to the new record?

We were given a *huge* education in rhythm, pure and simple. Rock & roll started out as dance music, but somewhere along the way it lost its hips and became rhythmically simplistic. The emergence of hip-hop and dance culture has upped the ante in the rhythm department, and there's no going back. Listeners aren't going to accept lazy rhythms anymore.

Did you take a different tonal approach on the new album?

In most cases, the tones and treatments have been kept as simple as possible. In the past I would often use effects as a tool to inspire a different way of playing and not be a traditionalist. But in many cases on the new record, my tone is just guitar and amp. That's kind of new for me, and it was a real challenge. I discovered a whole new side of what I can do, which was really fun.

Does playing guitar come easily for you?

I battle with it. I don't necessarily enjoy it so much as I see it as a struggle and a fight. Because I very rarely rehearse, at first I'm at odds with the guitar, but this means that my mind is open to new ideas. I haven't formed ruts down the fingerboard by playing the same things. It's still very much unexplored territory. Maybe that's one reason why I don't feel that attached to my instruments. It's almost like I'm going to dominate them in some sort of way. I don't feel like they're part of me; they stand between me and something new.

> "I find it to be an ongoing challenge to keep the guitar from becoming too traditional."

Have you ever considered working to build your chops?

I'm almost scared to do some really serious practice because of what it might do. Whenever I start working on a song, I immediately try to forget everything, to empty my hands and head of anything that may be hanging over from another song or album. I try to approach it like, "This is the first time I've ever played a guitar. What am I going to do?" That's one way of getting straight through the conscious mind into the subconscious layer where the true creative spirit lies.

Do you imagine parts before finding them on the instrument?

Not actual melodies; they definitely tend to be a product of playing. My parts come generally out of exploration; they come from improvisation and accident. My strength is seeing them when they come out and capitalizing on them. I have quite a good ear for music, so when I hear something that interests me, I normally stop to develop it and bring it to a conclusion. So the original idea very rarely comes before I've actually started playing, but ideas for new sounds and new approaches to the guitar do come before I start. I very rarely follow conventional paths in any aspect of my playing or writing. In fact, that's probably one of the most important things about why I play like I do. For instance, if I feel I'm getting into some sort of rut, I do something really radical, like change the tuning of the guitar.

The Unforgettable Fire *shows evidence of that kind of exploration.*

Yes. See, I was experimenting a lot with damping my guitar strings, using felt or gaffer's tape over the strings near the bridge to give zero sustain. Using echo, I found some remarkable effects. The intro to "Wire" is a case in point: Having damped the strings with gaffer's tape, and using a bottleneck and an echo setting, I got this incredible sound. It sounded quite Eastern, but really bizarre.

Can you play conventional styles?

I could play in any style, but not to a very high standard. It would be no contest to put me against a fast player like Gary Moore or any of those guys; I could not even begin to do anything like that. At a very early stage of my career, I just decided that for me that was totally irrelevant. It may have thrilled listeners, but as far as I was concerned, that was something that had been done before and there was no need to repeat it. I'm more interested in what Joe Blokes down the road in this garage band is doing than, say, what the new Jeff Beck album is like. Not that I don't respect Jeff Beck, who's an incredible musician. But I think we've seen what he can do, and there's a lot of guitar players out there that we haven't heard.

You don't seem to play standard guitar chords very often.

No. I don't play proper guitar [*laughs*]. For a start, I avoid the major third like the plague. I like the ambiguity between the major and minor chords, so I tread a very fine line sometimes between the two. I tend to isolate the chords down to two or three notes and then octaves of the note—like for an *E* chord, I play just *B*'s and *E*'s, including my big *E* string.

What's your approach to playing harmonics?

I don't play them in any unusual way. For me, harmonics are approaching the most pure sound available to a guitarist. There's no frets involved, so the tone of the harmonic is … I mean, I love it. It's one of the nicest sounds you can get from a guitar. There's something about the purity of the signal from a harmonic that becomes such a big sound when it's treated well—very bell-like in many ways. I remember Steve Howe used to play harmonics when he was with Yes. I was interested by that sound because it was very delicate. They seemed like natural components for the sound of the group when I was putting together lines for our songs.

Did you ever go through a phase of playing long solos?

No. From the beginning, our music was very trim. The solos that I took were very short. And unlike what most guitar players were doing at that stage, they were quite melodic. I used to use a lot of harmonized strings, even in my solos—like droning, say, the *E* string against something I was doing on the *B* string. It had an interesting sound, twelve-stringish sometimes. I didn't use a distorted tone; it was very clean. And our music really needed more than just one-string solos of the blues variety. That sort of thing didn't work, and it also didn't interest me very much, because it was being done so well by other people.

You played quite a few solos on All That You Can't Leave Behind.

Sometimes a solo will present itself as an option—or even a necessity—and I'll happily take one. However, for the most part, I'm a minimalist at heart. If a song doesn't need a solo, I'm not going to force one into it. It's always the music that dictates what I play. I never want to feel that I'm playing anything gratuitous. I get off on finding the perfect tone for the perfect part.

So the songs that have solos were just begging for them?

I think they were. For instance, "Kite" originally didn't have a solo. We had the tune almost finished, but we weren't quite happy with it; it needed a twist. So we edited in a section, I plugged my '64 Gretsch Country Gentleman into a cool fuzzbox—an Ampeg Scrambler—and a Vox AC30, and I came up with a solo for it. It really made that part of the song come alive. That's a case in point, where the decision to do a solo came from the sense that something was missing in the tune. On this record, though, I often found myself simply enjoying the pure tone of the instrument. That's kind of new for me.

Why do you think you enjoy the natural sound of the guitar more now than twenty years ago?

I suppose since we came out of this period in the late seventies and early eighties when punk was happening, some of the punk ideals really struck a chord with us. Things like moving away from the rock aristocracy of the time were a big part of how I played then. I wanted to step away from the prototypical rock guitar thing, and making the guitar tones more abstract was a way to do that. But now it feels so fresh to really explore the natural tone of the guitar.

"Walk On" has some very classic Edge-sounding parts.

I mostly used a white [Gibson] Les Paul that I've had for a long time, through the AC30. The solo on that tune is my Gibson Explorer through the AC30.

Your old Explorer?

Yes. I used it quite a bit on this record. It's the same one I used for all of the first record and most of the first three tours.

"I never want to feel that I'm playing anything gratuitous."

What's so special about that guitar?

It just has this unique tone. In fact, I was surprised by how much the guys in the band enjoyed the sound of it. Adam [Clayton, bassist] in particular was delighted to see it out again. He said, "This thing sounds like nothing else on earth!" It's a pretty special guitar.

It sounds like guitar still excites you.

I find it to be an ongoing challenge to keep the guitar from becoming too traditional—which can happen to even the best ideas and the best styles. They eventually lose their fire and their ability to reach you because they get overused. I'm constantly trying to find uncharted territories by looking for sounds and tones that inspire new feelings and stop me from becoming too staid. Ironically, on this record that meant plugging a beautiful vintage guitar straight into a lovely vintage amp. That was pretty inspiring for me.

How would you advise young guitarists to keep their playing fresh?

One of the best ways of developing an individual style is to start writing songs. It was actually in the development of songwriting that my playing style came. I would credit the other members of the band as having quite an influence, because there was a lot of chemistry. Being with other musicians is a very healthy thing. If you do what a lot of players do—pick up a guitar and start playing lead blitzes, copying Eddie Van Halen or whoever else—you set off on a path that for me is a cul-de-sac. It's far more interesting to empty your head of anything anyone else has done and just start feeling sounds and making musical figures you can call your own. What I'm trying to say through my guitar is that everybody is different and can sound different. There's no reason on earth why guitar players should copy one another and end up sounding the same.

What are your goals? Is there anything you still hope to accomplish?

As a band, we have a kind of image of what the perfect album is. We're always striving toward that. Innovation and originality are important, but we're not interested in the idea of a cult music form for the chosen few. We're interested in music that has the power to touch everyone. We're always getting closer to it, but we probably will never attain that standard. In fact, it's not really important that we do. It's the trying that's important. It's almost an impossible standard to attain. It's like all your favorite groups rolled into one, with none of their faults. If we ever did make the album, we'd probably stop.

Have other artists achieved that level of perfection?

In moments, but those moments aren't really consistent. "Strawberry Fields Forever" might be a peak, or [Bruce Springsteen's] "Born to Run."

Is the guitar getting phased out of pop music?

Pop music is a strange thing. I can't say guitar will always be a part of pop, but I think that guitar music will always survive and have a particular place in contemporary culture. I can't see that going away. It's the instrument that has always been at the forefront of rock & roll, and it *defines* it.

What is it about the guitar that still resonates with people?

I think it may have something to do with it standing for freedom in some weird way, somewhat like the automobile has meant for freedom for people over the last century. Since the invention of blues and rock & roll, the guitar has inspired that kind of feeling in people. It probably always will.

Tom Morello

The Search for Noise

Interviewed by Matt Blackett,
Guitar Player, July 2000

I had many reason for wanting to interview Tom Morello. His ability to wrench new and different sounds from the guitar is amazing, his sense of the groove is huge, and his tone and feel with Rage Against the Machine bridge the gap between Van Halen–style riff rock and streetwise hip-hop like nothing else. I was aware of his penchant for political discourse and, as a knee-jerk Berkeley liberal, I was prepared to go down that road. What I found when I arrived at his Hollywood home, however, was a normal, friendly rock dude who, despite his Harvard education and social consciousness, cut his teeth on Kiss and Zeppelin records, just like me. We talked and joked and laughed for a few hours, and he proved himself to be a funny, articulate guitar freak who is refreshingly humbled by his status as one of the few true guitar heroes to emerge from the nineties.

—*Matt Blackett, Associate Editor,* Guitar Player

• • •

It's tough to turn on the radio without hearing rap metal. What sets Rage apart?

Well, from a rhythm guitar perspective, my influences are Zeppelin, Black Sabbath, and Deep Purple. Some of the bands that might share our hip-hop influences seem to come more from the Pantera/Metallica school.

What about from a lead guitar perspective?

A lot of bands still have that Nirvana aesthetic where guitar solos aren't cool. They're young enough that they didn't have to endure that gunslinger mentality of the mid-eighties, where it was "shred or get off the pot." I was immersed in that. I had to run those races, and that informs my playing a little differently.

Who inspired you to develop your playing beyond the simpler, post-punk level?

Randy Rhoads. It was his dedication. I had a Randy Rhoads poster that I would stare at when I was practicing four, six, eight hours a day. I got a real commitment to the instrument from him. I picked up the guitar because of punk rock—the Sex Pistols made me want to be in a *band*. Their music wasn't about castles and dragons and groupie-filled limos. There were these regular, working-class guys playing simple stuff that was as powerful as anything I'd ever heard. I remember thinking, "I could do this *tomorrow!*" And I did—I was in a band forty-eight hours after getting *Never Mind the Bollocks*. I couldn't play an *E* chord, but I was in a band. So I picked up the guitar because of punk rock, but I got the desire to excel at it from Randy Rhoads.

What other players proved influential to you?

When I was twelve, Jimmy Page gave me the desire to rock. He created this vibe that was so much bigger than the stifling little suburban town that I lived in. Hearing his music made me aspire to greater things. What I got from Liam Howlett [of Prodigy] is the way he looks at texture, repetition, and tone. I love the way he thinks about sonic possibilities and creating songs out of sounds. And when Rage formed, Dr. Dre's *The Chronic* album was happening. I had been noodling around with the toggle switch, going after more eccentric sounds. All of a sudden I was able to emulate the things I heard on his records, which made me dig his stuff even more. Listening to Dr. Dre pushed my playing away from the traditional guitar approach.

Other than your approach to guitar, what makes Rage different from other bands?

It's the chemistry. Long before we got together, many of these riffs were in existence, and I jammed them with some of alterna-rock's finest players. But none of the riffs sounded remotely as heavy as they did at the very first Rage rehearsal.

Let's talk about your latest album, The Battle of Los Angeles. *What's that sound that opens "Testify"?*

That's my Tele in dropped-*D* tuning with a slapback delay, through a [DigiTech] Whammy pedal set to a flat-seven. I'm rocking a wah pedal back and forth to give it a tornado sound. As I go through the sweep of the wah, it creates all these overtones that make the sound pretty hectic.

How many guitars are on that tune?

On the main riff there are two: the Tele on the neck pickup, and a Les Paul overdub. I played them both through my 50-watt Marshall. For the disco part in the breakdown, I used an Ovation Breadwinner through a Line 6 Flextone amp. At the store where I got my very first Kay guitar, the Breadwinner was the top of the line, and I said to myself, "I'll have one of those someday." I now own two.

Do you use a time-based effect on the intro to "Guerrilla Radio" to create that sixteenth-note pulse?

Yes, but it was put on after the fact. I got the idea after we had tracked it, but we didn't play to a click, so there was no way to do it mathematically. We ended up triggering a delay and a gate to every snare hit. Live, I use a tremolo pedal to get that sound.

Do you ever record to a click?

Occasionally, yeah. It's really up to our drummer, Brad [Wilk]. Some of the more straightforward hip-hop grooves, such as "Mic Check," require a steady beat from beginning to end, so we'll track those with a click. For the most part, we just get in the room and play. My favorite rock songs speed up and slow down—I like that push and pull.

> **"I still have a lot of Al DiMeola in me."**

What are the other tones in "Guerrilla Radio"?

The phased sound before the solo is an Electro-Harmonix Small Stone. The solo is two tracks. On one part I'm using a Talk Box and triggering the notes with the toggle switch. The second part is the Whammy pedal set one octave up, with a wah and the toggle switch.

You do a lot of that toggle-switch gating.

Yeah, like a DJ thing. With the exception of my Tele, all my guitars have two volume knobs, so I can have one all the way on, the other all the way off, and then toggle between them.

What other songs do you use that technique on?

On "Calm Like a Bomb" I do it for the verse part, but it's a little different. I played it on this cheap pawnshop guitar that is miswired so that no sound comes from the *middle* position of the three-position switch. That gives it a much more rapid, hummingbird-wing on/off effect. I'm hammering and pulling off between an open B and the B at the twelfth fret, hitting the toggle switch, and sweeping the Whammy pedal over a two-octave range. In fact, you can hear the same toggled lick *without* the Whammy pedal in the breakdown.

Is it tough to keep those parts in time?

I'm not overly concerned about playing in time [*laughs*]. For some parts, I can take lots of liberties with timing, like the solo to "Sleep Now in the Fire." For that, I'm standing right up against the amp and getting feedback. I use my left hand on the vibrato bar to change the pitch of the feedback, and I hit the toggle with my right so these wild pitches jump in and out randomly.

What's going on with the weird section in "Born as Ghosts"?

That's one of my favorite solos of all time! I wanted it to lurch between two wildly different sounds. The first noise I call "termites"; it was done with an Ibanez guitar. I brought Ibanez one of my guitars that had really screwed-up electronics and asked them to figure out how it made all the non-guitar noises. I said, "Bottle that and put it into a guitar for me." They managed to harness the cacophony of a broken pickup and put it on a knob, like an internal noise generator. I turned that on and rocked the wah to give the termites some "teeth."

That has to be the least-requested option of all time.
Oh, yeah! It's twisted, all right.

How do you make the more ethereal sounds?
I double-tracked them with a Whammy pedal. I envisioned a solo that would combine the chomping-termite noise with a smoother, more melodic part. During the mix, I "conducted" the solo by switching back and forth between the two recorded parts.

How do you come up with all your sound effects?
I hesitate to discuss the process because they really just fall from the trees. I stumble upon them, then I record them onto my little cassette recorder. I have this noise chart where I write down the settings so I won't forget them.

How did you get started making all these noises?
When I was nineteen some of my friends were aspiring filmmakers. One day we just said, "Let's make a movie today." So we did a trilogy of horror films, and I did the soundtracks. At the time I was all about the Phrygian mode and scales. That experience really pushed me into creating sounds. It also made me learn how to get the most out of my little four-track. That was a formative experience.

What draws you to the whole weird-noise thing?
It's a wide-open road. One you get off the beaten track of chords and notes, any noise can be its own microcosm of songwriting. There is a deep library of songs that go from *G* to *C*. There is not a deep library of songs that use a toggle switch and a wah pedal. The possibilities are limitless with just those two things. Add an Allen wrench that you use to bang on the strings, and your options grow exponentially. I love that.

> "My favorite rock songs speed up and slow down — I like that push and pull."

What about adding pedals to come up with sounds?
Guitarists come up to me all the time and say, "Dude! I've got this amazing new pedal that does all this stuff!" And I'm here with the same greasy pedals I've had for years, because I'm still finding a tremendous amount of variety in this small setup. I like that challenge.

What makes a tune heavy?

It has to do with how deep the groove is. It's *not* about playing fast or scooping mids. I mean, all my super-heavy riffs were tracked with single-coil pickups, so the heaviness has to come from the playing. It's a totally natural, instinctual part of the band. From the first note we played, we instantly sank into this really heavy, funky groove.

Even though it's natural, are you aware of what's going on with the groove— like playing on or behind the beat?

That's another thing I consciously try *not* to analyze, for fear of losing it! I'll tell you a story of how to ruin a perfectly good groove. One of our records was produced by GGGarth, who is a great guy. He decided that I play behind the beat, and that was unacceptable. So, without telling me, he did some sort of calculation—"Tom plays *this* many milliseconds behind the beat"—and edited my tracks in Pro Tools until they were dead-on. I came in, took one listen, and said, "What happened? The tracks don't sound like me or the band anymore. Change them back!" He did.

What did you learn from this?

That it's how the music breathes when we're in the same room that makes the groove happen. *That's* what makes it deep and heavy and funky. Doing some calculation to concoct perfect time only sterilizes the groove.

So you guys must record with everyone in the same room?

With very few exceptions, it's guitar, bass, and drums cutting basics in the same room—sometimes isolated, but most of the time not. Every mic bleeds into every other mic, and we always record to tape.

> "It's how the music breathes when we're in the same room that makes the groove happen."

What do dynamics contribute to your sound?

Dynamics are a big part of the heavy factor for us. They've become an innate part of the songwriting process—the quiet parts that build the tension that makes for this huge release that makes 100,000 kids jump up and down.

Can you tell in rehearsal which parts will make that happen?

I can tell when I'm in my living room with an acoustic guitar. I can *see* it.

You really hammer the downbeat in most of your riffs. How much of a "rule" is that?

It's not really a rule, but you'd be a fool to stray from it—it's good enough for James Brown! Even though the "one" is a simple concept, it's not always played with the kind of conviction that makes for great rock and funk. In all the music that's richly

Tom Morello,
1996: Exploring
the chemistry
of rage.

satisfying to me, the "ones" are huge and unrelenting, and you don't have to be a guitarist to feel them coming. Everyone knows when the "one" drops.

Some of the repeating figures on your records sound like they're looped.

Nope, no looping. I always play them.

Who do you feel is doing creative work these days?

I really like the latest Nine Inch Nails record. I think it's an achievement. It was done totally differently from how we record—it's *very* meticulous. I really respect how Trent Reznor works, because that kind of work ethic is just not there for us. We get a couple takes down and then it's off to the Playstation!

We asked that same question to Joe Satriani and John Scofield, and they both named you.

Wow. Man, that is just over the top. I'm humbled. I mean, I got [Satriani's] *Surfing with the Alien* when I first moved to California, and I listened to it religiously. For him to say that is just amazing.

*On "Take the Power Back," from your first record [*Rage Against the Machine*], you play a "real" solo with lots of notes. Could you see yourself ever doing that again?*

Oh, I am absolutely not ruling that stuff out. In my heart of hearts, I still have a lot of Al DiMeola in me!

So are you the rock ambassador to the hip-hop world, or the hip-hop ambassador to the rock world?

That's interesting. Because we're a rock band with electric guitars—something you will rarely hear on an urban station—we're often new to the hip-hop bands we tour with, like Wu-Tang, Gang Starr, and Public Enemy. When those bands finally hear us, they're won over. So I guess we, as a *band*, are sort of rock ambassadors. I don't think hip-hop needed any help getting into the suburbs, though. It's done a pretty good job on its own.

You used to binge-practice on DiMeola and Yngwie Malmsteen licks, and then you went and did your own thing. What do you say to kids who use you as their starting point?

It depends on what your goals are. Guitar players start playing because they like other guitarists, and there's absolutely nothing wrong with emulating them. It's very satisfying. I remember the afternoon I could finally play the solo to "Detroit Rock City"—that was a great day! But if you want to be an artist with your own voice on the instrument, you've got to go after *that*. I discovered something after digging a big trench trying to follow in the footsteps of players I liked: The very thing that drew me to them in the first place was the fact that they were unique. It was their *personality* that made the music interesting. Having said that, I do hear a lot of bleeps and bloops that I recognize, but that's cool. It's a great privilege to be an influence.

Do you feel any added pressure or responsibility now that you are an influence?

The only responsibility is to be true to yourself—to make music you really believe in.

2

KEYBOARD

A t its inception, *Contemporary Keyboard* had a clear and simple purpose. It was a magazine by keyboard players for keyboard players—all styles, all levels, all instruments with keyboards on them. In short, we were to keyboardists what *Guitar Player* was to guitarists. In 1975, that meant we covered jazz, rock, classical, fusion, pop, avant-garde, zydeco, and anything else you could think of as played on accordions, pianos, organs, synthesizers, Clavinets, telharmoniums, and beyond. In the early days, we didn't have a direct competitor, so we were able to write about some of the wildest experimental music of the twentieth century. But whether we were covering John Cage's prepared pianos or Wendy Carlos's modular synthesizers, it was the music made on those instruments that mattered most.

While we didn't have direct competition, there were other music mags of the day whose coverage of keyboard playing served as our guide of what *not* to do. *Rolling Stone, Circus, Hit Parader*, even the venerated *Down Beat* all wrote about some of the same artists we did, but they rarely explored the technical nitty-gritty, and when they did they mostly just brushed the surface. Our goal was to dig deeper, to provide keyboardists with hardcore how-to details, to print accurate transcriptions of legendary solos, to discover both the hows and the whys.

By 1981 we'd dropped the "Contemporary" from our name, which meant we lost our nickname—*CK*—but we never lost our drive to stay as contemporary as possible. When the technology of keyboard playing went ultra high-tech—first with MIDI, then with digital audio, always with computers—so did we. But even as our coverage of music technology increased, we never took our eyes off the artists behind that machinery. Which is why, from our first issue, with its cover story on Chick Corea, to the latest editions, the people who make music remain at the heart of what *Keyboard* does best.

—Dominic Milano
Editor, Keyboard, *1985–1994*

CHICK COREA
The Joy of Creation

Interviewed by Tom Darter, *Contemporary Keyboard,*
September/October 1975, *Keyboard,* July 1983;
Robert L. Doerschuk, *Keyboard,* July 1988;
Greg Rule, *Keyboard,* November 1995

Throughout my seventeen years at *Keyboard* I had the pleasure of getting together with Chick Corea on maybe five or six occasions. Still, the encounter that stands out most in my memory took place before I came to the magazine. I was maybe twenty-one years old and scuffling around L.A. in search of work. One night I found myself at Doug Weston's Troubadour, where Chick's visionary quartet Return to Forever was headlining. (The opening act was comedian Scatman Crothers.) I was, of course, blown away, but I had the moxie to hang out after the show and strike up a conversation with Corea. We talked for about five minutes about his music and my dreams. His open, friendly attitude was laudable, though certainly not unique; there are plenty of good people in music. But what I remember to this day was that he grabbed a napkin, wrote down his address and phone number, and urged me to stay in touch. In the months that followed, while I was on the road with a cheesy lounge band, playing Ramada Inns and USO shows, Chick and I corresponded; I wrote about my frustrations with the gig, and he answered every letter immediately with words of support. Who knows how many other young players he was encouraging at the same time? He was, and he remains today, a rare spirit.

—*Robert L. Doerschuk*

• • •

How did you begin in music?

I got started very easily and naturally. When I was born I came into an environment with musicians and records around. My father had a band, a jazz-like band playing Dixieland for dances, but very nice music. He was into bebop at the time, and he had a stack of 78s. The music of Dizzy Gillespie, Charlie Parker, and Billy Eckstine used to be on all the time. By the time I was four years old I was playing piano, and my father was teaching me and showing me how to read and write music. That made for a musical, fun, aesthetic kind of environment for me. As a matter of fact, I remember the shock I experienced when I started going to school in the first and second grades, because I thought every kid was like that, and then I found out that my friends were in homes where they weren't supposed to be doing things, where they had to kind of sneak around. I never had to live that way. So the more I grew up, the more I realized that I was blessed with a great set of parents.

> "The amount of money people give you will be a reflection of how much confidence they have in what you're giving them. And their confidence will be a function of how honest your product is."

When did you start really digging into classical repertoire?

Ever since I was around eight years old I've been involved to one degree or another with classical music. There was one period early on where I was studying with a classical pianist, and he introduced me to traditional piano literature—the music of Bach and Beethoven. I got into classical music that way.

Do you remember being driven and focused on music back then?

Focused, yes. Driven, never. I think when someone pursues with persistence a direction, it gets interpreted as insanity or something [*laughs*]. But from very early on I fell in love with music and everything about it—the piano, and then the trumpet, and then the drums, and specifically improvised music and jazz. By the time I was, I don't know, in fourth, fifth, or sixth grade, my life was immersed in music. Going to school was kind of a vague background to the whole thing. I did enjoy hanging out with my friends when I was small, and I had some baseball partners. I used to really like baseball a lot. I didn't really practice a lot when I was young, but I spent a lot of time *listening* to music.

What about when you were younger?

I did a hell of a lot of hard practicing early on. There was one period of five or six years where I was at the keyboard from three to eight hours a day, some days longer than that, really hitting it. I spent a lot of time with all different kinds of scales and arpeggios and finger exercises. Then I would take a classical piece and begin to practice it, and if I ran into a passage I couldn't play, I'd find some drills for it. For instance, if there was a passage that had playing of thirds in one hand, I'd either make up an exercise or find one that dealt with playing thirds, and practice it. The classical literature really helped to show me what problems could exist in playing.

Did you consider yourself exceptionally gifted at that time?

My experience is that, first of all, I know that each individual's perception of infinity, of what may be the supreme moving factors of life, is very individual and different, no matter what they might name their religion. My own sense is that individuals have different dynamic drives and different amounts of life in them as a given quantity.

But sometimes you see a child prodigy, and it makes you think …

That part of it is not so much of a mystery to me, because it's not a new idea that a human being is not a one-lifetime thing. I think it's a real small view of life to think that any individual just kind of appears and then disappears at the end of one lifetime. Seventy years? Give me a break. I really believe that the spirit is an immortal, always-living thing, and that we've lived through lots of lifetimes. This way, we pick up experience. As far as our memories of previous lifetimes go, I mean that's pretty crapped out, but I really believe that abilities exist within all of us that are just part of our track, part of our experience. Whether they're available to us or not is really the trick. In a more practical way, I do find that no great things are achieved in huge, large strides. They're all achieved in very gradual, daily, persistent learning and growth and work.

There came a point when you moved beyond the old repertoire and became interested in more experimental contemporary music.

Yeah, for sure. [Karlheinz] Stockhausen mostly. I listened to a lot of piano music by Stockhausen, John Cage, and a number of others.

How do you feel about that music now?

Well, I haven't come across Stockhausen's latest efforts, but I think he's an incredible artist and composer. His kind of creation has a place, and the place it has is the place it has taken in life. The main difference between the way I want to approach my life and the way it appears that Stockhausen is doing it is that I'm more concerned with the priority of people and the effect I create on them with my art form rather than with the art form itself. The art form isn't precious to me. It could be anything: It could be electric or acoustic, fast or slow, consonant or dissonant, simple or difficult, or anything. What I'm trying to obtain is a genuine feeling between people. You have to have something inside that you'd like to show someone. When you put that into sound, then it becomes music. If you eliminate the idea of sending an idea from one person to another, then it really becomes abstract, and I can't understand it.

Do the increasingly technological aspects of creating music make it harder for listeners to hear that idea despite the distractions of all the bells and whistles?

Look, all the devices and techniques are very interesting to me. I'm a musician, so I have a lot of fun finding new tools and seeing how I can use them. But as interesting as all these developments are, it's a mistake to speak only in those terms without in

Chick Corea, 1985: Daily, persistent learning and growth.

some way discussing the purpose of art and how these tools can be used to create different emotional impacts on people. How do you use music? Do you inspire people? Do you make them feel good? Do you make them feel bad? Do you soothe them? Do you make them feel like creating? Do you put them to sleep? These questions never get dealt with, and I think they should. To show that any art form is a communications medium is something that must be done from the very beginning. From day one, before a person learns to play a scale, he must know that there is some reason for it, even if just to have fun with himself. Unless there's some talk about the fact that art is communication, the idea gets missed. I know that for me it did. I needed to have my coat pulled, so to speak.

Why?

I just wasn't interested in what people thought of my music. For a long time, I didn't care. It's okay, I guess, but it was kind of limiting. I would take the pursuit of technique to the point where I was feeling frustrated. I was learning techniques, but I felt that I was walking on a treadmill. I mean, I would pursue the techniques of art and not really have too much understanding of how the spirit and communication of art went along with it. I remember in my early days being very shy onstage—actually scared of audiences. I handled it by kind of ignoring the audience—not really wanting to see them there, and I concentrated all my effort on the space right in front of me.

How did you get past that attitude?

The thing that pulled my coat was reading L. Ron Hubbard's *Dianetics* in 1968. That really opened me up to looking at life in a slightly different way, by becoming aware of the fact that communication does exist between people. It's such a basic thing. It made me start to look at how I could take the technical skills that I was learning and that I enjoyed so much, and make them have some kind of relation to audiences, who in the end are the receipt points of what you do with music. Hubbard really opened me up to the human race as a social communicative, co-surviving unit, and I began to see art that way. The fact that I create something, or have something that I want to play, can't ever be divorced from the fact that it means nothing until I bring it to someone. I mean, it doesn't mean *nothing*, but it has a very different meaning when it's only in my head than when I finally put it on a record or play it for people. To me, the ultimate artistic experience is performing live, and he opened me up to that kind of thing.

Some people see performance primarily as a promotional activity for the album.

What an awful thought. I cringe at the idea of an artist thinking like that. Recordings serve a certain purpose in life. I have a record collection, and it's a fun thing to listen to recordings. But it's gotten so out of proportion; it tends to make the listener forget about real life. When you make music live and listen to others making music live, that's where the inspiration comes from. You see the act of creation going on right at that moment. A recording is a secondary thing. It's kind of like a document of an event. You can get quite creative in the studio, but the whole record business went crazy with it.

Have recordings made it harder for listeners to appreciate live music?

That is one of the problems of recordings, and radio as well, in society. A guy can just sit at home and play a record or turn on the radio without putting out the effort or the money to go where the music is. But that makes us kind of lazy. And it's not as much fun. You're not as close to the joy of creating.

> "It's a real small view of life to think that any individual just kind of appears and then disappears at the end of one lifetime. Seventy years? Give me a break."

Some people must certainly be tired of going to concerts to hear a band replicate a recording that listeners have already heard repeatedly.

That's an interesting subject, and an important one too: how music gets programmed. That's one of the big subjects in the classical world. How much should you stick with the old classics? How much new music should you play? It's all really just a problem of communication. For me, it comes down to a question of how to remain in rapport with my environment—meaning audiences, real people, and real life; how to continue to be personally interested in my work and have fun as an artist; and how to continue to expand my own horizons as an artist. I want to keep finding new ways of looking at art, and bring these new ways to people through my concerts. It becomes a question of balancing all this out, and there can be a million ways of doing it. You can completely lose an audience, or lull them into a soggy nostalgia, but the effect I like to produce is to create a carpet of relaxation and friendliness based on enough familiar factors to get people grounded and comfortable, then just to play around with lots of experiments and new ideas, always while maintaining some kind of rapport. It doesn't fulfill me to play something that people don't understand, or do something that shocks them in some way, like killing a chicken onstage.

So how do you present experimental music onstage without losing your audience?

My experience is that once that carpet of rapport is set up, and the audience has decided that you're a friend, not a foe, then they're willing to receive any sort of communication. At that point I've found that I can't do anything that's so out that they won't accept it. If the idea is presented with the joy of creation, rather than being forced on them, it's readily accepted. That was the idea that Return to Forever was based on: that normal people can enjoy high-quality experimental music.

> "It doesn't fulfill me to play something that people don't understand, or do something that shocks them in some way, like killing a chicken onstage."

How much of your interest in music as communication stems from a realistic interest in making money by playing commercially?

That's one of the perennial paradoxes. When you create something, it's a particular kind of flow that's very unworldly. It doesn't have to do with the usual things of day-to-day survival. You do it for what tend to become mystical reasons—but really there's no reason. You don't need a reason to make music. Asking *why* you make music is asking the wrong question, because the only answer, which is not really an answer, is that you do it because you like it. It's fun, and you like doing it. It sounds simplistic, but that really is the reason. So that's there, and on the other hand you have the music business, which has got very much to do with day-to-day living and survival and money and agreements and everything else that surrounds that. So there's always a paradox: How do you plug one thing into the other? If you just create and don't ever put yourself into the world to play it on a piano to another person, or make a record or something like that, it doesn't ever become a living art form, because no one ever hears it. My own view is that the person who is creating the art form has to get the people who are contributing to getting it out into the world—the management people—to understand or be in empathy with what the artist is doing, to understand that the artist is doing it just because it's a lot of fun. Then they can get creative from the administrative end, in thinking about how to get the art form heard and experienced by other people. It's that simple. If the intention remains to being of service, like wanting to flow out, and not one of money or personal gain or duty, then you've got it licked. But the world is topsy-turvy in that most of the motivation for working or creating is money. It's a lower motivation, and those two motivations are always knocking into one another.

Isn't there a median level where you know the things you want to do and realize that money is necessary in order to do them?

That to me would be less optimal, because that would be, to some degree, letting the need for money influence what you create. Optimally, what it would be is that you're doing exactly what you want to do, and then you're also making some money and surviving. In fact, if you continue to do it that way you'll make more money, because the amount of money people give you will be a reflection of how much confidence they have in what you're giving them. And their confidence will be a function of how honest your product is. If you're a baker, and you bake bread that tastes good and has good ingredients, the people who buy it are going to develop confidence in you. But if your product is worth shit, eventually you won't be able to get any money for it. In a weird way, there's a direct relationship between creating honestly, without a money motivation, and making money. The less you think about making money, and the more you think about just outflowing and being of service and having a great product, the more money you'll make, because those things create confidence in people.

KEITH EMERSON

Star Power

Interviewed by Dominic Milano,
Contemporary Keyboard, October 1977,
and Robert L. Doerschuk,
Keyboard, June 1992, October 1995

Lean and leather-clad, Emerson radiated charisma through his rakish good looks and gravity-defying antics onstage. He swigged regally from bottles of brandy, soared like an acrobat up and over his instrument, even hurled his Hammond L-100 to the ground and attacked it with a dagger. But he also played, with an exceptional technique and abundant references to classical repertoire. In our frequent encounters away from the stage, Emerson was a good guy to hang with: funny, irreverent, a perceptive listener. Still, it's those memories of glorious performances with Emerson, Lake & Palmer that endure. No other keyboardist has yet stolen the spotlight with the swagger and joy he achieved with that tempestuous, often pretentious, and always awesome trio. In fact, it's safe to say that of all the keyboard players we've seen, only one—Keith—qualifies as a real, true rock star.

—Robert L. Doerschuk

. . .

How did you develop the aggressive stage persona that would become your trademark with the Nice and ELP?

The whole thing about the organ routine actually started when I was with a band called the VIPs. We were playing in Hamburg, Germany. The band members had befriended the professional ladies there. I kept to myself, though; I was still very naïve, and I didn't want any part of that. The main hooker—her name was Bloody Mary, a very nice lady—saw how I was feeling, so she gave me a Quaalude and said, "This will cheer you up, darling." I took it, and I was awake for three nights. I offered to drive the band all the way through Germany to the next gig in France. During the course of that drive I crashed the vehicle, almost ruining all the instruments. We ended up playing this club somewhere in a vineyard. All the farmers there were getting really drunk. This fight broke out. I was watching it and going, "Yeah, this is great! Go for it!" I started smashing the organ. The reverberation unit was crashing, so I got on top of it and started going completely nuts. The next thing I realized was that the fight had stopped in the audience and they were all looking up at me, going, "What the fuck?"

Well, I slept all the way back to England because I was so knackered. When I woke up, the band was looking at me, and they said, "You've got to do that again." I said, "Do what?" "That great stuff you did in France." "You've got to be kidding. I'm not doing that in England. They're too conservative." So we played this little club, I think it was in Manchester. There was only a handful of people there, but the band was looking at me, going, "Come on, do it again. You know, what you did." So I did it. And everyone in the audience was looking at me with their mouths wide open.

Why did you adopt such an extroverted style?

I guess I've always been attracted to the unconventional. When I was ten or eleven, my father turned me on to the fact that Lionel Hampton actually played the piano with just two fingers. I thought, "That's neat!"

Not that this influenced your technique.

Right. But as far as that early stage act went, there was an organ player in London by the name of Don Shin. I don't know where he is today. He was a weird-looking guy, really strange. A very twittery sort of character. He had a schoolboy's cap on, round spectacles—really stupid. I just happened to be in this club when he was playing. The audience—you know, there were a lot of younger chicks down at the Marquee Club—were all in hysterics, giggling and laughing at him. No one was taking him seriously. He'd been drinking whiskey out of a teaspoon and all kinds of ridiculous things. He'd played an arrangement of the Grieg Concerto, and I'd already played things like that with the Nice—the *Brandenburg* and all [from *Ars Longa Vita Brevis*]. So my ears perked up. Somebody else was doing these things, playing it really well. And he got a fantastic sound from the [Hammond] L-100. But halfway through he sort of shook the L-100, and the back of it dropped off. Then he got out a screwdriver and started making adjustments while he was playing. Everyone was roaring their heads off laughing. So I looked and said, "Hang on a minute. This guy has got something." I guess seeing Don Shin made me realize that I'd like to compile an act

> "This fight broke out. I was watching it and going, 'Yeah, this is great!' I started smashing the organ. The next thing I realized was that the fight had stopped and they were all looking up at me."

Keith Emerson, 1984:
"I hate the idea of being
static."

from what he did. He and Jimi Hendrix were controlling influences over the way I developed the stage act side of things.

There was a story going around that Hendrix almost became a member of Emerson, Lake & Palmer.

Well, it was one thing that was suggested by [drummer] Mitch Mitchell when the band was first forming. At the time, Greg [Lake, bassist] and I were talking with Mitch about joining us. He was happy with the suggestion, and he said, "Well, I'm seeing Hendrix tonight. Maybe we could ask him to join too." Mitch said Hendrix thought a lot of my playing, and I told him the feeling was mutual. I thought it would be fantastic, although I was a bit skeptical about it. I thought Hendrix might take the attention away from me—I'm a bit of an egomaniac. If Hendrix had been interested, though, I'd have given it a go.

Were there any other guitarists you would have invited into the band?

The only one I really wanted to work with after David O'List [of the Nice] was Steve Howe. He came and auditioned and was very talented. We begged him to join. He hemmed and hawed at that. The first day he said yes, but then he said he had an offer to start his own band and couldn't join us. I don't know whatever happened to that. He disappeared for two or three years. Next thing I heard, he was playing with Yes. He was the only guitar player I wanted to work with, and I got so used to working without one that I was dubious of getting back and working with guitar players after that. I was willing to take the risk with Hendrix, though.

The guitar is so central to rock mythology. It must have been an uphill fight to implant the idea of the keyboard as sexy and dynamic.

Well, it wasn't easy. A guitar weighs less than twenty pounds, whereas with the organ you're looking at an instrument that weighs 350 pounds, and you've got to make it look as if it's part of your body. I hate the idea of being static, but the keyboard player is permanently locked into that position. That's why I wanted to get inside the piano, brush the strings, stick Ping-Pong balls inside.

The presence of a keyboard onstage creates an anticipation of conflict between the player and the immovable object.

That's why it's always pissed me off when I'm asked to be photographed at the keyboard. What can you do, put your arm around it like this? [*Emerson poses thoughtfully, chin in hand and elbow on imaginary piano, then laughs.*]

Describe your first gig with the Nice.

That was at the Windsor Jazz and Blues Festival. We were backing P.P. Arnold; she was a backing singer with Ike and Tina Turner, and she managed to secure a solo deal with Immediate Records. Her first single was "The First Cut Is the Deepest." She kind of rescued me from the VIPs when she asked me to form a band to back her. That was the Nice. We were allowed a thirty-minute spot of our own at the festival before we had to back her onstage. After playing the festival, the Nice managed to secure their own spot in a tent outside from the main stage. The outcome of that was that we were invited to do a residency at the Marquee Club. That was our turning point. Immediate Records was there, and they signed us up just on the strength that we had a residency at the Marquee Club.

What kind of material were you playing?

It was a mixture, a mishmash of things: a little bit of jazz, a little bit of blues, whatever we felt like doing. We did "Billy's Bag," a Billy Preston tune. We did things like "A Day in the Life." We did really weird stuff, like "Aries the Fire Eater," from some sort of astrology album that we'd gotten from America.

How did the music press respond to the idea of a rock band led by a keyboard player?

They welcomed it. You have to understand that English radio wasn't as formulated as it is now. You'd have the BBC dance orchestra in the studio, playing the latest Beatles hit live. Then they'd slip on a record. It might be Petula Clark singing "Downtown." But if you were very lucky, they might be risqué and play a Jimi Hendrix recording. It was wide open.

Is there a period you might point to as the glory years of rock keyboard?

The peak period, for me, was at the end of the sixties and the beginning of the seventies. The record companies allowed you free license to go into the studio and record exactly what you wanted to do. I hope the wheel will come around full circle, although I don't see that happening yet. Maybe that's because you don't find presidents at record companies anymore like Ahmet Ertegun. You have to respect a guy who has so much knowledge. He worked with people like Charlie Parker, Meade Lux Lewis, and Erroll Garner.

> "I had a need to get this sound. I wanted it to be big. I wanted the keyboard player to be out there in front, bigger and stronger than any of the Hendrixes."

You seem to have retained a respect for tradition in music. A lot of rock artists are much more iconoclastic.

Yeah. That's a shame. You've got to know the history and how your instrument came to be. That's why, when I hear someone copying me, I feel like telling them, "Don't listen to me. Listen to what I listened to. That's the only way you're gonna get the whole story."

The problem is that your style is so distinctive that, if one is influenced by what you do, it would be difficult to avoid the impression of imitation.

But how it came about is what matters. I had a need to get this sound. I wanted it to be big. I wanted the keyboard player to be out there in front. I wanted him to be bigger and stronger than any of the Hendrixes.

What was the first song you recorded where you felt you accomplished that, where you made the keyboard parts as strong as you would like them to be?

Without a shadow of a doubt, "Rondo," on the *Thoughts of Emerlist Davjack* album. I remember leaving the studio thinking, "My God, where did *that* come from?" Just the solo, on its own, is probably the only solo that would have been suitable for that cut, and it was totally improvised. I always wanted to achieve an orchestral sound, even on the limited equipment I had then. If I wasn't hearing exactly what I wanted at the time, as there was nothing available to play it on, I adapted. The [Yamaha] GX-1 was a turning point in that regard. It was like the Moog, but you could play chords on it. It took a while for the audience to accept the change in the sound it brought. I remember when the *Works* album came out. The main criticism was, "Why isn't he playing much Hammond organ anymore?" But I would never have even wanted to attempt something like [Aaron Copland's] *Fanfare for the Common Man* on the Hammond organ. It would have sounded ridiculous.

Where did you get your interest in arranging classical themes for a rock setting?

Simple reason: I like the tunes. I want to play these tunes, but I want to play them in a way that's acceptable to our audience—and will stimulate new interest in the original. You know, I started doing this back in the sixties, and that was my intention. But obviously, since that time, audiences have become far more perceptive [and] intelligent. One doesn't really have to do that now. I think people are going for classical music as much as for any other form. I don't want to be insulting the public's intelligence by saying the reason I'm playing *Fanfare for the Common Man* is because I want them to listen to the original. That may have been the case years ago, but since then it's become part of what people expect of me. My music has been tagged with the label "classical rock," which I guess is okay, but it's not a term that I want to really like.

What would you call it?

I guess it *is* classical rock [*laughs*]. It's playing classical music with a definite meter behind it. That sounds nicer. I call it playing classical music with the focus on the meter, a straight, rigid meter, one that's different from what the composer originally intended. But we only develop pieces that seem to demand that sort of treatment.

Your point is that you don't look on this source material as classical per se.

Right. It's pure music. It doesn't have to be classical. It could be a piece by Bob Dylan or the Beatles. I like to set myself the challenge of trying to draw out different qualities from the music. I even get a lot of fun from arranging Hoagy Carmichael; I did an arrangement of "Skylark" that I rather like. I also did an arrangement of Charlie Parker's "Au Privave," which is based on a bebop line, but I did it with the left hand playing counterpoint to the upper line. I certainly wouldn't get hold of a piece of classical music and really adulterate it. There are too many examples of people mucking around with classical music.

> "When I hear someone copying me, I feel like telling them, 'Don't listen to me. Listen to what I listened to. That's the only way you're gonna get the whole story.'"

The main difference between working with classical themes and, say, material by Dylan or the Beatles is that orchestral compositions suggest far more possibilities for creative treatment in terms of texture.

That's right. But to tell you the truth, when I first heard the original Prokofiev [ballet] *Romeo and Juliet*, what struck me about this particular music was the similarity between it and the way that Jimi Hendrix started "Purple Haze." The rhythm was so similar that I was sure I could make it work with the Prokofiev. Amazingly, you don't have to force too many changes to make it happen. It works quite naturally, the same as the shuffle rhythm works with *Fanfare for the Common Man.* [Emerson's arrangement of *Romeo and Juliet* can be heard on the ELP album *Black Moon.*]

When did it seem to you that the great years of rock keyboard were waning?

I may have had some premonition of it when we did *Brain Salad Surgery* and we used the Moog [modular synthesizer] as a sequencer. That was my first contact with the fact that you could actually walk away and have your instrument play on its own.

You suspected even then that this might be exploited by musicians who hadn't put in the time to develop their performance technique?

Yes, exactly. Then, of course, when the eighties came along, you got bands like Soft Cell going onstage and not disguising the fact that they're going *bink, bink, bink* with one finger. I mean, Lionel Hampton used one finger, but …

The eighties bands were adapting a punk attitude to the music technology of their time. Was that hard for you to accept?

No, it wasn't hard. In fact, if ELP had felt stronger or more positive as a unit, we probably would have ridden through the whole punk thing. Everybody says that punk threatened us, but it didn't. I really liked the Sex Pistols, because they were only doing what I had always done. People have this image of ELP being this conservative, polite band. Wrong! The Sex Pistols had nothing on ELP.

Those two sides of your music, the punk attitude and the respect for tradition, don't fit easily together.

But I think they do. We were three very competitive individuals. If I did something outrageous, then Carl [Palmer] would want to spin around on the drums. That's probably what pushed the band to the incredible peak of playing that we achieved.

Certainly ELP was a more balanced band than the Nice, in that you and Carl were able to give as well as you could take in complex arrangements.

That's right. There was a feeling that each of us had met his match. Carl would practice all the time. The thing that amazed me about Greg was that he never did. I never saw him sit down with his bass and practice a line. But back in those days I couldn't wait to get onstage. It was like, "I'm gonna show these guys. They're gonna eat their hearts out when they see me play." I remember Rick Wakeman watching me from the wings, and I thought, "Okay, Rick. Watch *this!*"

Do you write out those kinds of arrangements at the keyboard?

I don't need to. A lot of my best pieces were done away from the keyboard. The *Five Bridges Suite* with the Nice was written coming back from Ireland. I put my head against the window and heard the droning of these two turboprop engines. There was the fifth sounding, and I wrote part of that *Five Bridges Suite* listening to that drone.

Did you have manuscript paper to work with?

Not at all. I drew it up on an airsick bag.

RAY MANZAREK

Waiting for the Nubians

Interviewed by Robert L. Doerschuk,
Keyboard, February 1991

T he sixties marked the birth of modern rock keyboard, as a new generation of players stepped up to their electric portable instruments or planted themselves behind massive Hammond organs. Despite the differences between the reedy whine of the Farfisa and Vox machines and the meaty, muscular growl of the Hammond B-3, almost all of these artists were into playing aggressively. Only Ray Manzarek was different. His work with the Doors was a revelation: Rather than crank up the Leslie and jam down the volume pedal, he created long, sensuous lines that slithered from within the music or wafted aromatically through Jim Morrison's steamy, hallucinogenic vocals. When I met Manzarek at his home in Beverly Hills, the sixties were long gone; only a block or two away, Rodeo Drive teemed with shoppers more concerned with breaking out credit cards than breaking on through to the other side. Yet in his airy living room, with light streaming through tall windows and illuminating his collection of handsome framed prints, Manzarek hinted frequently at his unrepentant commitment to psychedelia; with conspiratorial whispers and sly glances, he made it clear that the Revolution in music and lifestyle that he helped pioneer is far from over.

—*Robert L. Doerschuk*

• • •

From your work with Jim Morrison in the Doors through your productions of the L.A. punk band X and on to your duo performances with Michael McClure, poetry seems to be a constant thread in your music.

If you're working with words, it's got to be poetry. I grew up with [the books of Jack] Kerouac. If he hadn't written *On the Road*, the Doors would never have existed. Morrison read *On the Road* down in Florida, and I read it in Chicago. That sense of freedom, spirituality, and intellectuality in *On the Road*—that's what I wanted in my own work.

How do you attain those elements in music?

Well, let me tell you one interesting story from Kerouac. There's one section in *On the Road* where he goes into a bar, and there's a quartet with a saxophone—maybe somebody like Gene Ammons, with that big, fat sound. Kerouac listens to the music a bit, and later he writes, "He had it that night. And everybody in the club knew he had it. That was what I wanted to get." I'm reading this around 1957 and '58, and I think to myself, "He had it? Had what? What did he have? And how did everybody in the club know he had it? What is 'it' anyway?" I never understood what "it" was until the Doors got together for their very first rehearsal. We played "Moonlight Drive." I showed Robbie [Krieger] the very simple chord changes, he put his bottleneck guitar on, we smoked a little cannabis, as people were wont to do in 1965 or '66, and we started to play. By the end of the song, man, it had all locked in. I said to John, Robbie, and Jim, "Man, I've played for a long time, but I never actually played music until right now." Then I said to Jim, "You know that section of Kerouac where he said the guy had 'it'? I know what 'it' is now: It's what we've just done." It's an indefinable thing, a sinking down into a lower state of awareness, so that your everyday consciousness is no longer in charge. You tap into, as Jim would call it, a more primordial consciousness. It's the collective unconscious that permeates all of our lives. We all slip right down into it, using all of our intellectual abilities and our knowledge of music to effortlessly play, and allowing ourselves to go into a heightened state of awareness. Boy, it was good.

> "You want to dance and sing and have joyous sex and men and women living together in beautiful loving harmony? Or do you want to fight and have war and chop the trees down? You know you can't chop the trees down. *Stop* it! Stop chopping the trees down!"

It also sounds very sixties.

When we were college students in the sixties, we were saying, "Why should we go along with the world the way it is? Why should we go along with the rape of the environment and exploitation of the workers? Let's change the world, give everybody a fair break, and nurture the planet." This is the Garden of Eden, if that's what we want it to be. We are the caretakers of the planet. We were not put here to dominate the earth; we were put here to make sure that it works perfectly in harmony. That's what the intellect can do. That's what our spirituality can do. That whole thing has been lost, but all you have to do is snap your fingers and say, "By God, we're gonna do it!" The future starts tomorrow, and it belongs to us. We can do anything we want with it. You want to heal the planet? You want to dance and sing and have joyous sex and men and women living together in beautiful loving harmony? Or do you want to fight and have war and chop the trees down? You know you can't chop the trees down. *Stop* it! Stop chopping the trees down! Stop putting artificial fertilizer on the ground! Stop eating junk foods! Eat what's in season! And the world will keep functioning. It's very simple.

Many of the current problems you describe were on the sixties agenda as well. Does that mean that your generation dropped the ball?

That's one of the big questions that my wife, Dorothy, and I talk about every once in a while. What happened? When we were in college, thousands of people ingested psychedelics and broke on through to the other side and experienced the timeless story of man's quest for enlightenment. Thousands of acidheads joined the ranks of the spiritual people. Then something happened. Materialism turned their heads around or squashed that spirituality out of them.

Maybe all these spiritual acidheads eventually got too old for college and had to start earning a living in the real world.

You're right. When you have to go out and get a job, then the little compromises begin. One leads to another, and pretty soon you've lost your soul, and kundalini has slipped back down. When that kundalini power uncoils itself up your spine and your consciousness, and your crown chakra explodes into the universe, and you realize that we are all one and we are all God and we are all the universe, it's a marvelous feeling. But it can slip back down into the lower three chakras, and I guess that's what happened. Plus, a lot of people wanted to get stuff for free in the sixties. Life was free, therefore everything should be free. People would come to our concerts saying, "Hey, we're hip! Let us in for free!" They didn't want to pay, but you must pay the piper. You can dance to the piper's tune, but you also have to pay the piper. So now the hero's journey is to fight the bastards, to fight the corruption, to fight those subtle things they lay on you for a couple of bucks: "Hey, come on! Ya wanna go for the big bucks?" Well, what the hell are you gonna do with those big bucks? Get a bigger car? You don't need a bigger car. The whole point is to get a smaller car that runs more efficiently.

The Doors confronted that same problem years ago, when you considered selling the rights to "Light My Fire" for Buick to use in a commercial.

We thought it would be a good idea, not so much to make money off of the song, but to get rock & roll on television. At that time, in '67, rock & roll was not on television. They had a couple of little Saturday afternoon dance shows, but for rock & roll to actually penetrate the mainstream, that could be one of the most subversive things you could do. Right in your living room, right in *America's* living room, here's psychedelic rock & roll! Jim Morrison, God bless him, said, "No, man. Let's not do it, because that's the ultimate trap." And, of course, he was right. Falling in with those guys would have led us to what's happening today. I mean, there's Eric Clapton, man, playing for a beer commercial.

So idealism and naïveté went hand-in-hand in those golden days.

Yeah. We had no idea how terrible it could be, and just how powerful the Devil could be—the dark, greedy, rapacious, grasping side of humanity. But now we're seeing it, man. We're cutting down the fucking rainforests! What are we gonna breathe? Where's the oxygen gonna come from? They don't care, man. Nobody cares. They just gotta get more money, so they can get—what? A bigger house? For what? I get scared in a big house. Night comes, and it's spooky. The wind blows....

How does this dark side of humanity manifest itself in today's music?

Well, for one thing, when I listen to songs on the radio, I can't tell who the soloist is anymore. Nor can I pick out the band. I can identify jazz musicians and classical pieces, but with rock I have a tough time saying, "Oh, that's so-and-so." For the most part, urban contemporary music has great dance beats and great synthesizer sounds. But who's playing it all? I have no idea.

Is that because the emphasis in music is on conforming to commercial ideas, rather than on developing riskier new approaches?

I guess it is. Or is it conforming to what we think reality is supposed to be? See, I look on this in psychedelic terms, and I see that it goes deeper than just conforming to what's going to sell. I think it's toeing the line of Western civilization—the Judeo-Christian-Moslem myth. Because the Millennium is coming. We're finished.

Exactly how is all of this reflected in modern music?

Spiritually, psychologically, you will not go over the line. *This* is how heavy metal is supposed to be. *This* is how rap is supposed to be. Contemporary dance music *must* be this way. You cannot vary that, unless you're an iconoclast. And if an iconoclast actually does vary these standard musical forms, he or she may actually be varying the standard forms of civilization as we know it. I don't think anybody is willing to take that chance, man. I don't think anybody is willing to take the hero's journey—to vary not only the urban contemporary dance mix [*falls into dramatic whisper*] but to vary the *whole ... fucking ... thing!*

So times are even tougher now for creative artists than they were in the Doors era.

Absolutely, because we broke through. For a moment, the young people said, "Hey, we're taking over, man!" It was a real battle. The adult world had no idea how much power we had. Now they do know. Now they know that these kids, these artists, must be stopped. The first thing a fascist regime must do is to stop the artists, because the artists are the free thinkers, and invariably along with free thinking goes free love.

If you think free, perhaps you won't consume. And if you don't consume, then commercial advertising goes down the toilet. Then what happens to our television and radio shows? They have to go off the air. But that's what we've got to do. We've got to have more public access. It's got to be unsponsored. Art should be unsponsored. Either that or give the artist some bucks and say, "Hey, support yourself, man!"

Your point is that although speed metal, for instance, might sound raucous and incendiary, it has very little disruptive impact within a society that has learned to recognize, label, and thereby emasculate it.

Exactly.

So since you can make practically any kind of music these days without being perceived as a threat, what would you do if you were a young musician again? How would you approach playing music?

I would go neo-psychedelic, and I would take every member of the band on Joseph Campbell's hero's journey. I would find the truth of the ancient myths in today's society. Jim Morrison had a great line: "Let's reinvent the gods, all the myths of the ages. Celebrate symbols from deep elder forests." Here's the good side of what's happening: World music is coming. World beat music is the most exciting thing I've seen in the past fifteen years. I can't get enough of this blending of India and Africa and Polynesia. Africa! The power of Africa! And the Nubians, our black brothers! Somebody said to me, "Ray, what do you think of rap?" I said, "I gotta tell ya, I'm waiting for the Nubians."

> "For the most part, urban contemporary music has great dance beats and great synthesizer sounds. But who's playing it all? I have no idea."

Are you talking specifically about people from Nubia?

No, Nubia meaning the American Pan-Africa movement. The people who call themselves Nubies. It's a generic term for the seeds of Africa, the pollen of Africa, the shaman of Africa, the pantheistic deities. It's time to let Dionysus and Pan break loose. When that starts to happen, it's going to be very scary for the Establishment, the same way the Doors and Stones were scary for the Establishment. We who are getting behind it are going to say, "This is a music of love and fun and excitement. Sure, there's danger, and there's weirdness in there, and it gets spooky, and you talk about death. But in confronting death, you find an incredible joyousness and strength to live your life in a harmonious way. Music has got to have that spooky element. It's got to have power. The music *is* gonna have the power, because the Baby Boom will be relinquishing power soon—certainly aesthetic power. They have financial power, and they'll come into political power, and they'll take over the corporations. But their younger brothers and sisters and their children are the ones who will look back to the sixties and say, "*That's* what we want to do. *That* is the spiritual emphasis that's lacking in our lives."

Yet it's the elder siblings and the parents, the targets of this youthful revolt, who defined that spiritual emphasis in their own adolescence.

Ain't that a bitch, man? Robert Frost came to the crossroads and took the road less traveled. And Robert Johnson too! The hellhound is there, and he's on your trail. The city lights are to the right, and the forest is to the left. You can run to the safety of the city lights, where the hellhound can't get you, or you might go off into the forest. As an artist, certainly as a reader of *Keyboard*, since everybody who buys your magazine is an aspiring artist, you have to travel the road less traveled. You cannot serve both God and Mammon.

When you buy a new instrument, you're acquiring the same sounds and features that get used by artists you can't distinguish on the radio. How do you use these tools to follow the less-traveled path?

First of all, you have to play the licks you've heard on the radio. You have to be as good as the guys who are playing, so you go for that. There's nothing wrong with imitating other people's styles when you're starting out. Then, at some point—it doesn't matter what age it happens—you begin to become an adult artist. Now, what does it mean to be an artist? An artist is a person who dares to bring the messages of his unconscious into reality. As musicians, we affect the body more directly than any other artist. The painter affects the eyes, the writer affects the mind, we affect the body. We have the ability to change the vibrational patterns of the body. We can harmonize with the body, heal the body, or put it into a negative state or a frenzied state. By echoing, through music, the status quo, we can even put the body into a strange consumptive state. But as artists, we have to go beyond the status quo. You do that by examining yourself and reading some books. Musicians have to read, man. I don't find enough musicians reading poetry. Somewhere in one of those books, either in philosophy or poetry, you're gonna find some passage that says, "The saxophone player had *it*." That is when you become an individual musician—when you begin to explore what 'it' is.

> **"The adult world had no idea how much power we had. Now they do know. Now they know that these kids, these artists, must be stopped."**

Is playing music a different experience for you in middle age than it was when you were a twenty-year-old rocker?

No, man. Once you hit that passion, it never changes. Once you've experienced the joy of creating, and how good it is to play music, and what a thrill it is to play it well enough that you think what you're doing is good, that never leaves. For me, that's the whole point: to bring as many other people as I can into that joyous state of creation. Whoa, is that fun!

Who is your best audience now—people your age or younger listeners?

I hate to say it, but it's the younger people. They haven't succumbed to temptation. Like Luke Skywalker, they have not been seduced by the dark side of the Force. Although it is good to talk to people in their forties: "Yeah, man! Remember how it was? Bunch of old guys getting together to kick around war stories, except we're talkin' psychedelic." Maybe our problem was that even though we broke through to the other side, it's up to today's young people to implement that breakthrough. They've got to keep runaway business in America from exploiting Third World countries. We're saying, "Hey, chop everything down, give it to us, and we'll pay you five cents." Take care of the Third World! The Third World is going to give us the healing plants and the healing rhythms. The Nubians are all out there. They're everywhere. They're *lurking!* Pan is always in the forest. When you go on the road less traveled, you're going to find Pan. You're not going into the city, because the city is bright lights, pollution, and a lot of money. What does that get you? You're probably going to become a dope addict. As Jesus said, "The Kingdom of Heaven is within you." And the enemy is within you too. Don't think that it isn't! That's what we, as artists, must fight: the enemy within us. The one who will give in, the one who will be soft, who will say, "I want to make so much money I can't believe it." *That's* the enemy.

BILL EVANS

Form and Substance

Interviewed by Jim Aikin,
Contemporary Keyboard, June 1980

S ince I don't do much traveling, many of my artist interviews, including the conversation you're about to read, are conducted over the phone.
About the time *Keyboard*'s June 1980 issue hit the newsstands, though,
with Evans on the cover, his tour schedule brought him through Northern California. At the Bach Dynamite & Dancing Society, on the beach in Half Moon Bay, he tore
through the theme from *M.A.S.H.* ("Suicide Is Painless") with his new trio. Between
sets, I went backstage and introduced myself. He was low-key and cordial, but what
I chiefly remember were his puffy, spotted hands. There was no doubt he was seriously ill—but remarkably, it had no effect whatever on his playing. From that gig, he
went on to a nine-day gig at San Francisco's Keystone Korner (the tapes from which
were recently released by Milestone in the eight-disc box set *The Last Waltz*). A week
after that, he was gone.

—*Jim Aikin, Senior Editor,* Keyboard

• • •

*When Scott La Faro, who played bass in your original trio, died in a car accident
back in 1961, what kind of an impact did that have on your work?*

When Scott was killed, it was not only a blow from the standpoint of a dear friend
dying, it completely cut off my feeling of realizing a lifetime ambition of having a certain kind of trio, with the kind of musicians that could take the music someplace because they had the taste, the creative ability, the responsibility, and so forth. When

that happened, I didn't know what to look forward to. There were no other bass players on the scene at that time that could do what Scott had been doing.

What was it that made Scott so unusual?

Well, see, at that time bass players accepted certain rigid roles and approaches to playing, like you had to walk here, you had to do this or do that. I think it's acknowledged that Scott was perhaps the fountainhead of modern bass playing. He was a rare talent, and you don't find those people that often. What we tried to do was loosen up everybody's role so that they were participating more, and with responsibility. This is the difference. It takes a really complete musician and a complete artist to be creative and have the responsibility to know *when* you can do something that's a little freer than it has been, and when you shouldn't. If you take this kind of concept and apply it to your playing arbitrarily or intellectually, it won't work. It takes a really musical approach, an artistic approach, to know when to be really simple, and when you should break something up. That's what I was looking for. At that time I don't think there were any bass players other than Scott who had the capacity to accept a concept like that. First of all, it had evolved with us over a period of two years, so it would have been very hard for somebody to step in at the end of the evolution and take over, even if they had the capacity. See, I believe in a steady group. I believe in a group where the people are right for the group, where they believe in the music, and they're responsible, and you stay together. That way, the music grows, and it grows in ways that you don't even realize.

When you say the music grows, what do you mean?

Different things have begun to happen with material that I've been playing for years. Things that were more or less static have gotten into motion and are developing. I don't know how noticeable those changes would be to anybody else, but we [Evans's last trio, with bassist Marc Johnson and drummer Joe LaBarbera] are getting a great response from people wherever we go, so I think it's not an imaginary thing. The music was actually progressing very much, and we were performing at a very high level without realizing it.

What is it that attracts you to any particular tune?

It's mostly a feeling. I can just hear a song, or see the music and play it, or whatever. I have a friend in London, a pianist whom I highly respect, named Pat Snipe, and sometimes I ask him to give me some tunes, because he works with a lot of singers and comes upon some good tunes. He's given me quite a bit of material that I've used over the past five or six years. "A House Is Not a Home" is one tune he gave me. I hadn't played it before the recording date [for *I Will Say Goodbye*] and I haven't played it since—frankly, it didn't snow me that much, but we got it together on this date and did it, and it turned out okay. Also on that date was a really special little Steve Swallow tune called "Peau Douce," which Eliot [Zigmund, drummer] brought in. So that's how it goes. We just bring in the lead sheets and put them together. Of course, it requires special kinds of musicians to handle this kind of thing at such short notice, but that's the way top jazz musicians are. They're used to it.

How big is your repertoire with the current trio?

There are about seventy tunes on my list that I can and do call.

How many of them are your own tunes?

About a third of them. It seems that the tendency today is for people not to play other people's tunes, but I would say that in a lot of cases the level of the music doesn't really merit that kind of approach. If you're going to play only your own things, they have to all be on a high level. I just play anything I like. I know Richard Rodgers doesn't need the royalties, and Jerome Kern doesn't need the royalties, and George Gershwin doesn't need the royalties, but if I love the music I play it.

> "I believe in a group where the people believe in the music, and they're responsible, and you stay together. That way, the music grows, and it grows in ways that you don't even realize."

One of your best-known solos, "Peace Piece," is also one of the least characteristic of what you usually do. Do you still like it?

Yes, I do, but it was a one-time thing. When I get a request for it in a club, I don't do it. The only time I've tried to perform it again was when we were playing with a dance company in Seattle. It so happens that the man who is the head of the dance company is named Bill Evans, and so we have done four concerts now together. He has selected music from my recordings and choreographed it, in some ways very freely, so that it's partially improvised. He wanted to do "Peace Piece," and that's the only time I've done it. I don't think that essentially is any different in feeling from what I do, but stylistically it would appear to be, because it's almost classical in its approach.

Do you still play classical music?

Yes, I do. I love it. I don't do a lot of it anymore. Until I was thirty I did spend a great deal of time reading repertoire, from Bach through contemporary. I spent quite a bit of time on Bach for the purpose of developing tone control and independence and so forth. Bach changed my hand approach to playing the piano. I used to use a lot of finger technique when I was younger, and I changed over to a weight technique. Actually, if you play Bach and the voices sing at all, and sustain the way they should, you can't really play it with the wrong approach. It's going to straighten you out in a hurry if you have a concept of what it should sound like. But I don't play as much at home as I used to. I'm trying to write a little more now. I feel in a fresh, creative period, and I've been coming up with a few things that I like.

When you write, do you start with melody, or chords, or what?

I've written a lot of different ways. At one period of my life I had a manuscript book that I carried with me everywhere. I read once that Gershwin said that he had to write twelve bad songs to get to a good song, and I also wanted to get away from the patterns that writing at the piano might influence me into. I went all the way back to, like, whole-note melodies and half-note melodies, basically on the pentatonic scale, trying to get back to the fundamentals of melodic structure. When I write away from the piano I don't think about harmony at all, and sometimes later I'm amazed at the harmonies that a melody will imply. I've written things at the piano.... I've written one thing where I wrote the harmony first and then the melody, I've written things that come easy and things that I just had to sit there and take it apart and screw it back together and saw it in half—and finally end up with something that sounds like it's natural.

I have notebooks filled with twelve-tone rows, and permutations and inversions of rows, and so forth. When I didn't feel like thinking music, I would use that as a sort of mental exercise. The peculiar thing about it is, I did a lot of that, and I don't think it has contributed anything to my musical thinking. There just doesn't seem to be anything natural in it, as far as it relates to me. Well, I've made a couple of little tunes out of rows, but that's all.

When I got out of the Army in 1954 I went back and did three semesters of post-graduate composition work at Mannes College in New York City, and the work and assignments that I was doing then fell into an entirely different idiom than the idiom

Bill Evans, 1975: Working on the problem of total language.

I play in. I think the reason is obvious: When you're improvising you must be able to move and to handle a certain area, whereas when you compose you can take a week to write three measures if necessary, so you can reach for areas of music that you ordinarily couldn't handle in a spontaneous way. Some of those pieces are interesting. There's a four-voice, twelve-tone canon. I wrote a song to a poem by William Blake that I liked very much.

Have you considered recording those pieces?

No. They're just little things, and they're so different. I would like to copy them sometime so they don't get completely lost. I just wanted to mention that when I compose I can get into an entirely different area. It's kind of interesting what comes out of you when you dig into yourself in an area that isn't something you can handle spontaneously.

How do you feel your music has developed over the years?

I would say that essentially my concept of form and sound hasn't changed that much. I'm working with a total language problem. What I'm trying to do is be able to say more in a way that a listener can relate to, and still have the roots of the music firmly in a jazz concept. I've really searched very hard and worked very hard to develop a kind of motivic ability, where one idea follows another, and I think I'm getting to the point now where it's happening quite naturally. It's surprising how this type of displacement, which when I'm playing seems so solidly in place, right where it should be, sometimes sounds so displaced when I listen to it afterward that it might even throw me if I weren't paying attention. That happens, for example, on "Jesus's Last Ballad" [from *Affinity*], where during my solo I displace an idea. It's happening over a regular meter, and yet it's a funny thing.

What do you mean by displacement?

You could call it displacement, but that really isn't it. I'm not really displacing ideas. What I do a lot is ... well, I could illustrate it by saying if a tap dancer or a soft-shoe dancer sort of takes a jump and lands and slides and then comes into a strong beat, it's as if he got there too soon, but then he slides into the strong beat. It's not exactly that; it's a way of keeping the music moving when you're using a regular metric form, by making the phrase accents and the motivic accents fall according to the content of the motifs—falling before it should happen, or maybe dividing it up in different ways as it happens. It's a way of propelling the music, making it have a great deal of forward motion, and at the same time saying something extra because you're getting deeper into the language of music. It's a very difficult thing to explain. If I could play you a tape of "Who Can I Turn To" or practi-

> "I'm still playing songs and eight-measure phrases, but I'm trying to find a type of freedom within that."

cally anything else we're doing right now, you probably would understand it, if you know how to listen. I don't know, frankly, how many people in an audience know that we're using a strict form, or how many of them think we're just playing a succession of abstract ideas that have no relationship to strict metric form and content. Probably not too many do know and not too many are able to follow, but this is where the real meaning of what we're doing is. A really sophisticated jazz listener would know that.

How much of your solo on a tune like "Nardis" carries over from night to night, and how much is new?

Our solos are different every time. A lot of people might not believe that, given the complexity of what we're dealing with, but this is the kind of challenge that we set for ourselves. In "Nardis" there are only two things that carry over. One is when we get to the chart at the end of my solo. That lasts for one chorus. And at the end of the bass solo we play a one-chorus sendoff for the drum solo, which also has the same figures in it. Other than that and the chart going out, everything is absolutely [different].

Chick Corea once said that when he plays a solo over a period of time it tends to settle itself, so that gradually it becomes less improvised.

Yeah, that can happen. The period I went through after Scott was killed was more like that. When I was with Miles [Davis] he would do songs that way, where he would develop a way of approaching a solo; maybe certain key structural notes or motifs or whatever, he would keep in. I try to accept the challenge and use the discipline in my playing to be fresh. You can't always be fresh, of course, and you rely on professionalism and craft to carry you through, but ideally it would be entirely fresh, and when new things are right, that happens. Now, I don't know what someone else would think is entirely new, because the structure I would keep pretty much the same; the form would be the same, but the melodic and rhythmic content, if it were a really high-level performance, would be entirely new.

Where did this approach to improvising come from?

I don't know exactly what my point of departure was, but I felt that the jazz melodic language should go in this direction because of all the roots and traditions that I felt and loved about it, just the natural language that you recognize—this is the language of jazz. I'm still playing songs and eight-measure phrases, but I'm trying to find a type of freedom within that. For instance, we've been playing "Nardis" for twenty years, and it has evolved into something, which is now rather abstract and

> **"You can pour emotion onto an audience without very much content. However, I have to judge my own work, and I feel that there has to be another kind of content than emotional."**

rhythmically strange. When we perform it I play a long solo section in front, and then we play the chart, and then the bass plays a long solo, and that goes into a sendoff for a long drum solo, and then we finally take it out. Now, we're definitely using the form very strictly, but I doubt if one person a year who hears it knows that. It's underneath, and we've gotten to the point where we relate to it in a very free way. To me, this is the most precious kind of freedom, gained by difficult dedication. I think following the form gives substance to what's happening. It brings return of idea, return of whatever, in the right places. Whereas if you say, "I'm going to start with nothing and go anywhere," you don't have that kind of fiber in the music. That's the way I feel. I know that most people react to music almost completely emotionally, and you can pour emotion onto an audience without very much content, and succeed immeasurably. However, I have to judge my own work and enjoy my own work, and I feel that there has to be another kind of content than emotional. There has to be an artistic and aesthetic and formal content as well.

WENDY CARLOS

One Big Cookie

Interviewed by Dominic Milano, *Contemporary Keyboard,* December 1979, *Keyboard,* August 1992, and Robert L. Doerschuk, *Keyboard,* August 1995

Among the many things I remember of my first meeting with Wendy Carlos is the awe I felt sitting alone in the basement studio of her New York brownstone, surrounded by all her tools: the modular Moog, her hand-built mixing console, the tape decks, the piano … Those tools were silent, but outside the rain did a modest imitation of Wendy's *Sonic Seasonings.* That first meeting yielded twelve hours of recorded interview and marked the beginning of a friendship that has lasted more than twenty years. If there's one thing to glean of Wendy's personality, whether through listening to her music or reading an interview with her, it's that she does nothing halfway. Her curiosity is tireless. And she's eager to share all that she discovers.

—*Dominic Milano*

• • •

How did you get your start in music?

My first keyboard was a roll of shelf paper that my father drew a keyboard on with a pencil. He measured some relative's piano and drew a keyboard for me. I had a book that had some facts about piano, and I actually practiced against that piece of paper. Then I got a Lester spinet; I had parents like many other parents who wanted their children to have what they couldn't have during the Depression. By age six I was on my way to playing the keyboard and taking lessons and, fortunately, learning the language of music, the physical as well as the aural, at a time when it was easy for me to get riveted into it. I'll never be anything but terribly grateful to my parents for giving me the motivation, even if that motivation might have been a slap against the hand. So I slugged through piano until I was thirteen or fourteen. I played a lot of Chopin and Liszt—unfortunately, not enough Beethoven and Bach, reflecting the prejudices of the fifties in a small backwater town in Rhode Island.

Then under the influence of a friend of mine I decided to go into physics because I had a good head for math. And I flunked out. I took two years and was put on probation, so I switched to music and had a 4.0 average. The faculty advisor, who had sort of invented the term biophysics, saw no harm in musical physics, so I spoke to the head of the music department and they concocted a course for me. So I took a lot of acoustics classes and physics classes while I was majoring in music [and] composing big pieces for the first time. I did well enough that I chose to go into graduate work in music. There were only two places to go for electronic music at that time: the University of Toronto and Columbia/Princeton. I picked New York because it sounded like an interesting town. Vladimir Ussachevsky gave me lots and lots of time to myself. I had all night long in the studio, because the composer-in-residence had just left and I took over his time slot at night. Every night around midnight I went to the tombs and every morning around six I got out, had breakfast, and went to sleep. And I got my masters in composition with a two-hour opera that was done as a very show-off stunt. It succeeded in getting a big laugh out of every other student. It was the thickest and heaviest score that had been turned in in a long time. I guess I am a show-off. I like to make things seem like magic.

> "I had fellow students tell me that I wasn't a serious enough composer because if I answered the question of what was more important, life or art, I would say, 'Life, obviously.'"

What types of music were you composing in those days?

I was never into the avant-garde. That kept me out of peer groups of students who saw eye-to-eye on the type of music that ought to be written. But they all got into serial mathematics and twelve-tone rows. Having a math background, I thought that it was all gibberish. I didn't go for that type of non-rhythmic, non-melodic, non-harmonic music. It seemed more concerned with what we don't do than what we do.

What was the first piece of electronic music you ever heard?

The first exposure I had was from a friend who brought me a recording of Pierre Henry's *Veil of Orpheus*. I was fifteen or sixteen, about the age where maybe late starters nowadays begin listening to the technological music of our time. But my exposure was more eccentric because I didn't know this type of music even existed. *Veil of Orpheus* is a theatrical melodrama with many clearly staged details: voices talking from the distance with echo, manipulated piano sounds, some oscillator sounds. At the time, it was presented to me as though it were being done by people at the Brown University Audio Research Laboratory. I asked an older friend who was going to Brown if he would find this laboratory for me. He went all over the campus looking for it, and then came back and told me he didn't think there was such a place. And indeed there wasn't; it was somebody pulling my leg. So kind of as a smart-assed answer and also because it seemed like a fun thing to do, I produced a *musique concrète* thing, using my parents' piano and some recordings of test tones that I had, howling into a microphone and feeding it through echo from the piano soundboard with the damper pedal held down, and copying it backwards from one tape to another and overdubbing other parts with tape-delay echoes. Very primitive, but that was the technology that was available. What Vladimir Ussachevsky was doing with Otto Luening at the time was not all that different.

Did electronic music immediately seem like something you wanted to pursue?

Well, it certainly wasn't at that time something that I wanted to do for the rest of my life. But it was fascinating. From that point on I started fooling around with tape-recorded kinds of music. When I finally went to college and decided to get into electronic music, I was already experienced at producing quite a few of these things in my parents' basement rumpus room.

How did the process of incorporating sounds beyond those generated from traditional instruments affect your creative method?

Although I've been playing the piano since age six, somewhere in my brain I'm hard-wired to be a timbre person. Orchestration was one of the things that moved me into writing music, which is why I haven't written a lot of solo works for any instrument: because there's not the interplay of timbres. The electronic medium seemed to lend itself very nicely to color, to the interplay of a muted sound and a bright but quiet one with one that's more rounded but loud, with a low-pitched sound that has very little fundamental but stronger harmonics in the upper region, which is the way acoustic instruments tend to interact. The areas of acoustics and physics, therefore, come into it, and the skill of orchestrating for instrumental ensemble comes into it. It's a misconception that the electronic medium is inherently all that different from regular orchestration.

Did orchestration classes in college affect your timbral approach in electronic music?

No. Taking orchestration was nothing more than picking up a skill. You'd learn that this instrument has this range. When it's in this part of the range it tends to be loud. Over in this part it can't play loud at all; it gets covered by the other instruments. It has to breathe roughly this amount of time. Or it doesn't need to breathe at all. It's only natural that you benefit from anything you do that broadens you and gives you the ability to think in a somewhat different way or develop a skill at some particular thing. But it's hazardous to consider things that might appear to be disparate to be *essentially* disparate. I don't find one skill to be something that sits in a little box, which is opened only when you're dealing with one particular thing in your life. It all flows together, like a batch of chocolate chip cookies I once made with way too much shortening. You don't have individual cookies anymore; you have one big cookie. Even having a degree of proficiency in a computer graphics program might allow you to reshape notes on a graphics-driven MIDI sequencer with finesse and artistry, because of the background you'd have with making beautiful shapes applied now to editing velocities and MIDI values.

Your point is that you draw more from the experience of life as a whole than from disciplines isolated from the context of life.

I had fellow students tell me I wasn't a serious enough composer because if I answered the question of what was more important, life or art, I would say, "Life, obviously." Does that make me less of an artist? They say yes. Myopia.

What path of development would be most useful for electronic music at this point?

The healthiest direction is hybrid. The idea of hybrids with instruments is that we can embrace many styles of making sounds, which ought to be a liberating experience. Modular is a good way to think. If we could plug in a module that uses the kind of controllers we want to use, as long as there are enough of them to define the pitch, the loudness, the timbre, the way the vibrato comes in and out, and a couple of other parameters, that's enough. Once there are six or seven things going, you've got a genuine instrument on your hands. Then you'd have a choice of sounds through what I call engines within a particular machine. You'd have an engine that takes in sounds from a microphone as samples, which you would treat as a waveshape or raw material to be modified. Another engine would do modifications, much like the old Moog and other analog synthesizers did, with filtering and distortion and cross-modulation. Then you'd have engines that are closer to the FM process or to the phase modulation of the Crumar GDS, so that these waves, be they sine waves and triangles or sampled drums and voices and car brakes squealing, can be subjected to these sorts of processes. Then tie it all together with some kind of additive thing so that you can have the ability to pop any of these things into a format where you can take everything apart, down to its overtones.

Wouldn't this kind of meticulousness operate against the idea of expression or spontaneity?

I've never been a fan of anything that tends to make music less expressive, less flexible, less human. Those things are very important. That's the whole reason why we did *Switched-On Bach*. We started that record because we were afraid that if we did all of the things we wanted to do with a synthesizer, people wouldn't understand it. So we thought, "Since somebody has to be tutoring, we'll do it. It's no big deal. We'll just show them that this is a nice method of making traditional-sounding human music, with regular chords and melodies. No reason in the world that it has to sound like what the medium has been limited to, more or less, up until now."

So Switched-On Bach *was a fundamentally commercial project.*

Absolutely. Of course, it was never expected to do what it did. It was merely intended to establish credentials that we could play music electronically, so that even if the next melody we play is with a strange timbre, it still is a melody. Don't lose sight of that—just because the novelty of the timbre might make you think this is all somehow intimidating and weird and unrelated to mainstream music, it *is* mainstream music.

> "I guess I am a show-off. I like to make things seem like magic."

Switched-On Bach *also planted the seed of what eventually became the home studio phenomenon.*

Yeah, but computers did that too. I can't take credit for this. I sometimes find it stifling to some extent to be a studio person. I wish we did more interactive work with other musicians. If it has to be done electrically, with modems, okay. But somehow I would like to see more interaction among musicians who have the new technology.

You've speculated in the past on the possibility of playing live.

Maybe it'll never happen. Nobody has made a good offer. I'm finding, to my dismay, that it's easier *not* to collaborate with others than to collaborate, and that it was easier to collaborate in the acoustic music days.

Is that a byproduct of the home studio routine?

Of course it is. But on the other hand, it also makes music part of the vernacular again, like it used to be when kids would take piano lessons and practice on Mom's upright, when music was something that was *done*, before radio and television took over as entertainment. In the evening, after dinner, what did you do? You would read poems to each other, or act out vignettes from famous paintings and have people try to guess which painting it was. Then somebody would play the violin or do some singing. Making music was not so much the passive experience of listening to others, so long live the home studio! There's nothing healthier than to make music an experience for everyone, so that kids maybe can read at least a treble clef melody in *C*. A little musical literacy would hopefully make the audiences of the next generation more hungry for gourmet music, because their tastes would be elevated through the awareness and sophistication you derive from making music, so they won't be happy just hearing a drum machine go *tunka-chunka, tunka-chunka*, on and on: a one-hundred-percent fast-food, fatty musical diet.

The scenario you describe refers to a time when there were clear divisions between what you might call high art and folk art.

Not at all. *The Magic Flute* was a real people's opera, if you want to call it that. The royalty was paying the tab, but people in the street were humming tunes from the latest great operas.

But in the States, let's say, for people who listen to blues musicians or the Grand Ole Opry, *music served a folk purpose. For higher purposes, they'd trot out Rachmaninoff or Rubinstein.*

Yeah, I see what you mean.

Then recording democratized all that. Suddenly Louis Armstrong could record in the same studio used by Horowitz. So a lot of the music we might describe as "bad" might actually be misjudged because we're applying high-art standards to something more rooted in the folk tradition.

Well, I think it's obnoxious to diss many kinds of music on merely stylistic grounds. Why shouldn't the blues as played by Louis Armstrong be as much art as something from a Romantic German, late nineteenth century?

Isn't there a continuum, though, from the blues tradition through to rap and other popular forms based on those tunka-chunka drum machines and loops?

> **"It's obnoxious to diss many kinds of music on merely stylistic grounds. Why shouldn't the blues be as much art as something from a Romantic German, late nineteenth century?"**

In rap, from a musical point of view—music only—there's very little happening. If you're that circumscribed, there's not much room for Art with a capital "A" to evolve. But blues is not limited in any way like that, so it's demeaning to even discuss whether it's low art, whereas Ravel, who happens to be one of my patron saints, is high art. If it's badly played, if it's poorly thought through from a compositional point of view, if it's a *C* major triad for four-and-a-half hours, then cynicism is appropriate. You could put yourself up as sort of a Dada hero, maybe like John Cage, and say, "Nyah-nyah-nyah, you take yourself so seriously with all that twelve-tone stuff, and I'm telling you it's all a crock." To some extent, that kind of person is necessary. But should we applaud snobbery? Only in the sense of quality. What you can be elitist about is quantity. If somebody uses the democratically available tools and does an amazing job with them, the type of elitism that acknowledges that they've done something better than average is not elitism at all.

Does an appreciation for high art make it difficult to appreciate low, or folk-based, art?

That's one of the funniest questions of culture and art. In one sense, it's circular reasoning to say, "If a lot of people buy this record and listen to it a lot of times, there must be some very important communication taking place, so it must be very sophisticated." That's a populist definition of quality. Then you can see somebody doing something very difficult, like Horowitz playing his arrangement of "The Stars and Stripes Forever," where it sounds like four hands going. Even if you're not a musician, you can see that there's a level of physical dexterity that reaches a point where you have to say, "There's a whole other stream out there." If you refine, as Ravel would do, to the point that there's not one extra note, there's something that must be acknowledged. Even if they're playing "She's Too Fat for Me" on a homemade concertina with a kazoo attached, but with a high degree of well-honed skill, that requires a nod. You hope to live in a society where you would gain respect if you could as an audience member say, "Hey, listen to that. Something really magical occurs in the middle of this piece." But this gets us into the quicksand of aesthetics, and that can't be described any more than you can teach somebody how to compose.

Can you teach someone to improvise?

It's the same gift. Improvisation is the first level of composition. In fact, it's the heart of composition. If you have composition without innate improvisation, it's not really composition.

Stravinsky referred to composition as frozen improvisation.

And so it is. But the blue pencil does play a role too. Remember that tragic outcry from a fatally sick Ravel at the end of his life: "There are so many wonderful pieces inside me that I can't get out!" My best musical ideas usually come to me through my inner ear. I frequently hear symphonies in my head as I'm trying to go to sleep. That's not kinesthetic. That's not the hand guiding; that's the inner ear guiding. If I'm sitting at the piano to follow what I'm hearing in my head, I'll try to play the notes I'm hearing.

That doesn't sound like an exercise in improvisation.

The improvisation is what you do on the first pass. You have the idea, you hear where it's leading. Yes, there's the excitement of doing it on the fly. That's why people love to go hear opera singers—because their voices *might* break. There's a circus quality to it, as Glenn Gould pointed out. But that's different from music *qua* music. Music doesn't need that theatrical side, although of course it must move you in other theatrical, humanistic senses if it's to be effective. Otherwise, it cuts itself off from the human experience, and therefore it has no emotion, and therefore it bores people. And therefore it ain't for me.

BRIAN ENO

Uncertainty Principle

Interviewed by Jim Aikin, *Keyboard,* July 1981,
and Robert L. Doerschuk, *Keyboard,* June 1989, March 1995

Brian Eno's impact extends far beyond the keyboard realm—not surprising, since he persistently describes himself as, among many other things, a non-keyboard player. He has none of the synth fanatic's obsession with new technologies, except in how their breakdown may lead to unpredictable collisions of intent and accident. On his ambient recordings he is the anti-Emerson, striving to express himself as slowly as possible. There's something subversive in his attitude, as there was in his manner on the occasions we spoke. He speaks quietly, takes his tea with milk, and projects a gentle bemusement. Nothing in his personality betrays the incendiary creativity that has drawn David Bowie, U2, David Byrne, and scores of other innovators into his circle of collaborators. No, Eno's power is in the content of his ideas, whether articulated in words, in sound, or even in the silences that, like breath, fill his music.

—Robert L. Doerschuk

• • •

How do you assess the impact of music technology over these past several decades?

As with all technological changes, the ones we've seen in music technology obey the most obvious momentum. I always criticize synthesizer manufacturers for making the most obvious technological choices, which are simply to multiply the number of options they put in the machine. If you're printing chips, the easiest thing is to make a few more options. The hardest thing is to try and solve the problem of making these machines interface better, or relate to human beings in new and interesting ways. How do we make them, for instance, anything like as responsive as some of the acoustic instruments—which, after all, are highly evolved? I would like to see two things. One is a type of synthesizer that doesn't offer huge numbers of options in terms of stored or possible available sounds, but does offer tremendous response to you as a player, so that you can actually start to feel what it's like to play this instrument.

And the other option?

The second one is that synthesizers have remained linked to keyboards. I feel that particularly because my first synthesizer had such a crappy keyboard that I never bothered to use it, except for effects.

Which instrument was that?

The EMS. I wasn't a keyboard player anyway, but that gave me an edge because, certainly in England, I was the first synthesizer player to use the thing as something other than a keyboard instrument. Until then, people used it as a kind of organ with a few funny sounds on it. I couldn't use it that way, even if I had been technically able to, so I started doing something else with it.

If you had started on a more sophisticated electronic keyboard, then, you might not have had to use your imagination to compensate for its deficiencies.

Well, clearly this is what's been happening with the big digital synthesizers. Now, the effect of this on the players—or at least the conspicuous effect, as far as I can see—is that the players move very quickly from sound to sound, so that for any new situation there would be a novel sound because there's such a wide palette to choose from. This seems to me to produce a compositional weakness. These players are working in terms of sounds they don't really understand yet—you know, the sound is too novel for them to have actually understood its strengths and weaknesses, and to have made something on that basis. It's like continually being given a new instrument. Well, that's exciting for the player. Every ten minutes somebody says, "Hey, here's another instrument. Now try this one." But from the point of view of the music, it seems to produce a rather shallow compositional approach. Frequently, in the studios, you see synthesizer players fiddling for six hours to get this sound and then that sound and so on, in a kind of almost random search. What's clear, if you're watching this process, is that what they're in search of is not a new sound, but a new idea. The synthesizer gives them the illusion that they'll find it somewhere in there. Really, it would make more sense to sit down and say, "Hey, look, what am I doing? Why don't I just think for a minute, and then go and do it?" You could contrast this approach to that taken by Glenn Gould, for instance. In the article in *Keyboard* [August 1980] he mentions the fact that he has been working with the same piano for years and years. Clearly he understands that piano in a way that no synthesizer player alive understands his instrument. You see, there are really distinct advantages to working within a quite restricted range of possibilities, and getting a deeper and deeper understanding of those. I really know the instruments that I have as well. My [Yamaha] DX7 programs are very good.

Yet your approach to sound seems to run against the sharp delineation represented by the DX and other digital synths. You seem much more interested in blurring sounds than in etching them out clearly.

Yes. In fact, the DX7 isn't the greatest synthesizer for my direction. But I've always thought that sound doesn't stop with the synthesizer. I'm always thinking in terms of using a whole chain of stuff to screw up the sound [*laughs*].

Why are you so interested in obscuring sounds?

Well, first of all, whenever you hear a real instrument, or any real sound in the world for that matter, you hear it in a container of some kind. If you hear a guitar being played, you're hearing all the formants in the body of the guitar, not just the strings. The synthesizer, on the other hand, is like [hearing] just the strings. It's a disembodied sound. Because of that, I've always enjoyed the opportunity to build a body around that sound. The problem is that the sound involves too few atoms. Once you get into the level of having a whole bunch of complex molecules involved, then you start to get into the richness that makes sound interesting.

> "Violin makers wanted to produce an instrument that was completely even in timbre at every pitch. Of course they failed, and their failure is what makes those instruments interesting."

Your mission, then, is to add electrons to the nucleus of sound.

That's right [*laughs*].

How do you feel about the synthesizer in general as a sound source?

There are two things that the synthesizer lacks. One is that it lacks a sound that is idiosyncratic enough to be interesting. By that I mean that all natural instruments respond naturally, which is to say they respond unevenly, and somewhat unpredictably. You know, a guitar sounds slightly different at each fret, and it has oddities, which are undoubtedly a large part of the interest of the instrument. A good player will understand and make use of those oddities. But synthesizers in general don't have that. The aspiration of synthesizer designers is to produce maximum evenness. And that was actually the aspiration of traditional instrument designers—violin makers, for instance. They wanted to produce an instrument that was completely even in timbre at every pitch. Of course they failed, because they were working with materials that wouldn't permit that, and their failure is what makes those instruments interesting.

Some non-European instruments embody these imperfections to an even greater degree.

And that accounts for a good part of their interest. Look at the *shakuhachi*, the Japanese flute. The intention in its development, in contrast to what we've been talking about, was to produce a quite *different* timbre at each pitch, and for each individual sound to have its own distinct character. As far as I'm concerned it would be much nicer if synthesizers began moving away from their perfection and through the violin stage of imperfection toward the *shakuhachi* stage. Now, in doing this you can move in one of two directions. In the direction of very high technology you can do that—with instruments like the Synclavier and the Fairlight you can program each note to have its own special idiosyncrasies. Or you can move in the direction of very low technology, which is the direction I'm much more likely to take. If I built a synthesizer, it would be fairly unpredictable. In fact, the synthesizers I own have already become fairly unpredictable because I've had them a long time and haven't had them serviced very much. I know a lot of people are into the inhuman cleanness of a synthesizer, but I don't like that, and I subvert it by laziness: I never get my instruments serviced, so they start to become a little more idiosyncratic, and I also use a lot of auxiliary equipment, which I also don't get serviced. Now this sounds flippant, this not getting things serviced. I actually do get things serviced sometimes, but a lot of the faults that develop are rather interesting, so I leave those alone.

What kinds of faults?

Well, for instance, on my little EMS a fault has developed whereby if I feed a loud input signal into the ring modulator it will trigger the envelope. This isn't supposed to happen, but of course it's very useful because then you can use the envelope to trigger any other function in the synthesizer, so I can follow the input sound with another sound if I like, or feed the input sound through a filter that's controlled by the envelope—that kind of thing. Now, this is distinctly a fault of the synthesizer, and when I do get it serviced I have to put little notes all over the thing, saying, "Don't service this part. Don't change this."

How can creative musicians make use of instruments with comprehensive technological capabilities, which tend to preclude the use of happy accidents?

By getting bored. Now, I get bored extremely quickly. I get nauseated if I'm doing the same thing over and over again. It actually makes me feel physically sick; I'm not being metaphorical. I then stop whatever I'm doing and go on to something else, or I think, "I've got to find some way of upsetting the pattern." Of course, there are

> "There are distinct advantages to working within a quite restricted range of possibilities, and getting a deeper and deeper understanding of those."

lots of people whose greatest pleasure is to do the same thing over and over. Perhaps they do have a real use in the world.

But you would suggest that musicians use their limitations to do something else with the ideas they've got.

Well, finessing is worth doing too. You might think of it as a two-stage process: Some people invent new words, but other people learn how to speak well with them. The people who exercise the vocabulary are doing something very important. I'm just not one of those. My fun is in thinking up other words to fit the vocabulary. It's like being a collage artist: You take this postcard, which somebody else made. You stick it next to that photograph. Then you put a bit of paint over the two of them and join them together. This is very in tune with what has been going on in painting for the past fifteen years or so, with people sticking together not just the abstract qualities of sounds but the references that carry with them. All the engineers working with rap bands are having a terrible time because the artists insist on leaving all the scratches on the records they sample. What they're saying is, "Hey, this *is* taken from somewhere else, from another time and place." So part of the message of the music becomes the fact. It's collage, binding together history as well as sound.

It also creates an impression you've described as "cultural ambiguity." What makes this postmodern approach more interesting than the traditional exercise of digging deeply into one's own native culture?

I wouldn't say that it is necessarily more interesting. Especially interesting is the fact that some people, like Ry Cooder or perhaps Neil Young, keep digging in the same little trench, as it were, and coming up with neat stuff. What's changed is that the overall dynamic of where you search and what you look for has widened. It is possible now for there to be music stars who, in terms of the range of their work, are something like Samuel Beckett: They stay in the same place their whole lives and get better and better at what they're doing. Or it's possible to be an eclectic gadfly. Neither of these choices was possible twenty years ago. You were expected to have a boringly predictable rate of change in your career, to vaguely embrace new ideas as they came out but not to lose your identity, as they say in marketing. So the possibilities of range have changed: You can be very focused, you can be in the middle, or you can be vague.

> "Audiences are probably sick to death with music. I know I am."

It seems odd in a way that while your concerns are so philosophical, the first way a lot of people became aware of you was through rock & roll. How do you see that? Do you feel that rock music is in a different world than this whole thing, or is it all the same to you?

No, it's not all the same, actually. The continuous discourse that goes on inside of me is the question, "What am I doing here?" That's the question, but the "here" can be either the rock music or the other one. I'm equally quizzical about them both. It's not as if I think there's a hierarchy involved where there's the respectable music with its background in La Monte Young and John Cage and so on, and then there's this pro-fane stuff. It's not that. It's that at various times I can be very heavily persuaded in one direction or the other, while at other times I can entertain both of them and they do seem to fit together. I hope this will stop at some time, actually. It's a waste of energy to be oscillating back and forth all the time. I would really prefer to be doing something that seemed to synthesize them, and I feel that I'm slowly mov-ing that way, but it's taking time, you know? You can't force these connections.

What changes do you see enhancing the experience of listening to music in the future?

Well, first of all, audiences are probably sick to death with music. I know I am. I don't listen to music very much. I'm sitting here, at a desk, and next to me I have three or four hundred CDs on a shelf. I only bought about six of those; all the rest have been given to me. It's just so much stuff! How do you navigate through all this? What is it that catches your attention? This is why I think there's going to be a role for curators.

What sort of curators?

I can imagine somebody putting together collections of music that he likes and selling them. You say, "Oh, that's a nice collection. I'll buy his next one as well." This person creams off a little percentage on the top, having put these things together. Sooner or later we're going to be deliver-ing music down phone lines, and there are going to be people, something like DJs are now, who package it for you. These curators are essentially two things: They're filters who save you from having to listen to everything, but they're also connectors in that they make taste connections that you might not have made yourself. Even-tually computers will be able to start doing this too. If you say to a computer, "I like Teardrop Explodes, Velvet Underground, Abba, Silver Apples, and Sinéad O'Connor," I can imagine a well-programmed database saying, "In that case, have you heard Elastic Pure Joy? You might like them." It would scan the groups of things that peo-ple like and spot certain regularities of connection, like the fact that people who mention Tony Bennett generally didn't mention the Velvet Underground.

> "Sooner or later we're going to be delivering music down phone lines, and there are going to be people, something like DJs are now, who package it for you."

Any other predictions?

You know the thing that happened with David Lynch and Quentin Tarantino? The music they put onto their records was given an extraordinary resonance by the fact that it was associated with their films. This was a trick I learned a long time ago. If you call something "music for film," that says to people, "Imagine what the film would be for this music." You evoke a whole set of imaginative skills that people have, and they think it's in the music. But it's not; it's in them. It's a trick, really, to use your own imagination to flatter your music. What Tarantino did with the soundtrack for *Pulp Fiction*, for instance, was very interesting. He's kind of sanctified some rather nondescript music, given it a real zing and a resonance. That soundtrack is great to listen to because you know there's a story there.

So the fact that this music is now in a movie changed your perception of it.

In fact, I've never even seen the film. I've only heard the soundtrack. But as soon as I heard it, I thought, "Oh, yes. I see. I see how this could fit here." This is the way in which a sort of multimedia form will come into being—through back avenues like this.

PHILIP GLASS

The Illusion of Repetition

Interviewed by Robert L. Doerschuk,
Keyboard, April 1987

I t was in the late seventies when I first called Philip Glass, the celebrated composer and performer credited with inventing the repetitive, detail-obsessed, high-tech style now known as minimalism. I identified myself over the phone as a writer with *Keyboard,* and Glass responded, "I was wondering when you were going to call!" What impressed me most in our subsequent conversations, and in this interview at his suite in San Francisco's Inn at the Opera, was the informality of his intelligence. For all his grounding in the classics, his populist instincts were evident, not just in the revolutionary character of *Einstein on the Beach, Satyagraha, Koyaanisqatsi,* and other landmark works, but also in his attitude. Breezy, approachable, ironic, there's still a bit of the taxi driver (a job he undertook during hungrier days) evident beneath the Glass surface.

—*Robert L. Doerschuk*

* * *

Traditionally, young pianists have aspired to be the next Horowitz. Do you find that today's keyboard players are not as fixated on building a concert recital career?

Well, I suspect you still have that aspiration. You still have a steady crop of people heading for the recital stage. It's a hard, hard business, and I don't envy anyone who sets their goal in that direction, because it's so competitive. Except for the handful of people who succeed at it, it can't be so rewarding. What really happens, of course, is that people who stay on as practical playing musicians begin to play a lot of other music, because that's how you make a living. If your predilection is toward new music, you might begin playing with some of the new music ensembles, which is another way to function as a pianist. It's very demanding, and it takes a lot of technique. You have to really be a good musician to play Elliott Carter, or a piece of mine, or whoever. But those are the kind of players you're most likely to run into.

Not long ago your choices were more limited; if you wanted to stay in music you were either a concert artist or a teacher.

I think that's true. There is another option now. My generation as a whole can probably take credit for that. We were the generation of composers who decided we wanted to play our own music. Whether it was the Sonic Arts Union, which was people like Gordon Mumma and David Birnbaum, or people like Richard Teitelbaum and Frederic Rzewski, or of course Terry Riley, Jon Gibson … I mean, there's a very big list of people, people about my age, who were not willing to wait for others to play our music, so we got involved with performance. What we're finding now, in the late eighties, is that there's a public for this music. In New York it centers around the Next Wave Festival, and Merkin Hall, and the Kitchen, and Roulette; we all know where those places are. There's an active life in the new music world. It's not about sitting around in a school and sending your string quartet [composition] to somebody in another school and hoping they'll play it, and then you'll play their string quartet. It's more about playing your music, and playing somebody else's music. It's attracted a new kind of performer and definitely a new kind of audience. We have a much more interesting music world now than when I was coming out of music school.

Much of the pattern repetition in your older writing seems to anticipate the development of arpeggiators and sequencers. Have you considered using devices of this sort in lieu of playing such parts by hand?

> "If my music would really repeat as much as some people think, it would be unlistenable."

Interesting, huh? But I've never really considered doing that. Of course, I'll use sequencers sometimes for programming percussion. It can be useful in the studio, but as a live technique, it isn't. If you actually look closely at my music, you'll see that it doesn't actually repeat that much. The kind of programs it would be necessary to write to produce that music would be so complicated that it's actually easier to play it. Now, sometimes in a recording studio, some things can be sequenced, though they're usually fairly simple parts, like percussion things. But if my music would really repeat as much as some people think, it would be unlistenable.

You do create an illusion of repetition, though.

And to do that, you have to change all the time.

Do you use repetition signs a lot in your written keyboard parts?

Sometimes, but I tend not to. My repeats rarely get above three, so most of my stuff can be written out in standard notation. I used to use what I called multipliers, which were brackets with numbers, but I've found that it's not a wise idea to have a multiplier outside of my Ensemble. Most people are just confused by it, so we just write it out.... No, that's not quite true. In some of the polymetric things, it's easier to write things out by having a group in the left hand repeating four times, and in the right hand repeating three times, then having the overall thing repeat maybe four times. So in polymetric music, I will use the shorthand.

Given all the overlapping rhythms in your work, a player could easily get lost when reading that kind of a score.

That certainly can happen. One of the Ensemble problems is to stay together. I've been playing with some of these people for eighteen or twenty years, so we've been able to get beyond any of the problems of simply falling apart. We occasionally have what we call train wrecks. Not very often, but it happens. But when you play together for as long as this Ensemble has, you achieve a level of performance that you simply cannot achieve with other players.

As a keyboard player, are you challenged by the parts you write for yourself?

Well, it's funny. When Martin Goldray came in as our third keyboard player three or four years ago, it was actually to pick up my parts. We needed someone who could play them better than I. It was the whole problem about practicing, because I don't practice as much as Michael [Riesman, Philip Glass Ensemble conductor and keyboardist] would want me to. The second parts are Martin's. Then I've written a whole series of other parts for myself, and mine are the easiest because I have to spend my time writing.

What kind of player would be an ideal performer of your keyboard repertoire?

Well, what you need is very steady playing in terms of tempi. You need real independence of right and left hand. That is axiomatic in my music: You have to be able to play twos against threes, sometimes fours against fives, and that's not so easy to do. *Einstein at the Beach* is full of that. And, you know, synthesizer playing is really different from piano playing. If you haven't developed that technique, you play much too hard on the synthesizer, as I'm sure your readers know. Someone who is just a piano player will have great difficulty playing this music on the synthesizer. I definitely write for synthesizer playing. That kind of rapid playing over extended periods of time cannot be accomplished on the acoustic piano. If you tried it, you'd be in shreds.

Yet you don't write synthesizer parts; your keyboard writing is pretty straightforward, without electronic effects.

Oh, yeah, of course. In a way that makes it simpler, but it also focuses a problem very clearly for us. I think that the people I work with and I are on the very forefront of people who combine electronic and acoustic instruments. This is, to me, the most interesting area. For example, we're recording the opera *Akhnaten* now, starting off with the Stuttgart Opera Orchestra, but by the time we get done there will be tons of overdubs on it. We're really learning how to extend and enhance the acoustic instruments with electronic means. The function of the keyboard in these pieces is to fill out the wind playing. I've gotten into the habit of writing very difficult wind parts for my own players, who can do it—someone like [saxophonist] Jon Gibson, who practices circular breathing. Here's a guy who can sit and play for literally ten minutes without stopping. Now, with orchestras, that's simply not going to be true. I write for a lot of parts sharing: Flutes 1 and 2 share a part. But even so, I found in some of those pieces where I was still writing more similarly to the Ensemble writing that it was a good idea to back up the parts with a keyboard. In those cases I programmed the keyboards to sound like the woodwinds. It was just a synthetic way of covering very difficult playing.

Some listeners at Ensemble concerts are surprised at how loud the group can be, especially since dynamic nuance is an important part of your writing.

Well, one of the things you give up with amplified music is exactly that. I don't know whether there's much you can do about it. It's a tradeoff; almost everything in life is. You gain in complexity of sound and timbre what you lose in terms of nuance and shadings. However, about half the music I write is acoustic. At the moment I have six operas around the world, and in any year three or four of them are done in different places, often within the context of very traditional presentation. The Philadelphia Orchestra with Dennis Russell Davies did two evenings of Wagner and Glass, and there you have people who are trained in the kind of dynamic and nuance playing you were referring to. It's very pleasing to me to hear what happens to music when it's done that way.

Wagner and Glass? That's an odd couple.

Yeah. One program was Act III of *Tristan* and Act II of *Akhnaten*. Nice, huh?

I can imagine the Wagnerians in the audience listening for leitmotifs in your work.

And it wouldn't be too hard to find them.

Has writing extensively for your Ensemble limited the chances for your repertoire to endure?

I haven't thought about that very much, although I'm very interested in phenomena like the [Duke] Ellington orchestra. What happens to an ensemble that's built around one person? I haven't made arrangements for the Ensemble music to be performed outside of the Ensemble, but the operas can be done by anybody. The opera scores are copied out by professional copyists, the parts are clean and in good condition. But it's not a question of documenting. It's a question of setting a standard for the music, so someone should *want* to play, for example, *Music in Twelve Parts*.

In any event, you're among the very few contemporary artists who have established comparable levels of credibility in the pop and classical worlds. Specifically, you've made it a point to show that the energies of both traditions can be used to create viable music.

It's so much fun to do that. And one of the reasons I do that is I don't see why the hell I shouldn't. Years ago I found out there were a lot of things I wasn't supposed to do, and I said, "To hell with that!" That started the very first time I played in a little nightspot called Max's Kansas City, back in 1972. I knew the guy who ran the place, Mickey Ruskin, and he said, "Look, why don't you play here? You can have the door." We made about three hundred dollars that night, and after that I said, "Gee, I'll play wherever anyone asks me." In L.A. I sometimes alternate between playing at the Roxy and at Dorothy Chandler Pavilion. It seems that we only have one chance to do this, so I'm interested in looking into it all. I'll tell you another thing: The people that I work with, like David Byrne or the Roches, these are very bright, talented people. It's crazy to deny yourself the opportunity to work with them for some imagined idea of propriety.

You worked with Byrne, the Roches, Linda Ronstadt, Paul Simon, and other pop icons on Songs for Liquid Days. *Was the process of composing music to their lyrics different than it might have been had the libretto consisted of solfège or numbers, as in* Einstein on the Beach?

It was. First of all, in the case of *Einstein*, the primary subject matter was conveyed to me in drawings; there was some text as well, but mainly the drawings that [director/set designer] Bob Wilson made. So I wasn't starting totally from scratch in a certain way. In other words, if I was doing the scene called "The Trial," I had dozens of sketches of the scene before me when I wrote the music. In writing the *Songs*, the words took the place of the drawings. In other words, the music related to a specific subject, which was the words, so that I began with the words and, literally, the words inspired the music.

The connection between lyric and music must have been more obtuse in some of the songs than in others.

That's true—for example, the last one, Laurie Anderson's ["Forgetting"]. I had that series of words to set. They came in groups of three, but I set them in rhythmic groupings of four. That meant that every line of three had a space in it; it would go *one*, rest, *two, three*; or rest, *one, two, three*; or *one, two, three*, rest, and so forth. I remember looking at the words and seeing that she had so consistently used this group of three that I could fit the three into the four and form a kind of rhythmic tension between the words and the phrasing. That's how I began

> "I definitely write for synthesizer playing. That kind of rapid playing over extended periods of time cannot be accomplished on the acoustic piano. If you tried it, you'd be in shreds."

writing that song; I set the actual words at the end. Then I took the second group—"They rushed slightly by, these lovers"—and I used that same music again. That left me the first group and the third group to set up. That became the narrative part of the song.

You seemed to depart from the specific written list of words at the end. The piece seemed longer than the written libretto.

Oh, yes, that's right. You see, it said, "So she repeats these words over and over again." I spoke to Laurie and said, "Since you say 'over and over again,' why don't we do it over and over again?" She said, "Yeah, that's okay." So I extended the four lines to maybe twelve lines. It's funny, because it was a disappointment to some people that the songs were rather overlong in terms of what one might have heard on the radio. But who would make a comment like that? It's not even exactly true. "Hey Jude" was about eight or nine minutes, and that was one of the most popular songs that was ever written.

Jimmy Webb's "MacArthur Park" ran for more than seven minutes.

Yeah, and the people who wrote those things were masters of popular music. I can hardly be called that. I'm someone who's stumbled into the song form. The length, to me, was determined by the words and by the musical needs. I wasn't thinking of the packaging aspect of it, which is like, How are you going to get it on the radio? There is one three-minute song on there, but that's by accident.

Which of these songs was the most difficult for you?

It's funny. I have this way of hardly ever remembering the hard parts. But I think "Liquid Days" was it. And "Open the Kingdom" [both by Byrne]. The difficulty was that it took me a devil of a time to figure out what the hell they meant. They were given to me as a pair. David is very helpful and easy to work with in one way, yet he often will not tell you the most important thing that you need to know. He just doesn't talk a lot. I looked at these two songs for a while, and I finally saw that they were both love songs. One was about domestic love, and one was about religious love. That was very interesting. Once I saw that I had the key to it; I realized that it was exactly like certain traditions of music. The vocal music of South India is like that. Songs are either to your lover or to your god, always one or the other. I saw that this was what these were, so I just decided to put them together. They form a range of human love, in a way, don't you think?

The music on the words "open the kingdom" certainly evoke religious choral singing.

> "David Byrne is very helpful and easy to work with, yet he often will not tell you the most important thing that you need to know."

Absolutely, yeah. Well, I saw it that way. And you take words like "days of fishes," "uncertain," "I'm asking," "open the kingdom" [all from "Open the Kingdom"] ... these are all religious images. Whereas the other one—"love wiggles on the floor," and "love could use a shave"—that's something that happens at home. Love becomes this kind of a comfortable person that you've been hanging around with. It makes it nice that the girls [the Roches] are singing it.

Several years ago, in talking about writing for voices, you told an interviewer, "I don't take plays and set them to music. Meaning is conveyed in language. That's not very important to me. I use language very much in terms of the sound. I like the idea that none of us can understand it." Yet, on Songs for Liquid Days *you did precisely "take plays and set them to music."*

It just goes to show you can't trust Phil Glass [*laughs*].

BILLY JOEL

Working Backward

Interviewed by Robert L. Doerschuk,
Keyboard, December 1981, January 1990

O
f the many artists I've interviewed over the years, Billy Joel stands
out for what I might describe as a kind of ferocious intelligence. You
can hear it in the craftsmanship of his songs; at their best, they reflect a quality of construction that's comparable to that of the classic writers of the
thirties and forties. But it's especially evident when you're sitting across the table
from him and witness his concentrated, intense, and sometimes combative conversation. And there was this: When we met in Los Angeles for our second *Keyboard*
interview, nine years had elapsed since our last meeting. In that interval Joel had
undergone innumerable experiences, played countless concerts around the world,
recorded with scores of musicians, gotten divorced and married, and so on. Yet as
we shook hands in the lobby of the Bel Age Hotel, he squinted at me carefully, then
said, "You've changed your glasses!" He was, of course, right.

—*Robert L. Doerschuk*

• • •

How would you describe your keyboard style?

A lot of it is actually based on ideas I have for the guitar. I've always wanted to
play the guitar, so what I do in a lot of my writing is to compose the guitar part on
the piano, then come into the studio and say, "This is what I want. I'd like to hear this
on the guitar." The producer or somebody will say, "Why don't you play that on the
piano?" And I'll say, "But it's not supposed to be for the piano!" See, I've never really
thought of myself as a stylist. I think I'm a lousy piano player.

Oh, come on.

Well, I took classical piano when I was growing up, and I know how good a really good pianist can be. My left hand pretty much plays octaves all the time. My right hand can play some flashy stuff, and I can play choppy chord things pretty well. I'm a better organist than I am a piano player. I can *scream* when I'm playing an organ! When I got my first Hammond organ I think I was seventeen. I bought every Jimmy Smith album there was, every Jimmy McGriff album there was. I got all the Groove Holmes records. I'd play that stuff with my eyes closed. Actually, I have more fun playing organ than piano. My favorite axe in the whole world, just to play for virtuosity's sake, is still the Hammond B-3. I've done David Letterman shows just to be able to play it, just to get my rocks off. Paul Shaffer was going, "Wow, he's doing sixteenths!" One of my fantasies was always to be just an anonymous Hammond organ player in some roadhouse blues band. I'd wear a hat and sunglasses; nobody would know who the hell I am. And I'm just groovin'—not singing, not doing nothin' but playing.

What organ did you play when you joined your first band?

It was an Estey, one of these little wooden things that had air blowing through it; it sounded like a big harmonica. No, more horrible than that; it sounded like a sick cow. I got it for Christmas when I was about fourteen. I thought, "Wow, this is the hottest thing!" Back then everybody played guitars, and there were really no keyboards developed. So we took an old Kent microphone and stuck it in the back of the Estey when I wasn't singing. When it was time for me to sing, we pulled the mic out and I used it. After that I got a Vox Continental, which I considered top of the line until I heard a Hammond organ, and that just wiped me out.

Why did you move over to the piano?

For writing, it's a better instrument. I've got to have the piano there. I'm always finding stuff out on it. See, I took classical piano for about eleven years, and a lot of what I learned there got in the way of my writing because I got hung up in these rules: "I can't do that. That doesn't make sense. I can't make that change, because that's too obvious." Then one day I just said, "Why *can't* I do these things? Forget the theory! Forget everything I ever learned and try to get innocent again." I'm still working backward to this day, still trying to write without any rules. Who says that when you go from a *C* you have to end up on *A* as the tonic? What's the word they use? The pivot chord? You have to hit a chord to get back to the tonic. The chord before the resolution.

You've got the tonic, the dominant, the subdominant …

I forgot all this stuff [*laughs*]. But before I forgot it I always would get hung up. How do I get back to the tonic? Finally I said to myself, "Why don't I just play any chord I feel like playing, if it pleases me?" You lose a certain amount of feeling when you intellectualize.

Does that apply to your playing too? Is there any conflict between your classical training and the way you play rock piano?

Yeah. My fingering has suffered with rock piano. I suppose I have a Mongoloid style. I played a lot of the classical stuff by ear anyway. I got tired of reading the music, so I'd go out and buy the record. I had to learn the Beethoven *Sonata in D Minor* [Op. 31], so I went out, got the record, and learned it pretty much by ear. I'm sure I missed a lot of notes; the teacher looked at me and said, "What arrangement is this? That's not on the music!"

How long did it take to learn it that way?

About two or three days, I suppose, if I sat down and listened for an hour and a half each day.

That's incredible.

Well, it was really laziness. When you're lazy you become very ingenious in certain ways. I just got tired of reading those black dots. To this day I can't sit down and sight-read. When I was about twelve I was able to sight-read great, but I just can't do it no more. It's too slow. My ear's a lot quicker.

What do you think about more modern keyboard gear—the synthesizers, the samplers, and so on?

In a lot of ways it's had a very good impact, especially for keyboard players, because it's brought keyboard players to the front. You've got these dominating groups on the pop charts that are keyboard-oriented groups. Look, I'm a keyboard player. I love to see the keyboard guy beat the guitar guy any day of the week. I remember the days when there was no way that you could get your Hammond or your piano or your Farfisa or your Vox above that son-of-a-bitch of a guitar player and his Marshalls. Now we have the technology. And let's be frank: Keyboard players usually have a more substantial background in the fundamentals of music than guitar players do. That's not to knock guitar players, but the keyboard players are the guys who've been pounding it out on the damn upright piano in the back room for an hour or two a day since they were kids. So I'm for whatever brings the keyboard player to the forefront.

> "One of my fantasies was always to be just an anonymous Hammond organ player in some roadhouse blues band."

However …

However, a lot of the technology has made it so easy for facile writers and inconsequential writers to play with the sound rather than write a great piece of music, that it's tended to water down a good deal of substance in composition. You can tell, if you're a musician: The whole record is based on that one little glowy, glitzy thing. To me, that's not the essence of composition. Look, Mozart wrote forty symphonies, and they didn't even have pianos in those days. I think he wrote all his crap on harpsichords! And Beethoven wrote some of the greatest music ever created on a fortepiano! It wasn't until Chopin that you had the real deal.

So you feel that songwriting has suffered because of this technology?

I don't want to sound like an old fart, but even though I've heard a lot of breakthroughs in sound, I haven't heard a lot of breakthroughs in composition. I mean, the most vital music now is rap, which has no melody in it at all. It's very little composition; it's rhythm, sound, and lyric.

Perhaps you're saying that the traditional disciplines of songwriting, not songwriting itself, have declined.

Well, there's an onus to that. The old songwriters are called craftsmen now. It's sort of like being called a liberal. I don't think there's anything wrong with craftsmanship. I'm *proud* to be a craftsman. Still, the underlying essence of the compositions is always spontaneity. I don't sit around and *craft* the ideas. The ideas are born of themselves. The craftsmanship comes from, "This is really good. I'm not gonna just drop the ball on this idea. I'm gonna make it as good as I can."

> **"Technology has made it easy for inconsequential writers to play with sound rather than write a great piece of music."**

That appreciation for craft is apparent in the bridges you write for many of your tunes.

Bridges are my forte. I think I'm better at writing bridges than I am at writing verses and choruses. You've really got to challenge yourself. If you come up with something that you think is really clever, and it's the impetus for completing the song, you often find that you've painted yourself in a corner: "How the hell do I get out of this?" *That's* where the real creativity comes in. The bridge is often looked upon as an unimportant part of the song, but I always ask myself how I can make it just as good, just as strong, as the rest of the song.

Without detracting from the power of the theme.

That's right—without going so far afield that you're not even dealing with the same theme. The first bridge in "Storm Front" [from *Storm Front*], which is in the key of *C*, starts with the minor third to the tonic in an old blues mode. But the second time we go to it, as an instrumental breakdown, it goes into the key of *E*. I don't know if anybody picked up on this, but the melody in the guitar is "Stormy Weather." Then we got away from it, and it was like "Sunshine of Your Love," where Eric Clapton actually played a variation on "Blue Moon" in his solo. To me, this is a little bow to a master songwriter, like, "Hey, this is such a well-written piece of music that I can translate this into a modern idiom."

You've been known to do more than that, by devoting entire songs to evoking the sound of another artist—the Four Seasons on "Uptown Girl," John Lennon on several cuts from Nylon Curtain....

Billy Joel, 1989: Grabbing attention, piano-bar style.

Yeah, there's a lot of that on *Nylon Curtain*. It's scary. See, I don't think of myself as any kind of stylist at all. I may have gotten a certain amount of critical abuse because I'm such a non-stylist, but I don't think that's necessarily a bad thing.

Do you write those sorts of songs with the intention of sounding like someone else?

I don't know if I necessarily write the songs that way. When the actual composition is going on, it's all me. A lot of times it happens during the recording process: The admiration I've had for the artists I've always idolized will come out. I reinvent myself every day, so on one particular day maybe I'm Hendrix. "Shameless" [from *Storm Front*] is an unabashed imitation of Jimi Hendrix. It is *screaming* Hendrix. I've never heard anybody re-create what Hendrix did. I don't know if I pulled it off, but I wanted to hear that myself.

Isn't there a commercial risk at making so much of your work so apparently derivative?

But that's the magic of composition! I mean, Mozart didn't limit himself to writing just sonatas. He wrote concertos, he wrote opera, he wrote symphonies. He wrote in every medium there was. He reinvented himself every day. And he was *thrilled* that he could transcend what Salieri, the hack of his time, was doing. Jimi Hendrix said the same thing. He said, "One day I wake up, and I'm an Indian chief. The next day,

I'm an astronaut." To me, that's the essence of music. When you get lost in your own style or your own image, whatever it is that you think has made you successful as a sonic personality, I believe that you lose the essence of whatever it was that made you successful in the first place.

Because you wind up imitating yourself?

No. You wind up doing sequels. You wind up becoming a hack. The joy of music, to me, is that self-discovery process—never limiting yourself to being a stylist.

In between your days with Long Island bands in local clubs and your emergence as a concert attraction, you spent some time working at a piano bar in Los Angeles. Did you learn anything in that gig that you can apply to your performances today?

I suppose I learned how to develop attention-grabbing stuff. What you're doing in a piano bar is basically playing for tips, so you try to pick out what will get bread out of the audience. Is this guy Italian? You play the *Godfather* theme or something like that. Is this guy Irish? You play "Danny Boy." You try to get those five-dollar bills in the brandy glass. So I guess I picked up a certain amount of smarts. The main thing I learned from working in the piano bar was that I didn't want to do that any more. Now I know what I don't like.

What exactly didn't you like about the piano bar?

It was just … depressing. I suppose "Piano Man" says it: drunken people sitting around, asking for requests. I had to do standards, and I actually learned how to fake a lot of standards that I didn't know. You just play a lot of major seventh chords in a stock kind of progression, and you can play any standard in the world. There was always somebody trying to grab the microphone and sing, and drinks were pouring all over you.

Audiences are wasted at rock shows too.

That's true, and the bigger the place, the more people who are going to be out of it. But we really haven't had that much of a problem. The audiences we get are usually pretty lucid, although at the end of the show there's always a pile of puke somewhere. Playing in coliseums can be a burnout too, but this doesn't mean we want to go back to little clubs. We tried that last year, and it's always crowded onstage, and the monitor system isn't right, you know. We spent so many years in the clubs that I can't really say we miss 'em. A lot of times they're a pain in the ass.

What advice can you give to young players who are trying to survive the kind of bar gig you used to play?

> "I may have gotten a certain amount of critical abuse because I'm such a non-stylist, but I don't think that's necessarily a bad thing."

Let me think. Tips for guys at the Holiday Inn. This is going to require some thought.... Okay. If you're working in those places, number one, you know you want to get out of there and go on to something better, so you might as well have fun while you're doing it. It's actually a good place to develop original material. Try out original stuff, but don't lay too much of it on people, because they're gonna mainly want to hear familiar things. What I used to do is, I used to goof, like if somebody asked for a Sinatra song I would get into doing a whole put-on of the Sinatra thing. I'd be having a blast, and they would think I was really into it. So I suppose a certain amount of sarcasm helps in those situations. You'll end up doing some things you really don't want to do, but I would stay away from songs like "Feelings" or "Jeremiah was a bullfrog" ["Joy to the World"]. If you want people to come back and see you, if you want an agent to get interested in booking you, try to do something different from what everybody else is doing. Like, don't be in a wedding band.

You mean, don't play wedding gigs?

Well, actually, I'm talking to wedding bands too. I mean, don't play the stock repertoire that wedding bands do. Don't just go to the fake book: "Okay, let's do Number Fourteen, three beats...." You've got people listening to you, you've got an instrument, hopefully you've got some kind of P.A. system, so it's a good time to see how your material hits people. That's an advantage that I don't have anymore. Somebody in my position doesn't have the opportunity to test new material. I just put it out, and if it bombs it fails big. Whereas you have a better chance to develop your own stuff slowly.

How can creative musicians keep their heads together in essentially uncreative situations like that? There are lots of good players who are stuck in unrewarding gigs.

Well, one thing I know about working in those places is that outstanding musicianship usually goes right over the heads of people who go there. They want to be entertained, not overwhelmed with riffs, so you develop some kind of stage rap that does get people's attention. I'd just say, take all the things you can get out of it and turn it into something positive. Keep in mind, though, that you really want to get the hell out of this place. Jeez, hopefully you're getting free drinks.

TORI AMOS

Pain for Sale

Interviewed by Robert L. Doerschuk,
Keyboard, November 1994

Though she inspired a legion of female singer/songwriters to expiate their angst in rainbow images and intricate melody, Tori can't be mistaken for any of those who followed her lead; from the first notes of "Silent All These Years" on to her latest intriguing examination of characters from other people's songs, she is an artist of absolute distinction. Her performances are unstable balances of strong musicianship and unpredictable emotion. In our conversations over these past ten years, especially during one extended stay with her and her crew in England during their *Boys for Pele* sessions, Tori would shift on a dime from cryptic, parable-like pronouncement to wicked humor and on to tremulous fragility. She never closed the door that led toward her soul, but she didn't always make it obvious where that door was, or what you might experience after going in.

—Robert L. Doerschuk

. . .

Why do you write songs?

[*Long thoughtful silence.*] I remember walking down the hallways of the Peabody Conservatory and hearing the same piece being played in ten rooms, pretty much all the same. I knew that I couldn't play this piece better than any of these people. It would probably be very different: You'd know where the redhead was, you'd figure out which practice room I was in. But I'd never win any competitions, ever, because nobody was interested in my take on Debussy. I never won anything. I always got marked down. Always. I had big arguments with these people, that these guys were pushing the limits of music in their time, just like John Lennon in his time. To understand their music, you have to understand the time. You have to know what's going on around them, especially when there's no lyric, when it's all music. Nobody, I thought, ever got the feel right. So I knew that if I was just gonna be playing some dead guy's music for the rest of my life, I'd probably never get a hearing, because their impression of what the dead guy should sound like was not mine at all.

But going even further back, was there ever a time when something in you said, "I want to make my own notes and words"?

I was seven [at Peabody]. I already knew what I was going to do. It was over when I was seven, a done deal. I was already writing. I didn't know how good or not good I could be. I knew that I could probably figure it out musically, but word-wise I was writing "The Jackass and the Toad Song." But I've always been a bit of a romantic. I'd be five years old, lying on my bed, with the afghan over me, squeezing my legs together and thinking, "Something should go here one day." I wanted to run away with all those guys, with Zeppelin and Jim Morrison and John Lennon. I [recently] told Robert Plant that I really wanted to pack my peanut butter and jelly and my teddy and my trolls and come find him.

So even then the power of the songs being done by the people who wrote them was something you could feel.

Yeah, I was totally conscious of that at five. It's funny, because I think I'm more affected by those writers than the ones who were happening when I was in high school. I wasn't really affected by what was going on in 1979. I had checked out; I was listening to my old records. Somebody played me the Sex Pistols after they had come and gone, and I wee'd in my pants. I said, "Shit, my father never showed me that *this* existed." I felt absolutely inadequate when I heard the Sex Pistols and the Clash, going, "Where was I?" I mean, I made Zeppelin and the Beatles and all those people when I was five.... Actually, Zeppelin didn't happen until I was nine or ten, when I started to bleed, so it was totally perfect; I was all ready for Robert.

> "Lucifer understands love better than anybody. You know he's done a mean tango with Greta Garbo a few times."

How did those sorts of influences affect your growth as a songwriter?

First of all, I cannot contrive a song. I'm not nailing people who can. I know some very good writers who I respect a lot. They're called to do something for a movie, and they come up with it in two weeks. They're not schlock writers; I'm talking about people who don't do hack jobs. They've got two weeks, and they're watching the film, and they're getting inspired. And I'm like, "How do you do that?" I don't care what you offer me right now: If the fairies don't sprinkle their little wee on my head, it's not gonna happen. I can't make it happen. Now, say I'm walking down the street, eating a banana, and something happens—four bars, with a sketchy lyric. If you gave me two weeks, *maybe* I could develop it, just on my skills and craft alone. I'm not telling you it could be great. It might be passable. But there are certain songs I look at and say, "I would not change a breath."

Those who can produce songs on demand tend to rely on certain formulas. Are you saying that it's best to avoid formulas in order to write more personal material?

Well, we have to remember that hit records and good songs are not synonymous. Maybe in the old days, a little bit. But now most hit records are not great songs. I'm not saying that those formula writers cannot stumble on something. But at a certain point, it's not about formula writing. I know I'm going back to the Beatles, just because that's a big point of reference, but how consistent can you get? "Eleanor Rigby"? "Norwegian Wood"? How many great songs and hit songs do you get? I remember John Lennon talking about listening to songs that he loved, then changing them to make his own versions. He would say, "God, I love this song. I wish I'd written this song." Then it would come out totally different. You might not even know what song it is that inspired you to do something, but there is that ingredient. Sometimes I do think that we're really just rewriting songs. There are only twelve bloody notes, you know. So I'll listen to some song and say, "Why didn't *I* write that?"

Because it speaks to you …

… as if I would have written it. I could name five songs, right off the top of my head, that I would have given my right arm to write. [Joni Mitchell's] "Case of You": You don't get it any better. A better song hasn't been written. I don't care what female singer/songwriter you throw up in my face: None has done anything in the league of "Case of You," *me included.* For a woman to be able to say what that says, with that kind of addiction and yet that kind of grace, is just not done. Even Zeppelin and those guys listened to Joni. It kills me when the metal guys or the hard-rocking guys who are more poseurs than anything will show up and say, "You know, all the guys in my band are embarrassed to like you, because they're into Zeppelin." And I'll say, "That's kind of funny, 'cause I just did a duet with Robert." I don't think people understand that with songwriters, it's not about volume, you know?

Commercial songwriters can be like caricaturists who scale complex emotions and issues down to bite size. You and other more personal writers are more like abstract painters.

You're right, but my intentions for writing have changed. There's a time when you want people to sing your songs with you. If you didn't, you'd keep them in your living room. Let's not lie to ourselves; that's the truth. Even though I could tell you I'm writing because it's my form of expression, there is a need—that is a fair word, I think—to have them shared. Sometimes I'll listen to work that I've done, and I'll go, "I'm not in that place anymore. I couldn't write like that if my life depended on it. But I do understand an element of it that I would like to have in, say, this next piece." I do like that approach of, like, peeling your skin off. Although the whole concept of *Under the Pink* is about peeling the skin off, that's more of an abstract work, whereas *Little Earthquakes* is more like a diary.

There must be a limit to how far you want to open that diary in your work.

> "Led Zeppelin didn't happen until I was nine or ten, when I started to bleed, so it was totally perfect; I was all ready for Robert Plant."

Funny you should say that. Since before I wrote *Little Earthquakes* I've had a pact with myself of no censorship. See, if you're a songwriter and people don't really know who you are, that's one thing. But if you're singing your own songs, it's a little different in this respect: I've found that the more known a writer gets, the less powerful and exposing their work gets, because the more they get known, the less they want to expose. I've caught myself trying to censor recently, going, "Oh, my God, they're gonna know who *that* is. And they're *definitely* gonna know who *he* is." But this is not about putting names next to things. That's irrelevant. If people want to speculate, they've missed the point.

The paradox in this kind of writing is that the more you personalize, or Tori Amosize, your songs, the more universal they become to those who work to get inside them.

But I don't ever think that these are Tori Amos songs. I translate them in such a way because of Tori's experiences that would be different from so-and-so's experiences. Emotions are very simple. I don't find them complex at all, to be quite honest. Everybody understands basic emotions: feeling like a coward, wanting to kill some cunt and having no remorse about it. It's like, "No, I don't feel guilty about this. What I feel bad about is that I don't feel bad about this." That's what I have to look at. I try and crawl into my unconscious, and it's not that different from what's inside any of us. All of us have a bit of the vampire and a bit of the nightingale. But don't tell me that the hardest cats rockin' out there right now aren't afraid of pain. I'm just saying that, whatever your lifestyle, they're all bummed out that Mom's gone.

In his last work, John Lennon even turned domesticity into art.

Well, who says that just because you fall in love and you open your heart to somebody that you're not gonna have more passion, more angst, more to look at than you ever had? The more you expose yourself to different feelings, the more you have to draw on. Obviously, if you're in a complacent relationship, your work might sound that way. But why does growing have to be synonymous with complacency? There's so much self-destruction on the artist's side. Not necessarily on the hack's side. Hacks aren't self-destructive, because they've got a business to run. But the artist will do anything to keep the machine going. We're so afraid to write things that won't be accepted. Well, I believe that audiences get bored very quickly.

Bored with someone's output over a period of years?

Yeah, at a certain point. Maybe you know it even before they do, because you feel it.

How do you keep in touch with real life from within the cocoon of fame?

Look, if my whole life was …

Not your whole life.

Wait. If most of my life was about going into the studio, making the record, doing the video, doing the tour, living and breathing only that, at a certain point, what would I fucking write about? I *know* that. Now, there are some very good ones out there whose work is still about one kind of energy. Say it's anger: That's *all* it is. Well, guys, hello? Can we have maybe a different angle on your anger today? All the angry boys out there talk about how they can't have this stuff. Now, I adore angry boys. I'd make 'em all apple pie with cinnamon ice cream. But they all talk about how they can't have this and they can't have that. They've got this whole movement based on what they can't have. And I say to them, wrong. It's a choice. They've chosen not to have certain things. And none of them takes any responsibility for that. Those boys are gonna get interesting when they start to go, "I *chose* not to have love." Come on, boys. Let's say something interesting for a change, instead of, "I can never have this or that." *That's your choice*, because you think you're shit. There's very little responsibility for their part in it. They don't own up to, "The reason I can't have love is because I think I'm gonna shrivel when I'm with this woman, because I don't think I deserve her." Let's go into the *why*. To go into that, you have to *live*. You're not gonna get to these answers by I–IV–V–fucking–I.

And it's not just the boys. Some of the girls do it too. Ay-yi-yi, can we stop blaming the guys here? We can blame them for what they've done, but then we have to balance in what we've done. The work isn't interesting when people aren't constantly discovering. We're stopping our lives as writers because we think we won't make great art. Who has put this thought out there? It's like a virus.

> "The music business is packaging darkness, but for the most part I think it's just a parody of darkness."

You're saying that there's a loss with respect to talented writers who could have said so much more before getting stuck on a single riff.

Totally that's what I'm saying. It is such a sense of loss. I'm not gonna mention names, but I'll watch something and go, "I know that this is very calculated." Once you've been on the other side, you know what it is and what it isn't. You just smell it.

You're like, "This person has so much. They could go further than they ever thought they could go in their pain and their darkness." I've always said that Lucifer understands love better than anybody. You know he's done a mean tango with Greta Garbo a few times. Really understanding love is the only way you get to that side of things. Otherwise, you're just renting videos. It's HBO. These guys and girls who write about one more torture device over and over again? That doesn't scare them. That's not a challenge. And that's not challenging those kids who really are screaming. Talk about pain: If they want to experience pain, they should go hold hands with the Little Mermaid. Then they'll get scared shitless because they'll have to be real.

The pain industry that you're describing …

That's a great term for it. I guess I'm part of it too, in a sense.

… strips real pain of its validity. When people tire of hearing songs that tell them how miserable they should be, they're robbed of the opportunity to feel real misery.

And they become parodies of themselves. It's so theatrical. Where's the *real* experience, so that when you take it to theatrics the foundation is still strong? But when it's just about anger for anger's sake …

… you're describing the fashion rather than the guts.

It *is* a fashion, and it isn't really that deep. We can all be a bit seduced by it. There's a masochist in me too, but my masochist is getting a little bit bored. It's not getting satisfied by those guys anymore. It's like, "You think *that's* painful?" My God, Baudelaire and Rimbaud were talking about and experiencing the *heart*. But it's so easy to contrive something. You know, "We're marketing dismemberment this week. That seems to be what kids want, so we'll do it. No problem." The whole point is that dismemberment isn't darkness, is it? It's just dismemberment. It's like, that's why God created video, so that you don't have to do any work on yourself. It's just a good distraction, an alternative to getting to what darkness is. The music business is packaging darkness, but for the most part I think it's just a parody of darkness.

Look, I'm just saying that the writers' community has been given a drug. "Tori takes another step in her life, so she won't be able to write songs like 'Silent All These Years' anymore." Guess what? You're right. She'll never be able to write that again. So why is that a bad thing?

TRENT REZNOR

Positively Negative

Interviewed by Robert L. Doerschuk,
Keyboard, April 1990, and
Greg Rule, *Keyboard,* March 1994, December 1995

ome people say **Trent Reznor** saved synthesizers from extinction. I
say they're not far off the mark. In the late eighties and early nineties,
when keyboards were practically banned from rock, Trent and his Nine
Inch Nails bandmates brought synthesized salvation to the head-banging masses.
Their industrial sound was tough as nails yet proudly electronic, and it found favor
with millions. Trent's work was simply the best of its kind: masterfully written, produced, and recorded. At the time of these interviews Trent was on top of the world,
but it was a place he loathed. He stayed as far from the limelight as possible, kept
the shades pulled, and poured his intensity and dark energy into his music. During
our first in-studio interview Trent had transformed the recording confines into a
dimly lighted, creepy temple of sorts. For Round Two we met at a hotel in Hartford,
Connecticut, where NIN was about to embark on a tour with David Bowie. Trent
had checked in under the name of Dr. Hannibal Lecter. Both of us couldn't help but
chuckle when we heard a knock at the hotel door midway through our interview:
"Room service for Dr. Lecter—we have the wine you ordered."

—Greg Rule, Editor in Chief, Keyboard

•   •   •

*You're best known for your production work, sound design, and sample process-
ing for Nine Inch Nails and other bands. But you're not thought of that much as
a keyboard player.*

I can play. I was classically trained. I have technique at my disposal. But I've
kind of abandoned technique and tried to approach music more from the by-ear

147

method or by impulse rather than by theory. [On the debut NIN album *Pretty Hate Machine*] I played pretty much everything into the sequencer, but to offset the perfectly quantized drums and bass, I tried to use the elements of vocals and guitar as totally rough, usually on the first take, so that the record didn't feel too perfect.

Why?

I enjoy working by myself, and I hadn't found anyone I really wanted to collaborate with. Rather than whine about not having musicians at my disposal, it was a challenge to figure out what I could do myself. I've always composed on the computer. I don't know how to do it any other way.

Was there something about your classical training that got in the way of your emotional expression or creative process?

"I would find lyrically a lot of the things on *The Downward Spiral* more dangerous than the gangsta rap stuff."

Maybe. It got to the point in high school or junior high where it was like, "Why don't you take fewer classes in school, and practice ten hours a day?" To sacrifice a normal life to become a concert pianist really had no appeal to me. There's a beauty in being able to play back someone else's music with incredible technique, but in another sense you're limited to, "You shouldn't play that with rubato because it wasn't written that way." I began asking myself, why am I playing this instrument? Is it to excel in technique? To me, that's a bit stifling. Rather than be great at one instrument, I'd rather have a general knowledge of a few, and work in a more composition-oriented environment. Also, I had that teenage rebellious streak, so it was like, forget it. I didn't look at another piece of music. I started approaching things differently. I could lay my fingers on the keys, and if I thought about it I could figure out what that chord would be. But I started trying to go more from instinct: "I know what it's gonna sound like without thinking about what it is."

Did you draw any inspiration from listening to more experimental bands?

Keyboard-wise, I was really into the Cars. The way they approached synthesizers, melding them with the guitar, was cool. That's about the level of alternativeness I was into. Growing up in rural Pennsylvania, I didn't have access to the true underground. There was no college radio around there, and no bands. You had to find outside influences through osmosis. So I grew up liking Kiss and bands like that. Those are my roots, shallow as they may seem.

People who know you only through your records, videos, and stage appearances perceive you as a deep, dark, troubled individual. Are you really as angry as your public image suggests?

Right. [*Long pause.*] First of all, did I conceive Nine Inch Nails to be this monstrous, negative entity? No. I think because Nine Inch Nails is focused on a certain element of my head, usually the more negative regions, people get the idea that that's all there is. But it's not. Now, that's not to say I don't have a lot of problems to work out in my brain. But I don't stay in a dark room all day with a sheet over my head.

So why does NIN still project this essentially negative vibe?

It started from: What can I say, if anything? I noodled around with some shit that didn't mean anything to me, but I liked the Clash so I tried to write lyrics like that. Then I got to a more intimate level and I realized I had a lot of things I wanted to say. So I started to put things on paper, how I really felt, like journal-type entries, and it came out being about things that bothered me: I don't fit in, I'm not good-looking, I want this out of life and I don't think I've gotten it—things of that nature. I'm not saying any of those feelings aren't things anybody else hasn't felt, but my way of exercising and expressing this frustration was through my music. I realized that I had more to say in that department than anything else. It was also kind of embarrassing because it was right to the bone. It wasn't like Lenny Kravitz's lyrics, for example— rock lyrics, probably well-written. But with my lyrics it isn't a character saying it, it's *me* saying it.

You certainly don't do much to dispel your image in concert.

Onstage, it is a conscious decision to not talk between songs— "How's everybody doing tonight?" First of all, that's not what I'd normally say. If I based my stage persona on David Lee Roth I would feel a need to do that, but I don't. You do become an extended caricature of yourself on the stage because it's surreal. You're in front of all these people, and there's this energy, and you're allowed to do whatever you want. So it becomes this distortion.

> "With my lyrics it isn't a character saying it, it's *me* saying it."

Will we ever see you on TV, smiling gleefully, singing about a mountain stream or whatever?

That's a hard one to answer, but if I felt that way, that's what my music would be like. If I went through such a sudden change, though, I think Nine Inch Nails would gracefully bow out as an entity and I would become whatever else.

How would Nine Inch Nails sound unplugged?

[*Grins.*] I had a few theories on that. My favorite one was us onstage with our equipment, and I'd look at Chris [Vrenna, ex-NIN drummer] and say, "Start the tape." He reaches over and pushes Play, and of course it's not on. It's unplugged; you can see the plug hangin' there. And I say, "Start the tape, Chris," and he pushes the Start button, and … nothing. So we just smash our instruments and leave [*laughs*]. But I've thought about interesting ways to … the thought I've had is, I've hung with Rick Rubin a lot, who's most likely going to produce a new Nine Inch Nails album, because I think it's an anti-Flood mentality, which is good because I need to have a new change. I know he's much more traditional-song-oriented [than Flood, producer on

Trent Reznor, 1995: Ridding his system of angst.

NIN's *The Downward Spiral*]. So as a writer I've been thinking more in terms of seeing what it would be like to go in that direction a bit. I don't mean becoming more conventional, but maybe starting with a song and then arranging it in any fashion—just little games you play to trick yourself into things. At the same time I also like the idea of removing those elements and seeing how far removed from a traditional song you can get and still have an element of something catchy about it.

Your keyboard player, Charlie Closer, programmed a bunch of tracks for White Zombie on songs that often have only one or two chords.

But there are choruses hidden in there, and that's the thing. You can have one note go through the whole song, but when he [Rob Zombie] starts singing "More human than human," that's the chant-along chorus. Most of Ministry's songs are one riff for as many bars as you can stand it, but it's still catchy because it does relate to something, as opposed to, say, some vintage Skinny Puppy, where what you think might be a chorus never comes back, which I think can be either rambling nonsense or an interesting format. I'm into songs that are breaking out of the mold that I've fallen prey to: verse, chorus, verse, chorus, bridge, solo section, chorus, chorus. Almost every one of my songs fits that same structure. I heard a track by Shudder to Think and I thought, "What the fuck? The meter's weird. Nothing repeats until the very end, where there's this little chant. It's fuckin' cool shit." So I went out and got the record. The structure of that was weird, but it worked.

So what do you think now when you go back and listen to The Downward Spiral?

After we finished it, I didn't listen to it for a while. I was too close to it. Then we went on tour and started playing some of the songs from it, and about midway through that tour I started listening to it again, a lot, and I was pleasantly surprised. I thought it held up. There were some things that I'd even forgot I'd done. And about a month ago, I started listening to it again. As with everything I've ever done, there are things I wouldn't do again, but generally I'm pretty pleased with it.

What things wouldn't you do again?

[*Pause.*] When I'm working, I try to maintain a spontaneous element and not overanalyze everything. Usually what I'll do … like, with *Pretty Hate Machine* I knew I only had X amount of time to get that whole record done in the studio, so I had everything completely done in advance. The studio was just a formality of putting it on tape. There was very little spontaneous studio energy coming from me because I just didn't have time. One day it had to be recorded and the next day it had to be mixed, for every song. So there wasn't a lot of, "Hey, let's try …" The opposite danger occurs when you're under the false impression of, "Hey, we're not paying. Let's fuck around." You can get off track that way. We could spend a week mixing a song when it was probably good the second hour of the first day. So I try to keep an element of spontaneity going, but at the same time what I've learned is, do something, don't think about it, and then come back to it a couple weeks later and just listen. If you like it then, usually it's okay.

So toward the end of that record [*The Downward Spiral*] I knew I was winding down, and I had a last little burst of energy. I did some things that didn't have that check time. One was "Big Man with a Gun," and the others were "Downward Spiral" and "Hurt." Listening to it later, there were a lot of things about "Big Man with a Gun" that I wouldn't put on there now. It fit an emotion I thought needed to be on the record, but there was probably a better way of accomplishing it now that I've had time to look back at it. And little, dumb things about the mixes. Unlike mathematics, which is an absolute … you reach the end, and either it's right or wrong, and there's something about that that's beautiful. It's absolutely over. But if you're doing a mix or something creative, you don't get that "I'm done" signal. You have to learn to say, "This is good, but could it be better?" Maybe. "Could you write a better lyric?" Maybe, maybe not.

> "We could spend a week mixing a song when it was probably good the second hour of the first day."

"Closer" was a big hit from Downward Spiral, *despite its hook line: "I want to fuck you like an animal." Did it bother you when you heard that song being played with the f-word bleeped out?*

That song kind of came about … it just started with that line, and then the music built itself around that. That was the scariest song to write, because there would have been a time when I wouldn't have allowed myself to be that obvious, because I would have been afraid that it wasn't tough enough, or it was too disco. When I was writing it and I came up with that bass line, I thought, "This is so obvious, but fuck it." I mean, if you listen to the whole album, that song, musically, is the most digestible if you're trying to pick a single, but it's also crippled from the start because of the chorus. But I'm not going to change it to try to make it a single.

So was bleeping the f-word the best solution?

On one hand, yes. I mean, I saw somebody's little kid singing it, a five-year-old kid. I've got to question my own intentions in that department. But aside from that, what I've tried to do is subversively sneak some things in. I realize we have a pretty big audience now, so can I take that position and slip some things in that are potentially dangerous ideas? Not to decay the moral fiber of America, but to have something of substance to think about other than just fluff. With all this controversy about song lyrics, I was surprised that we didn't get blasted sooner than we did. But their own idiocy and lack of knowledge crippled their argument. I would find lyrically a lot of the things on *The Downward Spiral* more dangerous than the gangsta rap stuff.

But when the song started to take off, it surprised me. What I hoped would have been a higher art thing became a frat-house, date-rape, strip-club anthem thing. Sad. I mean, it is an ugly song, no doubt. It's not nice. It's not life-affirmative. It's probably the ugliest one on the record, which is why I dressed it up in nice easy-to-listen-to music. But as culture moves on and people become less inhibited by religious oppression and are encouraged to think for themselves, if people get over the silliness and the tools and mechanisms of organized religion that are used to invoke fear, things will get a lot better. I think censorship has been causing a lot of problems in a lot of different departments in terms of human evolution. But, hey, that's what this country is based on—the ridiculous, right-wing, keep-you-in-line, don't-think-too-hard mentality.

Does that in fact make it easier for you to reach audiences that might be fed up with these sorts of things?

I think so. In some respect, it's an awareness of universal problems that young people have while growing up: waking up, seeing that it's not all as you were trained to think it would be, grasping that you're not part of the perfect yuppie world—a universal postpunk mentality. You see a lot of bands in the industrial movement who seem able to play upon this personal alienation and also get into the environmental issues that go hand-in-hand with it. Some of it is legitimate, but a lot of it is following the leader, even though these guys don't truly know what they're talking about or what they believe in. I'm trying to distance myself from that mentality. Nine Inch Nails is not here to change the world. I'm not out to make any great statement about politics, or "Don't put plastic on the cover of *Keyboard*." Really, it's about personal angst. My music is a way for me to get it out of my system.

3

BASS PLAYER

When *Bass Player* was launched as a regular publication, we had a big advantage. We were following in the footsteps of *Guitar Player*, the magazine that had originated the "by musicians, for musicians" category and set the rules for all the musical instrument publications that followed. And we were being guided by Tom Wheeler, *GP*'s venerable editor and our editorial director. So it wasn't surprising that our articles featured the kind of detailed "nuts and bolts" information that *GP*'s readers had come to expect.

But we had a vision for *BP*'s long-term success, one that would take it beyond being a *GP* clone. As a longtime bassist myself, I knew that the electric bass wasn't just a big guitar and that its players formed a distinct community, one quite different from the community of guitarists (or any other group of players). There were also all those musicians who played the acoustic upright bass, either exclusively or along with the electric bass; we wanted to include them too. There had never been a magazine that addressed every kind of bassist, in every style of music, and *Bass Player* was going to be that publication.

153

We also wanted *BP* to have a unique point of view—and a unique sense of humor. (Bass players, in my admittedly biased opinion, are often the funniest guys in the band.) We sought writers, both staff members and freelancers, who were serious about bass playing and irreverent about almost everything else. We wanted to be as entertaining as we were informative. And we tried hard to forge a bond with our readers, listening to their ideas and using them to continually improve the magazine. That, more than anything else, explains how *BP* was able to grow from a quarterly startup to a successful monthly in little more than five years—and why it's still going strong.

— Jim Roberts
Editor, Bass Player, *1989–1996*

RAY BROWN

Father Time

Interviewed by Richard Johnston,
Bass Player, March 1993

R ay Brown stands astride the past half-century as the single most significant figure of jazz bass. His career began in the forties, when he carried the influence of Duke Ellington bass virtuoso Jimmy Blanton to
the new technical demands of bebop, and it continues to the present as he nurtures
the next generation of jazz musicians in his own trio. Along the way he has brought
his powerful and eloquent upright style to jazzers ranging from Charlie Parker to
Diana Krall, while delving successfully into television, film, and pop music. After pur-
suing Brown over several months for a *Bass Player* interview, I finally hooked up with
him by telephone from his home near Los Angeles. Our talk started inauspiciously—
he was obviously finishing his dinner, and my first questions got only one-word answers. But eventually the dishes got cleared and he grew more expansive on his
history, musical concepts, and opinions.

—*Richard Johnston, Editor,* Bass Player, *1998–2001*

• • •

When you were first starting out, a bass solo was still a fairly unusual thing.

Well, you didn't get a lot of them. You couldn't hear 'em anyway, unless you played
a rhythm solo or some kind of slap thing. There were no amplifiers. I started playing
solos with [pianist] Snookum Russell. Jimmy Blanton had put out all those solos, so I
had something to go by. Then there was Slam Stewart's stuff; he had some records out
with Lester Young and Benny Goodman. They were the two most prominent soloists
at the time. Later on, there was Oscar Pettiford.

155

You were just in your teens when you started playing with saxophonist Jimmy Hinsley. What was that like?

I was on the road then. Most guys either left to go on the road as soon as they got out of school or before, if they could get away with it. My folks said I had to finish high school before I went out. But as soon as I finished high school, I was *gone.* Jimmy Hinsley played nightclubs, and we would sit down for a month or two months at a club. When I joined Hinsley in the summer of '44, it was in Buffalo. We stayed there maybe twelve weeks in a club called the Moonglow.

How did you get that job?

He came to Pittsburgh and heard me at a jam session at the [Musician's] Union. He offered me a job, and I told him I was in school and couldn't take a job until after I graduated.

Had you taken any lessons on bass?

No. I had formal lessons on piano but not on the bass. Four or five years later, I had a teacher in every city. I had a different symphony guy I went to see in Seattle, San Francisco, L.A., Denver, Chicago, Detroit, New York, Philadelphia, Toronto, Boston, and Washington, D.C., so wherever I went I took lessons.

Was there an advantage to having so many teachers?

No. I think you're better off to go to one teacher, but I didn't have that choice. If you're traveling, the next best thing you can do is get a bunch of teachers. But the idea is to keep studying.

> "My folks said I had to finish high school before I went out [on the road]. But as soon as I finished high school, I was *gone.*"

How did you land your job with Dizzy Gillespie?

That's a famous story. I got to New York and went down to 52nd Street the night I arrived—my cousin took me down there. I was walking around, looking at all the different joints, and I saw Hank Jones. I had met Hank in Buffalo; we were both staying at the YMCA, and we would jam together in the afternoon. So I went in and started talking to him. While we were talking Dizzy Gillespie came to the door, and Hank said, "That's Dizzy Gillespie." I said, "Oh, yeah? Introduce me to him; I want to meet him." So he called Dizzy over and told him I was a good bass player who had just gotten in town. Dizzy said, "Oh, yeah? You want a job?" [*Laughs.*] And that's how it happened.

Was Dizzy's music a challenge?

It was different, but I found it very exciting. I think it was just what I needed to get my attention, because I hadn't played anything like that. I had to listen and ask

Ray Brown, 1970: Meeting
the challenge of bebop.

questions. That's the way it was in those days. I was always inquisitive, so I think I learned most of my stuff by asking questions. Dizzy was the kind of guy who would show you stuff if you asked questions, so I learned a lot.

What was it like then, to play unamplified and compete with the rest of the band?

[*A big laugh.*] Well, by comparison it was a lot tougher. You had to put the strings up high, and the gut strings broke a lot when it got hot, if you had acid in your perspiration. But somehow we got it done. When I listen to some of the records we made before we had amplifiers, it sounds pretty damn good.

Do you think you've changed the way people play bass?

I guess I've influenced some people. I think most people who get prominent on any instrument influence a certain amount of people automatically, just by making records and being heard.

What does it take to keep going strong, as you have, over six decades of making music?

I think first you have to have a desire to play the music—a love of music. That's like the pilot light you need to have that never goes out. Then it's a matter of what you put into it is what you get out of it. You have to spend a lot of time practicing and playing.

What does it take for a drummer and bass player to work well as a team?

I think it's a growth thing. Once in a while you'll meet up with a drummer, and the first day you play together you hit it off right away. But that doesn't happen all the time. That happened to me when I was in L.A., and Quincy Jones was going to New York to record the album that had "Killer Joe" and all that stuff....

Walking in Space.

Yeah, *Walking in Space*. So he said, "Why don't you come to New York and record?" I said, "Oh, man, they got plenty of bass players in New York. You don't need me." But he said, "I think I need *you* on this one. It's something I got in mind." He kept after me, and finally I went to New York with him. We got to this record date, and the first track we did was "Killer Joe," and it was Grady Tate playing drums. We just hit it right off together. When we were in the booth, listening to the playback, and everybody was nodding their heads and patting their feet, Quincy looked up at me and said, "That's what I had in mind! I wanted to hear you guys together." So sometimes that works. But normally it's like a marriage: You play with somebody, you begin to think the same; your time becomes one. You could play across the street from each other and still play good time together.

Have you done much else on electric bass?

Yeah, but not that I want to remember [*laughs*].

Why not?

I don't think I really like that instrument. I played it because at the time it was necessary in the studio. At first in most sessions they would have six bass players, and you'd be playing all day. Then they were down to two: one string bass player and one electric bass player. Now they've gotten to the point where they call and say, "Okay, bring both [instruments]"—one bass player. So to keep all the work going, I had to double. But I never did fall in love with the instrument. I think you need to love what you're playing, and I love the string bass.

Are there any electric bass players you like?

Oh, yeah, there are a lot of them. It goes back to Monk Montgomery, probably the first guy to play it. Then James Jamerson, Chuck Rainey—and there's a bunch of young guys now who play the hell out of it. They play upright too, like ... what's that tall boy's name?

Stanley Clarke?

Yeah, Stanley Clarke. And John Patitucci. [Guitarist] Phil Upchurch used to play good electric bass. I ran into another guy ... you know, I can't think of his name now. I did a TV show with him.

Victor Wooten?

Yeah! [Brown, Wooten, and Edgar Meyer appeared together on PBS's *Lonesome Pine Special*.] Played the hell out of it. We had a lot of fun on that thing, because we just met the morning of the show. We had breakfast, and the guys came up to my room and we put the thing together, just before going to the studio.

Would you consider doing sessions full-time again?

No. It was fun while I was doing it, but I don't think I'd want to do it again. The sessions I do are very, very limited. I'm on the road most of the time anyway. The few times I'm not on the road, I'm home relaxing. A session like a Linda Ronstadt or a Natalie Cole is a little different; it's a special thing. But regular commercial stuff, I don't do. I'm enjoying writing and playing for my own group; I don't think I could beat that.

What about live TV work?

At times it can be all right. I did a lot of shows—*phew* [*laughs*]. Basically, the thing about TV is there's not enough to play. There's too many days when all the guests are writers, movie actors, something, and there's nothing for you to do but play on and play off. The rest of the time you're just sitting around. You do that long enough, you forget how to play.

How do you feel about the improvements in recording upright bass?

You're saying it has improved? I don't agree with you there. You get too many engineers now that don't know anything about string bass. All they know is electric bass. They all want to put you through the "blue box." It means they don't have to sit there and watch the needle while you're playing acoustically. They can take you direct; it saves them a lot of time and trouble. Sometimes I go into the studio and I have to fight with the guy about my sound. He'll say, "I got too much to do; I gotta take you direct. I don't have time to *pay attention* to you." Well, that makes you feel good, you know?

What would you tell someone who wants to be a full-time jazz bassist?

Practice ten hours a day, and you got no problem. That'll fix everything. The big deal is knowing songs. It's the same thing in classical music. If a guy applies for a job, they want to know how much repertoire he knows. In jazz, the leader wants to be able to call any kind of tune, from Ellington to Rodgers and Hart. The more you know that stuff, the better off you are. Plus, if you don't have any hassles with what key it's in, that's even better. I don't know where I learned all the tunes I know, but I know a lot of them.

> "You play with somebody, you begin to think the same; your time becomes one. You could play across the street from each other and still play good time together."

What about adapting to the concepts of different players?

You have to be flexible. When you get on the gig, you can easily tell whether they're going to listen to you or whether they're going to listen to the guitar player or the piano player. Somebody usually winds up leading the section. But a lot of times there's six to eight ways to play a tune, and you just have to see which way it's gonna go. Maybe the first time down there'll be some clashes, and the second time down you'll go where somebody else goes or they'll come to where you're at. It takes a few choruses sometimes. When you play a song, the guy who *has* to commit himself first is the bass player. He has to play the first note. He has to commit to the chord as soon as the song starts. *Bam!* If he doesn't play the downbeat he's wrong, or if he plays a first or third inversion, most times he's gonna sound like he doesn't know the tune.

> "Sometimes I go into the studio and I have to fight with the guy about my sound. He'll say, 'I got too much to do. I don't have time to *pay attention* to you.' Well, that makes you feel good, you know?"

What do you do when you don't know what chord is coming?

You've got to watch the piano player's left hand. If you can't see his hand, you've gotta fake your way through it until you can hear it.

Is it the same kind of give-and-take with the drummer?

When you play with a drummer, either you're gonna follow him or he's gonna follow you. This is not done by the spoken word, but by the way you play your instrument. I tell bass players, if you play like you know what you're doing, with a strong beat, good intonation, and the right notes, everybody will follow you.

What about learning how to solo?

Copy somebody. It doesn't have to be a bass player, but it can be. You ought to listen to horn players, because they don't approach solos the same way. When I was young I used to take all the Charlie Parker things off records. I loved the way Bird played solos, so I would try to steal his stuff.

What makes a solo great?

I like to hear a guy play a solo that when I go home I can still remember some of the things he played. Melodic, not just a lot of notes for notes' sake. A bass player has to think of the chord changes even if he doesn't want to; it's automatic. But a horn player has the bass and piano playing the changes for him, so he doesn't have to think about it. It's good for a bass player to listen to that approach. And different guys have different styles. Coleman Hawkins played all the changes. Lester Young played no changes, but he played little melodies on top of the changes. If you start listening and playing all those things and put it all into your "computer," something will come out eventually that will be yours.

Are there any current bass soloists you especially like?

Oh, yeah, there's a bunch of great soloists around. People like Niels Pedersen, George Mraz, and Eddie Gomez. And some of the younger guys: Charnett Moffett, Christian McBride. There's a whole slew of good young bass players now. I think bass players nowadays are more free and melodic than we used to be. I think that's the ultimate way to play a solo.

Would you like to see more young players start on acoustic rather than electric?

I'd like to see that, but you gotta face what's going on in your time. Guys are taking up electric bass because that's what all the jobs are for. Hell, most of the TV shows nowadays are done by machines, so the music can't be too important to them.

What styles of music do you listen to?

I like all kinds of music, as long as they're done well. I wish that every radio station had to play, within one hour's time, some classical music, some country & western, some jazz, some rock—not batter your ears down with the same goddamn music. People in this country don't listen to music with their brains; they listen to it with their behinds. It's our own doing. I think we should listen to everything; we'd all be better off.

JOE OSBORN

AKA Anonymous

Interviewed by Chris Jisi with Anthony Jackson,
Bass Player, May 1992

What unsung electric bass pioneers need to have their stories told?"
I asked my collaborator, Anthony Jackson, who has a keen interest
in the history of his instrument. "Joe Osborn," he instantly replied,
referring to the sixties L.A. session great. We flew Joe from his native Louisiana to New
York City, and on entering his hotel room we were greeted by a thick Bayou drawl, a
warm handshake, and a cold six-pack. The look on Anthony's face mirrored my own
momentary doubt: Did this easygoing, fifty-something Southerner remember any of
the artists he worked with 25 years prior, much less the details of his penetrating pick
lines on dozens of Top Ten hits? Two hours later we had learned more than just the
answers to all our questions. In an era when producers believed bass was meant only
to be felt in an almost subliminal support role, Joe Osborn arrived with a new instrument and let everyone know that it was okay for the bass to be heard and to be an
active part of the music.

—*Chris Jisi, Senior Contributing Editor,* Bass Player

• • •

You've always played with a pick. Why?

Osborn: Roy Buchanan and I were playing guitar in Bob Luhman's band at the
Showboat Hotel in Las Vegas in 1959. While we were there, we borrowed an electric
bass, and Roy started playing it, since Bob liked the way I played his country licks.
Later, Bob added a female vocalist who sang a lot of pop standards; I didn't know
all the chords, so I told Roy he'd have to come back to the guitar. I went down to the

local music store and bought a [Fender] Precision Bass. The next night I was the bass player—same amp, same settings, same pick and technique. I played it just like I played the guitar.

A few years later, when I got out to L.A. with Ricky Nelson and began working on records and publishing demos, people would say, "Wow, we can hear the bass all of a sudden." All the notes came out clearly, and I had no idea why. Eventually I realized that my bass, played with the pick, had its own frequency space. Instead of competing with the kick drum at the bottom, there was more of a blend. Plus it held up on any kind of record—even if the bass was EQ'd different, there was an attitude about it, a certain tone that you couldn't lose.

Jackson: Did you know immediately that the bass guitar was for you, or was there a period of strangeness, of indecision?

Osborn: I didn't give it much thought, because I was playing both instruments. It wasn't until Ricky Nelson's band that I officially became a "bass player." I guess it was strange at first, because I still visualized the guitar. In fact, I never have figured out what to do with the *E* string. I play mainly on the middle two strings for rhythm and up high on the *G* string for the lick.

Jackson: When you began playing, the upright was still the dominant bass instrument in popular music. Virtually no one playing the bass guitar had much of an idea how it should sound or how it should be played. When did you first become aware that, including yourself, there were a few players who were beginning to develop unique voices on the instrument?

Osborn: I never really listened to anybody else—but then, as you said, when I started out there weren't many people to listen to. Later on, I became aware of my peers: [L.A. studio players] Carol Kaye, Lyle Ritz, Ray Pohlmann, Max Bennett, Chuck Domanico, Ray Brown, and Red Callender. I loved James Jamerson's work up in Detroit. But I didn't listen to other musicians that much. The producers used to ask us to make it sound like this group or that feel; I'd turn to someone and say, "What is that?" and have him hum me the rhythm.

> "A studio musician is, after all, a prostitute. You're hired for a certain length of time to do what the producer wants, and you're not getting paid to like it."

Jackson: Did people consider you and Carol Kaye interchangeable, since you both played with a pick?

Osborn: Probably. But most contractors called everybody two weeks in advance and put them on hold, and then as they filled up their dates they'd cancel the rest. Quite often players were shuffled around with little regard to the style of music. I'd be on a session that Max should be doing and vice versa. Some producers were waiting for me to be available. If I couldn't make a date, I'd always send in the best player I knew of. A lot of people wouldn't do that, for fear of losing their gig.

I've heard that studio guitarist Tommy Tedesco encouraged you to learn how to read music.

Osborn: He said, "I see you on sessions for Johnny Rivers or the Mamas & The Papas, working your ass off to create those parts. If you learn how to read, you can do all the easy dates where you come in, read the chart, and split. You'll double your money, and you can still do the creative things." That made a lot of sense, so I got a book and worked my way up to page twelve—and my work did double!

Another fellow who helped me was an arranger named Al Capps. He didn't care if I played his written line, but he always wrote out the part with the chord symbols above, so if I tried to read it and got lost, I could just look at the chords. That gave me a chance to practice without any pressure. Inevitably, while I was still learning, I'd come across some arranger who would say, "Excuse me, is there something wrong with the part?" I'd say, "I certainly hope not, 'cause I'm having enough trouble if it's correct!" [*Laughter.*]

> "The Association got up and made a speech one morning: 'Please don't tell anyone you guys are doing all our records.'"

John Phillips was known for having all-night recording sessions at his home in Bel Air. Was that a creative atmosphere?

Osborn: Yes and no. John was great—he gave us a lot of freedom to create parts, and sometimes he'd come up with good things, like the bass fill at the end of the verses on "California Dreamin'." But as he's acknowledged, he had his problems with drugs, and it would get very boring after a while. It might take from two in the afternoon till daylight the next morning to get one track done.

Jackson: How were the 5th Dimension sessions by comparison?

Osborn: They were more structured in terms of time and what was either written or dictated for us to play. One of the few times I got to stretch out was when the producer, Bones Howe, told me to get real busy in the fade of "Aquarius/Let the Sunshine In."

How did you meet Karen and Richard Carpenter?

Osborn: I had put a four-track studio in my garage to mess around with on weekends, and someone sent over a trumpet player for me to check out. Karen and Richard came along to accompany him; she sang "Ebb Tide" and it knocked me out. I encouraged them to come back and record a bunch of songs that Richard had written. Some of those tracks ended up on their first album.

Yet you were only credited—and probably compensated—as a sideman, with no regard for your production efforts. Was that a sore point for you?

Osborn: Not really. I got irritated with Richard for some reason or other, and I told him to take his tape and go get a deal. Then again, I suppose it's got to be something of a sore point, because I'd like to think that if it were the other way around I'd have shown some sort of appreciation. But I ended up playing on a lot of their records anyway. In fact, to this day, Richard will bet you $1,000 he can hear one note and tell if it's me.

Jackson: I'm sure you played on plenty of records by famous bands that were supposedly using their own bass players. Did any of them swear you to secrecy?

Osborn: Oh, sure. The Association got up and made a speech one morning: "Please don't tell anyone you guys are doing all our records." But the producers didn't care. They'd go in and make a hit record and then put a band together to go out on the road. We recorded for a lot of groups: Gary Lewis & The Playboys, the Monkees, the Grass Roots, Spanky & Our Gang, the Partridge Family. I was talking to a keyboard player in Nashville about some of the projects that Hal [Blaine, drummer], Larry [Knechtel, pianist], and I played on, and he said, "Man, I just found out my five favorite bands are all the same people!" [*Laughter.*]

Jackson: Why did the concept of the group that does everything—the industry rhythm section—disappear? Was there a backlash on the order of, "So-and-so uses Hal, Larry, and Joe, so we've got to use someone else, even if they're the best"?

Osborn: Well, we were a little different, because people hired us individually—unlike, say, Muscle Shoals, where in that studio you got those four guys. A lot of times I'd show up with Hal, but there were people who liked me with [drummers] Jimmy Gordon or Earl Palmer. And, of course, there were people who wouldn't hire me on a big bet. When self-contained groups started to appear, one or two of us would be called in—Larry played with Bread, and Hal and I worked with the Carpenters. Hal has mentioned feeling a backlash personally, but I never noticed any. Then again, you have to remember that we were one rhythm section but we never sounded the same from record to record, even with the same artist.

Even so, were there certain basic things you did in approaching a track, and has that approach changed over the years?

Osborn: Not really. Aside from the given of locking with the drummer, I always play for the song. If you listen to the song—the lyrics, the feel, the vocals—it will feed you and tell you what to do. What it all comes down to, in the end, is attitude. You can learn the notes and the form, but ultimately you've got to just put both feet on the floor, dig in, and play.

Jackson: What about extreme cases, where no matter what you try the producer feels it's not happening? Or, just the opposite, when you're hired to fill in all the holes and basically finish writing the track?

Osborn: Both are okay with me. If a part isn't happening, there's always something you can do—bring it way back or try something extra busy. I don't mind criticism; what I don't like is people who say nothing at all. Heck, I can remember Art Garfunkel telling me, "Make it sound like a horse galloping through a spring meadow," but at least that gave me something to go on. As far as someone saying, "Joe, come up with an intro for this song," which is what happened on Johnny Rivers's "Memphis," or "Play a fill in this space," like I did on [the Mamas & The Papas'] "Words of Love," that's all right. A studio musician is, after all, a prostitute. You're hired for a certain length of time to do what the producer wants, and you're not getting paid to like it. Now, is that prostitution or not? The gratifying part for me has always been hearing a good playback. That's why I never really enjoyed playing live: I could never hear myself or anybody else. I've always preferred the environment of the studio.

> "Don't reject any idea that comes along from another musical avenue, because the session business will retire you before you know it."

Were you busy when you decided to leave L.A.?

Osborn: Yeah, but I was sick of the whole scene. I was mad all the time for no reason. It was just burnout. If I had learned how to cut back that might have made a difference, but I didn't know how to turn anything down. I thought if they called, you had to go. After I moved to Nashville it was different; I wouldn't take a morning session if I'd worked the night before.

Jackson: Looking back, what would you have done differently?

Osborn: I tried to hang on to the session situation a little too long, because it was comfortable: Just wait for the phone to ring and tell you where to go that day. For a long time I didn't try to make anything else happen. People would ask me if I'd like a shot at producing or writing some songs, and I'd tell them I was too busy. Then when things started to slow down and I tried to get into those areas, I found it was harder than I thought. It took me a while to get it going. The moral is: Don't reject any idea that comes along from another musical avenue, because the session business will retire you before you know it.

Jackson: How would you hope to be remembered?

Osborn: I'd like to think that maybe the way I played and the way my bass sounded changed the way records were made—indirectly, by making it acceptable to hear the bass cut through in a melodic way. I hope that when people listened to me doing things they hadn't heard before, it inspired them to try new things and to develop their own styles—just as you did, Anthony. I'll tell you, it's very flattering to learn that I influenced you.

Jackson: Well, I'm sure there are many more who feel as I do. After decades of listening to your work, I consider myself very fortunate to have finally had the opportunity to meet and talk with you.

Osborn: The pleasure was all mine.

BILL WYMAN

Stone Simple

Interviewed by Gregory Isola,
Bass Player, May 1998;
Jon Sievert, *Guitar Player,* December 1978

D rawing ham-handed comparisons between a musician's interview personality and his recorded work is a hoary critic's cliché at best, a flaming cop-out at worst. Still—and these instances torture the conscientious writer—sometimes the comparisons ring too true to pass up. For three decades—on the world's biggest stages, in the world's finest studios, and at the world's wildest parties—bassist Bill Wyman lived the life of a Rolling Stone. Called upon to anchor the greatest riffs in rock, he always came through. He played simply, stoically, but make no mistake—Wyman held together the World's Greatest (and often world's loosest) Rock & Roll Band at every turn. The comparison? Our interview was no different. From fond recollections of favorite instruments to poignant tales of passionate young men chasing their blues to pointed anecdotes that skewered his famous former bandmates, Wyman answered question after question with the relaxed enthusiasm, congenial good humor, and timely insight of a favorite neighbor—but he elaborated only as necessary. In other words, he let me call the tune; he simply supported everything I said with just the right notes.

—*Gregory Isola,* Bass Player, *1994–1999*

• • •

How did you get interested in music?

Basically, I think my parents wanted me to study piano just because we had one in the house. The fundamental music lessons in school were actually quite good— the theory lessons. They were good for teaching you about crotchets [quarter-notes]

Bill Wyman, 1989: Doing what comes from inside.

and minims [half-notes] and all of that. I was always messing about on the piano instead of doing the right things. I used to speed them up and slow them down and put twiddley bits on and all of that, and my parents used to get very angry.

Did you have access to much recorded music?

Only on the radio. And if you would listen to the BBC in those days, there was really nothing on there. The first person I heard who I thought was really amazing was Les Paul. He was the guy who turned me on to the sound of guitar music. I was listening to singers before that—mostly English ones, doing covers of American hits by people like Frankie Laine and Kay Starr. Johnnie Ray was one of the first to make me really open my ears. That was like two or three years before Elvis. A few jazz records made it across, and though I'm not really interested in jazz, I do have some nice memories of some records by Dizzy Gillespie at the time and by a band led by Kenny Graham called the Afro-Cubists.

What about blues?

There really *wasn't* any blues music in England. You couldn't buy the records, and they never played it on the radio. But in London there was a very small, underground cult, about thirty or forty people, who were into buying stuff abroad and swapping tapes. Brian Jones was in that scene, and Mick and Keith got into it a bit later. I was sending off to Chicago for Chuck Berry records in '57 and '58, but Mick was sending off for bluesier stuff—Muddy Waters, Jimmy Reed, Slim Harpo—by the very early sixties. And Brian was really into Bo Diddley and Elmore James. So even though my band at the time, the Cliftons, was covering R&B artists like Jerry Lee Lewis, Ray Charles, Larry Williams, and Sam Cooke, I'd never heard of Elmore James and Slim Harpo! In fact, when the Stones gave me a Jimmy Reed tape a week before our first rehearsal, I thought it was a bit slow and dull. But it was fresh; there was something nice in it I'd never heard before, apart from early jazz-blues things like Jelly Roll Morton.

How do you explain the immediate appeal of the Stones in those early years?

Every band in England in '63—the Beatles, Gerry & the Pacemakers, the Hollies, Herman's Hermits, the Dave Clark Five, you name 'em—they were all playing [*sings straight-eighth groove*] *dut-dut-dut-dut*. Every song they played was like that. The Stones were the only band in England—the *only* band—playing shuffle rhythms. We really swung onstage very early on, and it surprised people. Older jazz musicians could do it, but no one expected young kids to play like that—and people just couldn't keep their feet still. Of course, when we went to America Jimmy Reed was on all the jukeboxes, especially in Texas, so the shuffle wasn't such a revelation [*laughs*].

Who did you listen to for bass inspiration in those days?

Except for the Chicago stuff with Willie Dixon, most of those records didn't have bass on them. So I tried to find something that fit the music, and I ended up with a style that's quite sparse. I leave lots of holes, because I found the best thing to do on a slow blues is as little as possible. Then when I first heard Booker T. & the MG's in '62, Duck Dunn became my favorite player. I just loved his simplicity; he never got in the way. I knew most people were listening to Keith and Mick and didn't really notice the bass, but that's the way I think it should be.

What did you think of the work being done by bass players in other bands at the time?

I heard all these incredible, magical bass players in those days—Jack Bruce, John Entwistle, John Paul Jones, Felix Pappalardi—but they're all too busy for me. I totally admire their technique; I just can't stand the way they play! It's like another guitar; there's no *underneath*. Ronnie Wood plays like that too. He'd play on the odd Stones song here or there if I wasn't in the studio, and he'd always ask me later, "What do you think of that, Bill?" And I'd always say, "Bloody horrible! Where's the *bass*?" [*Laughs.*]

> "Every time we'd rehearse 'Satisfaction,' Keith would play it wrong."

You and Charlie didn't play off one another as much as you played together, like one big instrument.

I think I was one of the first bass players in England to understand I had to play along with the bass drum and really concentrate on what Charlie was doing. Jazz people were doin' it, and all the Americans were doin' it, but in England you didn't think like that; you just played along with the tune. I realized very quickly, though, that I should lock in on whatever Charlie was playing on his bass drum, and that's why we fit together so well so early on. The thing is, there was no one to teach you such things. You had to learn by trial and error. Luckily the band learned all these little tricks very quickly.

> "I finally said, 'Maybe someone else can bow it while I finger the notes.'"

How much input did the other Stones have on your bass lines?

Well, Keith runs the band; that's old news. But Mick always had the funniest way of suggesting bass lines. He'd come up to me during sessions and start making playing motions, like Joe Cocker does when he sings. And he'd say, "Play it like [*sings busy, atonal bass line*]." But he wouldn't sing the actual notes, so it was useless! When he'd walk away, I'd turn to Keith and ask, "What should I do?" And he'd mumble, "Play exactly what you played before." So I would, and afterwards Mick would come up and say, "That's better." [*Laughs.*] Mick's got his greatness in many ways, but sometimes he wasn't quite with us musically.

Keith Richards and Charlie Watts are formidable rhythm section mates, but your bass lines really drive "Satisfaction" and a great many other Stones tunes.

"Satisfaction" is a good example: I'm the only one who changes chords. Keith doesn't change, and there are no keyboards on it; there's only me. I just thought walking up to the next chord made it that much better. But when everybody else plays it—Otis Redding did a great cover—they play it on the same chord throughout. And of course the Otis Redding version caused all sorts of trouble because they played the riff in the wrong place, on the root of the chord instead of on the V. And the bass just doubled it, staying on the same chord. No one else thought about that at the time, but for years and years afterward, every time we'd rehearse "Satisfaction," Keith would play it wrong. He'd always start the riff on the root. I used to correct him all the time, and he'd say, "What do you mean I'm fuckin' playin' it wrong? Who wrote the song?!" "But you're playin' it like Otis Redding! It should be … [*sings the "Satisfaction" riff*] "Oh, oh, oh, yeah. That's right." [*Laughs.*]

What gives the Stones their characteristic sound? Why does no other band sound like them?

That's something I've tried to analyze with a lot of people. We have a very tight sound for a band that swings, but in amongst that tight sound, it's very ragged as well. Leon Russell and I finally came up with a theory that goes something like this: Every rock & roll band follows the drummer, right? If the drummer slows down, the band slows down with him or speeds up when he does. That's just the way it works—

except for our band. Our band does not follow the drummer; our drummer follows the rhythm guitarist, who is Keith Richards.

And that makes the difference?

Yes. Immediately you've got something like a one-hundredth-of-a-second delay between the guitar and Charlie's lovely drumming. Now, I'm not putting Charlie down in any way for doing this, but onstage you have to follow Keith. You have no way of *not* following him. You know there's no rigorous twelve bars and then we break and do that bit and then we come in with four more bars and then Mick does his part—it doesn't work out like that. The tune is basically worked out, but it changes all the time; it's very loose. So with Charlie following Keith, you have that very minute delay. Add to that the fact that I've always been able to pick up chord structures very quickly, so I tend to anticipate a bit because I kind of know what Keith's going to do. We've been playing together for so long that I know without even thinking about it. That's why I might be standing there looking at the ceiling when everybody else is looking at Keith to see when the final thing is coming down. I mean, we all make mistakes, but basically I don't need to watch Keith as the other guys tend to do, because I can feel when it's coming. That puts me a split second ahead of Keith.

What's the result?

When you actually hear that, it seems to just pulse. You know it's tight because we're all making starts and stops, and it is in time—but it *isn't*, as well. That's what we think is the reason for our sound, apart from our style. And yet sometimes the whole thing can reverse. Charlie will begin to anticipate, and I'll fall behind, but the net result is that loose type of pulse that goes between Keith, Charlie, and me.

How did that begin to happen? Was it a conscious decision or just a matter of personality?

Probably a matter of personality. Keith is a very confident and stubborn player, so he usually thinks someone else has made a mistake. Maybe you'll play halfway through a solo, and you'll find that Keith has turned the time around. He'll drop a half- or quarter-bar somewhere, and suddenly Charlie's playing on the beat, instead of on the backbeat—and Keith will not change back. He will doggedly continue until the band changes to adapt to him. It doesn't piss us off in any way, because we all expect it to happen. He knows in general that we're following him, so he doesn't care if he changes the beat around or isn't really aware of it. He's quite amusing like that. Sometimes Keith will be playing along, and suddenly he becomes aware that Charlie's playing on the beat, and he'll turn around and point like, "Aha! Gotcha!"

Like Charlie made the mistake?

Yeah, and Charlie will be so surprised and suddenly realize he's on the beat for some reason, and he hasn't changed at all. Then he'll be very uptight to get back in, because it's very hard for a drummer to swap the beat. So it's a mite funny sometimes, but it does happen, especially on the intros. Some of the intros are quite samey-sounding. I mean, if you're doing a riff on one chord with the inflections that Keith uses, and you're not hearing too well with the screaming crowds, you cannot tell if you're coming in on or off the beat.

Still, few bands have ever played together as well as the Stones.

That's because everything we did came from inside. We didn't think about it; we *felt* it. But we are all—Keith, Charlie, and I—quite naïve musically. This might amaze you, and it might disappoint a lot of people: If someone says to me, "Go from *G* up to *D-flat*," I have to think about it because I don't know where the notes are on the bass. Honestly, I don't. I play totally by feel and by ear. So I'd much rather just listen and *learn* the song than be told, "Go from *D* to *F*, then to *G* for a moment, and then back to the *D*." I can't think like that, and Keith and Charlie are the same way. If you say to Charlie, "Don't play your bass drum boom-ba *boom*, boom-ba *boom*. Instead play ba-*boom* boom, ba-*boom* boom," he'd say, "That's exactly the same thing!" [*Laughs.*]

That naïveté must have led to considerable experimentation in the studio.

Oh, yeah. Brian [Jones, founding Stones guitarist] and I used to try different things all the time, just to see what would work. For instance, we wanted a percussive upright bass sound for our version of Chuck Berry's "You Can't Catch Me." But my hands are just too small to play upright, and even my semi-acoustic Framus Star with flatwounds didn't sound quite right. So I borrowed Charlie's sticks and overdubbed a track of me playing my bass strings with drumsticks. It sounded great.

How did you tackle the bowed upright line on "Ruby Tuesday"?

Once again, my stretch was a problem. I knew where the notes were, and everyone in the studio was saying how right it was for the track—but I just wasn't able to get it together. So I finally said, "Maybe someone else can bow it while I finger the notes [*laughs*]." Keith said he'd do it, so we ran through it once to show him what strings to play and when to watch my hands, and then we just did it. And it worked perfectly.

> "Mick's got his greatness in many ways, but sometimes he wasn't quite with us musically."

Did you record any other acoustic bass parts with the Stones?

I did play upright on "Factory Girl" and a few other tracks on *Beggars Banquet*, but I had to play very simple bits. Years ago Sting bought one of those electrified things, and he told me to try it out. But it was the same problem: I just don't have the hands for it.

As far back as your first gigs with the Stones, you were playing what looks like a homemade fretless bass. What model were you using?

I think it's Japanese. I was playing in an R&B band in 1961 when I bought it from this bloke our drummer knew. Before that I'd been playing bass on the bottom two strings of a detuned guitar, so I was glad to finally have a "real" bass. Unfortunately, it was bloody horrible! The body was this great big wide thing. But I'd seen Gibson and Fender basses in pictures of Little Richard's and Fats Domino's bands, so I drew a shape like one of those on the back of my bass and had my next-door neighbor saw it down. Then I beveled the edges, took off all the paint, and put in a new Baldwin pickup. Still, it rattled with every note because the frets were so worn. I figured I'd just pull out all the frets and put in new ones when I could afford some. But when I pulled 'em out, it suddenly sounded really good! So I never put the frets back in, and I think it was the first fretless electric ever. I used it on every Stones album and many of the singles up to 1975. Even without an amp, it sounds wonderful; it's got *the* sound.

In the eighties, though, you began playing Steinberger L-2 headless basses.

No one liked the looks of it, especially Keith. But the sound was really good. The bigger problem was that with the headstock chopped off, I had nowhere to put me cigarette! We ended up gluing the top of a ballpoint pen to the end of the neck. It was a perfect fit!

JACK BRUCE
Magnificent Misfit

Interviewed by Jim Roberts,
Bass Player, Spring 1990;
Chris Jisi, *Bass Player,* September 2001

I n the late 1960s, Jack Bruce pioneered a new approach to the electric bass, one that established a higher standard of creativity for an entire generation of bassists. Classically trained and an accomplished jazz player on upright before he took up the bass guitar, Bruce was fiercely determined to push the limits of his instrument. In Cream—the first "supergroup," with guitarist Eric Clapton and drummer Ginger Baker—he had the perfect vehicle for creating bass lines that were melodic, rhythmically sophisticated, and endlessly inventive. (And let's not forget that he was also the band's lead vocalist and most prolific songwriter.) Cognizant of Jack's legendary temper, I was a bit wary when I went to interview him in his San Francisco hotel room. But he couldn't have been more congenial—although he did insist on wearing sunglasses while the tape was rolling—and he proved to be a thoughtful and engaging subject.

—Jim Roberts

• • •

Will Cream get back together?

Well, we've been talking to each other a lot more than we did for a while. There's a chance of it happening. Eric expressed a desire to make a record, which I think is the only valid way of doing it. A lot of people are saying, "Go on the road. Do the stadiums." But I don't think I would be up for that. It would be a challenge to make a record that could stand up to the other records, though—and I do like a challenge.

Would it be new material?

Yes, I'd be happy to do it that way. I can't say more than that, because there's not much more to say. We're friends again, which is a very big step—not that there were any deep problems, but because of things that were in the press over the years, we tended to think there were. When we actually got together, we said, "What *are* these problems?" And there were none, basically. So even if nothing else happens, it's been worth it from that point of view.

How do you feel about being inducted into the Rock & Roll Hall of Fame?

Well, at least I know what I am—I'm rock & roll! At first the three of us were somewhat cynical about it. In his acceptance speech, Eric said he thought rock & roll was about rebellion and not about receiving prizes. I thought he was quite brave to stand up and say, "I don't like this thing!" But as the evening went on, we got sucked right in. The thing that knocked me out the most was the recognition for the music, because Cream was a trio of *players* more than anything else. To be recognized after all these years and to know that people still love that band—it was very moving. I know I broke down when I was trying to make my little speech, and so did Eric. Ginger was the funniest. He got up and said [*imitates Baker's Scottish accent*], "Well, I fink everythin's been said. I fank you very mooch [*laughs*]."

After Cream, you played with Lifetime, which was one of the most influential of the early fusion bands. Is it frustrating for you to be pegged as a "rock star," even though you've worked in many other styles?

No. I think of it as the price for what I'm doing. I'm fortunate, because the fame and the money from the Cream experience have given me the freedom to do the things that are close to my heart—although I must admit that some things have been overlooked, like Lifetime. Lifetime was, in many ways, a high spot for me. Cream was too, of course, but you could say Lifetime was a later version of what Cream was doing. I was very proud to play with the late, great Tony Williams, and Larry Young was an absolute genius—one of the few I've worked with. He's like the Coltrane of the organ. I'd have to say Lifetime was the most amazing band I was ever a part of. That band was ahead of its time. It was also ahead of the *technology* of its time, unfortunately. We were playing really loud, and the sound equipment and recording equipment couldn't handle it.

You started out in classical music.

As a child I sang in the church. Because I had a rather good soprano voice, I was chosen to sing solos for Benjamin Britten's works and stuff like that. I got into classical music, and I was awarded a scholarship to the Royal Academy of Music in Scotland. But I came from the wrong side of the tracks. Britain is a very class-ridden society, and it wasn't acceptable for someone like me to be involved in that kind of stuff. I wasn't taken seriously. I was listening to jazz, and I would play jazz things for the teachers. But they had this idea that music finished with Richard Strauss and there was nobody after that who was worth listening to. I was into people like Bartók and Stravinsky and even Olivier Messiaen, who wasn't very well known yet. I was trying to get them to teach me about those things. I just wasn't able to fit in, to become what I thought I should be.

Maybe the experience at the Royal Academy was your introduction to the blues. Don't you think that the blues has something to do with feeling like a misfit?

It's also within yourself. I hear the blues in Indian music and African music, and even in Scotland. There's something called the Free Church of Scotland, which is so strict they're not allowed any musical instruments, so they only can sing—and you can hear it in there too. I know that whenever I'm in a situation where I get too comfortable or feel too accepted, I usually do something about it. I'm kind of a rebel, you know. You have to have people who are going to make waves. Mingus was a perfect example. He wasn't going to settle into things; he was always trying to extend his horizons.

And he was ready to thumb his nose at anyone who got in the way.

I think there's a little bit of that in me—the old nose-thumbing! But the funk is just in my bones; I've always been naturally open to it. I attribute it to growing up in Glasgow, which is not much different from Detroit or Chicago with its poverty and urban industrial setting, along with my early love of black music. I did a couple of TV shows with Marvin Gaye when he came to London in 1965. We hung out all night talking music, and he asked me to join his band, which I couldn't do, because I was getting married. I was getting a lot of criticism at the time for playing freely and melodically in pop and rock settings because of James Jamerson's influence, so Marvin's approval meant a lot to me.

> "The electric guitar is kind of a bastard instrument, but the bass guitar is a *real* instrument."

Did you and Jamerson ever meet?

The first time I met James was in 1974, at the Record Plant in L.A. He was there to do a Stevie Wonder session, and I was next door, coincidentally doing a tribute-to-Stevie track called "Keep On Wondering," for my album *Out of the Storm*. I was overdubbing my part in the control room, and suddenly the door burst open. It was James, who was late and had come into the wrong room. He started listening and said to me, "No, no, that's not the way you do it," and he grabbed my [Gibson] EB-3 and started playing the part to show me how it should be done! I was there for months doing my record, so I saw him a lot. We had some good talks, and he eventually asked if I wanted to do some of his session load. He was a really nice guy, but he was a little bitter because he felt exiled from Motown.

When did you make the switch from cello to bass?

I always wanted to be a bass player. My father took me to see the Modern Jazz Quartet when I was young, probably eleven or twelve, and we sat in the back row of this old concert hall in Glasgow. Percy Heath just filled the whole place with his sound, and I thought, "That's for me!" I asked to learn the bass, so at school they brought in a teacher, a wonderful old symphony player who must have been in his seventies. He said, "You're too small! Go away, grow up, and then come back." So they got me a cello and I started to learn that. A little later, I went back to the bass, and I was studying both instruments at the same time.

Who were your early influences on acoustic bass?

I wanted to play jazz. There was Mingus and, not too long after that, people like Charlie Haden and Scott LaFaro. There were a lot of things happening in jazz at that time.

When did you discover the electric bass?

That was in 1962. There was a guy called Roy Babbington, an English bass guitar player who was in a band called the 4 Macs. He was the first person I saw playing the instrument who made me think, "Well, it's not all *that* bad." I had known about the bass guitar before then, but I was very much a jazz purist. Then I got asked by [producer] Chris Blackwell to do a session, just when Island Records was starting up. It was a jazz session with a fine Jamaican player called Ernest Ranglin, and he wanted bass guitar. So I went to a music shop and borrowed a Guild semi-acoustic bass. It had those nylon tape-wound strings that kind of went *boink*. I took that in and did the session.

> "I hear the blues in Indian music and African music, and even in Scotland."

What was your first impression of the instrument?

I fell in love with it. I thought, "Wow, this is easy and it's *loud!* Wait till I play with Ginger!" It was an instantaneous thing. Steve Swallow says the same kind of thing happened to him. Cream was playing at the Fillmore West in 1967, and Gary Burton's group, with Steve on acoustic bass, was on the bill with us. Steve saw me playing, and he tells me he went out the next day and got a bass guitar and never went back to the acoustic. The bass guitar is a fine instrument on its own. The electric guitar is kind of a bastard instrument, but the bass guitar is a *real* instrument, a unique instrument. And I especially love playing fretless, as I've done for years now. I'm in love with the fretless, and I find it much more difficult to play a fretted bass now. The frets get in the way!

Aside from Roy Babbington, which bass guitarists caught your ear?

Before him, there hadn't been any. But around about the time I started playing bass guitar, I began to hear James Jamerson. Listening to those Tamla records, I began to see the possibilities of the bass guitar. [Motown records were issued in England on Tamla.] It wasn't limited to playing root notes four to the bar; it could actually be a melody instrument, which it very much was in the hands of James. There were a couple of other people around too: There was a guy named Cliff Barton, who was the first person I saw playing fretless bass. Later I wrote a song for him, called "Over the Cliff"; it's on *Things We Like*. He was playing fretless with [English bluesman] Cyril Davies.

What's your basic technique?

I pluck with my two right-hand fingers and occasionally my thumb. On the left hand, when I started playing short-scale basses, I went from using upright technique, with no third finger, to using all four left-hand fingers. I've also gone back to studying the veena again. It's a 200-year-old, bass-like Indian instrument with a large gourd at one end, a beeswax fingerboard with brass frets that you move for your own tuning, four playing strings, and three drone strings. The sound is intense; it just fills a room. Much of my bass technique with Cream came from playing the veena during that time: going back and forth with the index finger, à la Jamerson or Chuck Rainey. I did that a lot for a tremolo effect.

> "Whenever I'm in a situation where I get too comfortable or feel too accepted, I usually do something about it."

Do you still practice on bass, and how has your style evolved over the years?

I play mostly piano at home. I like to get away from the bass so I can come back fresh and find new ideas with it. I suppose my approach is more melodic nowadays from playing mostly fretless. I've also developed in the singing-while-playing aspect; there's a unity now I didn't have quite together with Cream. Being the top and bottom is fun.

From your earliest recordings up to the present, there's a certain consistency in your sound. Even with all the different instruments you've used, it always sounds like Jack Bruce.

The sound comes from your brain and then from your fingers. That's the secret, I think. The difference in tone between two piano players such as Thelonious Monk and Tommy Flanagan is vast, for instance, yet they're both playing the same instrument. It's touch. It's what you do with the instrument.

You've played all kinds of music, yet it all seems connected. That kind of versatility is very rare. Today, many musicians limit themselves to one style while they're still teenagers. What would you say to them?

That's really shortchanging yourself. I would hate it if I had to restrict myself to one kind of music, no matter what it was. I mean, my record collection is insane. When I'm at home, I'll go from Van Halen to North African frame-drum music to Pakistani *qawwali* music. I love the fact that music is an international language, and I hear the same kinds of things in all the music I like. It's up to people to choose their own paths, but I love the fact that I can move into different situations and be comfortable. It refreshes me. This year I'm working on a string quartet, and I'm doing a concert with a huge orchestra and choir, and I'm playing some rock & roll. That's the way I am.

Your most recent album, Shadows in the Air, *explores Latin rhythms; that seems to be a new area for you.*

I must admit that the current crossover popularity of Latin artists plays a little part in it, but mainly I got the idea to do a trilogy of Latin-influenced albums because I've just grown to love the music. I was a big fan of Chano Pozo's work with Dizzy Gillespie in the late forties. Dizzy brought Afro-Cuban music to jazz, and in my own small way I'm trying to do that now by bringing it to rock, the same way Cream brought the blues to rock.

Was it intimidating to play within the clave with the all-star Latin musicians you brought in for this project?

No. I'm not totally knowledgeable, but I've learned how to play and sing in the clave and to play a tumbao. On this album, though, it's about those guys coming over to my music and bass playing. It's kind of like I paid my dues playing their music with them over the years, and now they're reciprocating. I had some odd meters and other things they don't normally do, but they were bursting with ideas and enthusiasm. And incredibly, once we started playing, I never had to say a word or direct them; it just happened.

What are your plans at this point?

I'm excited to be going out with a nine-piece band in support of the album: Vernon Reid, Bernie Worrell, Robby Ameen, El Negro, Milton Cardona, Richie Flores, Alfredo Triff, acoustic bassist Mick Hutton, and myself. We'll begin in the fall [of 2001] and cover the States, South America, Japan, Australia, and then Europe next year. I'm also doing some shows with [former Scorpions guitarists] Michael Schenker and Uli Jon Roth, and I'm one of twenty-five bassists who contributed a track to Gov't Mule's double-CD tribute to the late Allen Woody. I enjoy participating in all kinds of different projects—but my passion is standing on a stage with a bass guitar and a mike.

Phil Lesh

Days of the Dead

Interviewed by Karl Coryat,
Bass Player, June 2000, July 2000

When I was first applying to be an editor for *Bass Player,* I was asked to interview an artist on spec. The first guy I thought of was Phil Lesh. Ten years later—after having hidden the words "Phil is God" in numerous *BP* graphics, Al Hirschfeld style—I finally got the opportunity. But I made it a point not to tell him straight out that I had spent several years as a dedicated, tape-collecting Deadhead. Instead, I tried to win him over by asking about the theoretical nuts and bolts of building bass lines. From the way his eyes lit up, I realized it was new for him to field questions about his uniquely staccato, bouncy bass feel rather than things like Deadheads and drugs. He became one of the most engaged interview subjects I had met: leaning forward, rattling off anecdotes, laughing uproariously. About halfway in, I made the confession: "You know, I went to twenty-five Dead shows." He seemed genuinely surprised. Then he just smiled and said, "That's a good number."

—*Karl Coryat, Senior Editor,* Bass Player

● ● ●

Your style is so different. It seems there's a standard way to play bass, and a Phil Lesh way.

There's only two [*laughs*]? It probably has a lot to do with the musicians I played with for thirty years. We all pretty much started out together and learned together; even Jerry Garcia had just picked up the electric guitar when the band started. Then we learned to weave our talents together.

180

Garcia once said he never understood your bass playing until he heard a tape accidentally sped up, and then your approach finally made sense.

That's one way to hear it. It surprised me when he said that, but looking back I'm glad he finally figured it out!

When you're improvising a line, are you planning where it will go?

Yes and no. In the short term I like to mix it up; from one bar to the next I may not know exactly what notes I'm going to play in between, but I know where I'm going to end up. There was a Formula One driver named Ayrton Senna who didn't think only about the turn as he was going around it, or even as he was coming into it. He had a vision of the entire track, and he always knew exactly where he was. So he planned his laps around the whole track, not just on this turn or that turn. He was World Champion three times. Similarly I try to think about the whole verse or chorus or even the whole song. In a jam I think, "How can I get this to go to another key? How can I fit in a certain rhythm, or interpolate something into the rhythm, to make the jam go somewhere else?" I'm really looking at the music on the long view. I'm zooming out.

Few bassists can make a groove bounce the way you can.

I picked that up from Garcia. His playing would imply this sort of [*vocalizes off-beat-heavy rhythm*]. I love the offbeat groove. "Not Fade Away" is my favorite example of that: The groove goes *bum-bum-bummm-ba-dum-bum*, but I like to play the *ba-DAM-ba-DAM-ba-DAMM-ba-DAM-DAM*. The first time I did that, Bill Kreutzmann looked at me like I was nuts, but I said, "Keep playing! Just keep playing! Do your thing and let me do mine!"

I also think about playing for dancers. I love irregular rhythms and meters, and one of the most fun things I can think of is playing a rhythm part where the downbeat doesn't fall with somebody's foot. That offbeat thing is a way to sort of confuse the dancers, so they don't know what foot they're on. I'm trying to get them to fly, to leave both of their feet off the ground.

Some Grateful Dead songs were incredibly slow. How challenging was that for you?

Immensely challenging. My trumpet teacher used to tell me it's infinitely harder to play slow and quiet than it is to play fast and loud. It's more effective too. In the Grateful Dead, the slower it got the more interesting it could become, because the divisions inside the beats were that much further apart, so you could put more in there. When I do really slow songs now, I encourage the band to put some interior rhythm into the rhythm, always implied rather than overtly stated.

When you're playing, are you thinking more than the average bassist?

In certain circumstances yes, because I'm trying to make the music go into a particular key or rhythm. I didn't do that so much with the Grateful Dead, because I wasn't driving the music as much, but in the bands I'm working with now, I'm driving it. It's been a revelation playing with all the wonderful musicians out there. It's also been a revelation to learn how many excellent musicians love Grateful Dead music, are delighted to get a chance to play it, and are willing to bring everything they have to it. The music is rich enough and has enough depth that it can support many different interpretations. In fact, some of the music I've been involved with lately has been more interesting than the stuff the Grateful Dead did. In some ways, the Grateful Dead was all just preparation—thirty years of preparation!

The first music you got into was classical and jazz. As a kid why weren't you interested in pop music?

I hated it, but you have to remember how old I am. I was born in 1940, and in the forties pop music was swing bands, small groups, and occasionally vocal music. Vocal music didn't become really popular until there was a general musicians' strike in 1944: You couldn't play on the radio or on records unless you were backing a vocalist, because the vocalists belonged to a different union. When the musicians came back, everyone was listening to vocal music because that's all that had been on the radio for a while.

I was four years old when I got turned on to music. It was a Brahms symphony. My grandmother would listen to the radio broadcasts on Sunday, and one time she noticed me sitting in my room, which was next to hers, with my ear against the wall. So she said, "Why don't you come in and sit with me?" I did—and the music just blew me away.

I took up violin at age eight, and at ten I started performing with the Young People's Symphony Orchestra in Berkeley. We played the great classics: Beethoven's Fifth, Schumann's Piano Concerto, Wagner's *Meistersinger*. I played with them until I graduated from high school, but by age fourteen I had switched to trumpet. I was a much better trumpet player than violinist, so I got to play in the Oakland Symphony, a semipro organization at the time. There I got to play my favorite symphony—the Brahms First—as well as some Sibelius.

When I graduated from high school I started getting turned on to jazz. I loved big bands, with their five trumpets, five trombones, and five saxophones going *wham-bam-bammm!* Very powerful. But I hated fifties pop, and I hated rock & roll when I first heard it. I thought it was just mindless; I was completely deaf to its nuances. I had my idea of what music was, and when you're fifteen or sixteen you have your opinion.

At a certain point I decided I wanted to compose, so I went to college and ended up in a graduate-level composition class taught by the famous Italian composer Lu-

> "In the Grateful Dead, the slower it got the more interesting it could become, because the divisions inside the beats were that much further apart, so you could put more in there."

Phil Lesh, 2001: Patrolling the space between the beats.

ciano Berio. In the class were guys like [future noted composers] Steve Reich, John Chowning, and Bob Moran. But I realized there's no future in composing unless you follow the academic path, and I wasn't willing to put the time and effort into what I considered grunt work [*laughs*] to make my way in the academic composition world.

Who would you recommend for a novice who wants a taste of modern classical music?

My hero, Charles Ives. Try his Fourth Symphony—that's what I always play for someone who wants to know what good modern music sounds like, since everyone knows Beethoven. Also, Elliott Carter's *Concerto for Orchestra.*

How did you start to appreciate rock & roll?

By the time the Beatles came in, I guess I had grown up enough to have a little tolerance, and I started listening in a new way. I was working for the post office, and I had a Beatle haircut—I was one of the first men in San Francisco to wear their hair down to their shoulders. But then some business type on Market Street wrote a letter to the United States Postmaster General complaining about my hair. So they called me in and said I'd have to cut it, and I said okay. Later they called me in again and told me it wasn't short enough, so I said, "See you later!"

When did you first consider playing bass?

One of my best friends, Len Lasher, was a fabulous bassist who later played in the San Francisco Symphony. One day I asked if he'd teach me bass as a second instrument. He said, "I would *never* teach anyone to play bass as a second instrument!" Gee, sorry! Then at a party five or six years later, I mentioned to Jerry Garcia that the electric bass was an interesting instrument, that I thought it had some potential beyond what I had been hearing.

How did you start playing with him?

The word started getting around that he had put together a rock & roll band. At the time he was the best banjo player on earth—or at least he was the most interesting and had the most potential. I thought, "That's an interesting concept: Garcia playing electric guitar." So we went down to Magoo's Pizza Parlor in Menlo Park to see his band, the Warlocks. The Warlocks had a bassist, Dana Morgan Jr. I don't know what his approach was, but I know Jerry wasn't satisfied with it. During a break he took me aside and said, "Listen, man. You're a musician. I want you to come play bass in this band." I told him I'd do it, but I said, "Look, you have to give me at least one lesson." He told me the four strings on the bass were the same as the bottom four strings on a guitar, only down an octave. Then he said, "That's all you need to know."

> "I hated rock & roll when I first heard it. I thought it was just mindless; I was completely deaf to its nuances."

When did you first pick up a bass?

June 7, 1965. Or close to that, anyway; that's the date we use for the formation of the Grateful Dead. I borrowed a bass from the music store where Jerry was teaching banjo. I had been playing around with the guitar a little, figuring out where the notes were. My roommate gave me some good advice: "Never play an open string unless you absolutely mean it."

You eventually got interested in moving from four- to six-string bass.

I had known about the Fender Bass VI [tuned *E-A-D-B-G-E*], but then around '81 I heard someone was making a true six-string bass, tuned from *B* to *C* in fourths. I thought, "Now, *that's* an instrument." I saw a Modulus Graphite ad, called them up, and asked, "You guys make fiber-graphite, neck-through-body, six-string basses? I want one."

Anthony Jackson's Fodera Contrabass six-string had been around a few years.

Right, but those instruments were wooden. At the time I thought a wood neck wouldn't be rigid enough for tension from all of those strings. When I heard they were making necks out of carbon fiber, the same material they use in spacecraft, that hooked me. I've played Modulus basses ever since. My early Modulus basses had a balance problem: They were peghead-heavy, so they wouldn't sit on my body. Finally I got Modulus to make a special body that had more mass down toward the tailpiece.

Did your playing change when you went from four strings to six?

At first I played mostly on the middle four strings, with an occasional foray to the top string. I used the *B* string mostly to get a fretted low *E*. The bottom string is difficult to play in tune above *E*, and it's so heavy it's hard to get the right amount of overtones so you can hear the pitch. So I can't use all six strings all the way up the neck, because it doesn't sound right. But I can go up the neck and treat it like a five-string tuned *E* to *C*, which works well. Basically, playing the six just made it easier for me to stay in one position, because before I'd be going up and down the neck all the time. That was a boon—and I just love the instrument's versatility.

What motivates you to venture below the low E?

Dramatic effect! Rarely will I go below *G* on the *E* string, but some situations just call for it. You can't stay down there for long, though, because it gets muddy. Also, the notes don't like to stop: You can't just lift your fretting finger to stop the note; you have to stop the vibration with your hand. That's true of all the strings, of course, but the bottom string has more inertia, so you have to make more of an effort to stop it, making it difficult to play fast down low. But for "dropping bombs," it's great.

How much did you influence the Grateful Dead's musical direction?

My biggest influence was in the beginning, when we were an experimental music band. Then we started concentrating on songwriting. It was a natural development: We explored the psychedelic jam pretty completely, and then as a reaction to that we wanted to bring things down to something very stated and complete in a short time period. That was a wonderful move because it gave us the material to combine those two approaches, which is what we finally did in the late seventies through the early nineties.

> "We played better at Monterey Pop, but we were sandwiched between the Who and Jimi Hendrix, so nobody remembered us. We've always blown the big ones."

What career moments do you consider highlights?

Playing at the Pyramids in '78 was a highlight of a certain kind, although we didn't play very well. But everything tends to roll together into one; it was good and it was bad. I can tell you the particularly bad moments, like Woodstock. We had some excuses: The stage was sinking, and the equipment was starting to roll toward the edge. The P.A. went off, the lights went off, and radio signals from the Air Force were coming out of my amp. It was not an atmosphere conducive to good music. I don't think anybody played well that night, but we were the worst. We played better at Monterey

Pop, but we were sandwiched between the Who and Jimi Hendrix, so nobody remembered us. We've always blown the big ones, as Garcia once said.

Do any recent performances stand out?

I did a bass duet with Mike Gordon when I sat in with Phish. I generally abhor bass duets, but it was marvelous—it was actually *beautiful.*

Did you have predetermined roles going into it?

No, we just played by ear. He knows how to get out of my way, and I know how to get out of his. It was like two hippopotami humping!

How did the Dead arrange sets?

The first set would be pretty spontaneous, but there would always be gaps. We'd do a song and stop; somebody would think of a tune and play a few chords, and we'd all know what it was and do that one. In the second set we'd say, "Okay, we'll start with this, go through some transitions, and end up here and go into 'Drums and Space,' and then we'll close with whatever ballad and rocker." That got to be a little tedious after about twenty years. We talked about trying some different things, but in the end nobody wanted to do any work to experiment.

What's your personal favorite studio performance?

There isn't one. "Help on the Way" [from *Blues for Allah*] is okay; it's not particularly probing or expansive or adventurous, but it's a nice bass line. I pulled that out of the implications of what Jerry was doing.

Any favorite performances on live records?

I don't know. There's so much on record that I couldn't possibly remember. My favorite performance is always the last one I did. Understand that the Grateful Dead played 2,500 concerts; it's in the *Guinness Book of Records.* And they all tend to run together. For thirty years it's been one big gig.

Are you listening much to contemporary popular music?

Some. I've been getting into Latin music, and for the last five years or so I've been deeply into African music. That's the hippest shit on earth. [Senegalese bandleader] Youssou N'Dour sometimes has three meters going on at once—6/4, 12/8, and 4/4—but they all fit together. Also, every beat is the *one.* The most exciting thing about pop music today is it's starting to become really international, with the rhythmic vitality of Latin and African music. I don't like a lot of stuff I hear on the radio, but every so often something comes on that really grabs me. The science fiction writer Theodore Sturgeon once said ninety-nine percent of everything is crap—but boy, when you get that one percent, it's a diamond.

BOOTSY COLLINS

Playing the "Ands" and the "Ifs"

Interviewed by Bill Leigh,
Bass Player, December 1998

I didn't expect my interview with William "Bootsy" Collins to go well. Fiercely protective of Bootsy's time, his wife and manager, "Sweet Lipps" Patti, had negotiated hard for allowing only a very short conversation with the funk bass pioneer. Fresh from a European tour supporting his 1997 hip-hop-flavored album *Fresh Outta 'P' University,* Bootsy just *had* to get back to cutting tracks at the Bootzilla Re-hab P-Form School, the studio attached to his Cincinnati, Ohio, home. Though the heyday of Parliament, Funkadelic, and Bootsy's Rubber Band had become the stuff of "back in the day" legend, along with his legendary year with James Brown, Bootsy continued to keep funk alive as he knows it—through constant experimentation and collaboration. To my surprise, once our conversation began, Bootsy was very patient and forthcoming, cheerfully explaining in his buttery downhome tenor why he stayed so busy: "You've got to keep it going while you got it going, right? Oh yeah!"

—Bill Leigh, Editor, Bass Player

• • •

You've been playing funk bass for a long time. Has your understanding of funk changed at all?

Funk to me is where I came from. It's the way I grew up. It's even deeper than the music. It's the way we communicated—actually, the way we lived. It's like ten people in a small room, and it's 110 degrees outside and there's no air conditioner. It's when the bill collector comes and you don't have any money to pay. It's when you've had as much as you can take and you can't take no more. What do you do? Funk it. That's when you grow into the funk.

What is the essence of funk bass?

It started off with the "one." Then the "ands" and the "ifs" were added—all the in-between things. That's pretty much what I started doing. Nowadays it's been developed to a whole other level; people are doing different things with the "ands" and the "ifs." It's their interpretation of what funk is for them. But as long as the "one" is there, your "ands" and "ifs" mean something. If the "one" is not there, it's kind of like daydreaming [*laughs*].

What is the most significant event from your early career that helped you develop into the person you became?

The first group I was in, the Pacemakers, or Pacesetters—we were kind of confused on which name to use—helped me start searching for who and what I wanted to be. That was when I started dressing crazy. I must have been thirteen or fourteen, because I met up with James at the studio when I was around fifteen.

James Brown has a reputation for being quite a disciplinarian bandleader.

Oh, he was! But you know, as a kid, I didn't really care about that. I respected him, but at the same time I had this kid inside me who felt like he was the baddest cat in the world. You know how cocky kids are, man! I had that all over me—and James knew it, so he treated me like his son. Everybody was calling him Mr. Brown, but I was calling him James. I figured I could get away with a lot of stuff, and I pretty much did. I never really thought I had it going on. I didn't even think about it until after I wasn't there. Then it was, "Man, what are you *doing?*"

Tough as it was, working with James Brown must have been a dream gig for you.

We were with James Brown—we were on top of the world! But we started thinking of things we wanted to do once we weren't with James. And the urge was coming on quicker than we anticipated. We weren't sure what we wanted to do, but every day it was growing in us. Each show we did with James took us more to the point of thinking, "Wait till we get a chance to really do *our* thing." We didn't have a plan; I only knew we weren't going to be with James Brown forever.

The song "What So Never the Dance," from Back in the Day: The Best of Bootsy, *is from the period between James Brown and P-Funk, when you went back to Cincinnati. Your bass is so out front—were you the leader?*

I guess. I couldn't hold that boy back, man; that boy was crazy!

Your big brother Phelps was playing guitar on that date. How is it that he let you step in front?

Bootsy Collins, 1990:
Above all, keeping the bottom.

I think he was having more fun with it being on me than on him. For some reason he's always wanted to be in the band and watch my back. I didn't know what the heck was going on; I just wanted to be out there. It was the girls, it was the wine—you know, getting high. But he was acting as the group's manager and booking the shows. He was the older brother, and I was the fool kid.

There you were in 1971, stepping out in front with the bass when few players had done that. What made you different?

Jimi Hendrix is the one I was looking at. I was freaked out about what he was doing, and I thought, "Wow, maybe I can do that with the bass!" That's what did it. I was probably going to do something crazy anyway, but hearing Jimi put the icing on the cake.

You knew you wouldn't be with James Brown forever. Is that how you felt about George Clinton and P-Funk as well?

Well, George and I had an understanding going in: If I did Parliament and Funkadelic with him, then he would help me do Bootsy's Rubber Band in return. I didn't have a plan when I was with James, but George helped me plan things. That made it totally different. James was more like a father; he really acted like a father. George was more like a brother. I could have fun with him in ways I couldn't with James.

Your musical role was probably pretty different too.

George really wanted me involved. He gave me free clearance to do anything and everything I wanted, while James wanted to look like he did everything.

You weren't P-Funk's only bassist; Billy Bass Nelson and Cordell "Boogie" Mosson were also around. How did you decide who would cut which track?

If they came up with a song, they cut it. If I came up with a song, I cut it. That's pretty much the way it was, unless George stepped in and said, "Bootsy, I want Billy's bass on this one." I was probably on more of the commercial stuff. I did some stupid stuff too, but that's me on most of the Parliament hits, and on the Funkadelic hits "(Not Just) Knee Deep" and "One Nation Under a Groove." Most people don't know I actually played drums on those too, as well as on "Flashlight," "Stretchin' Out in a Rubber Band," and "Bootzilla." If you see my name on it as a writer, it's generally me on bass.

> "When I played the Mu-Tron for some girls in the studio, they said, '*Ooh*, what's that wet, watery sound? That's *sexy!*' That made me want to play every song with that sound!"

How did you get into using effects?

Again, I have to credit Jimi. When I listened to his records I didn't know what he was using, but I knew he was using something. So I went out on a mission to find something to make the bass sound different and develop my own sound. I tried the wah-wah, but that wasn't really happening. I tried this box called the BassBalls that was all right. But until I found the [Musitronics] Mu-Tron I never heard anything that totally made it wacko. When I played it for some girls in the studio, they said, "*Ooh*, what's that wet, watery sound? That's *sexy!*" Oh, man—all of that rattle made me want to play every song with that sound! I would say I started using it around 1976.

Did you know any other bass players who were using pedals?

Larry Graham was the only other one I knew of that was even thinking about it. He was using a Maestro Bass Brassmaster, which gave it that sustain. But I had started wanting to use pedals when I was with James. I actually tried using a wah-wah with James, but he wasn't going for it! I knew I'd have to wait until I was away from him to really get off into it. And when I did, I went crazy with it.

As the founding father of bass effects, how do you feel a bassist should use them?

Go through them one by one and check out what they do. How you hit the note, the fingers or thumb you use, tells the gadget what to do. If it seems like it doesn't work for a certain song, it might work if you play differently, if you change how you talk to the pedal. And certain pedals sound better on certain songs. You have to search it out and find the right ingredient.

Not only did you just use some pedals, you used a lot of pedals.

Aw, yeah, and I still do. I was hooked on the Mu-Tron—that and the Electro-Harmonix Big Muff. Of course I started adding a whole lot of other stuff: MXR digital delays, Electro-Harmonix Bass Micro Synthesizer, the Morley pedal with the fuzz and the wah built in—it goes on and on. I had a board built for all those pedals. Nowadays it's a much bigger pedalboard, and I've got the old pedals mixed with the new ones.

With all those effects, how do you avoid losing the bottom end?

Well, the Space Bass has four different outputs: the lows, the mids, the highs, and the ultra-highs, each from a different pickup. My low output is straight, so I never lose that bottom end. The other three all go to different effects, and then I use four different amps and four speaker systems. I've got two Crown Micro 5000s for the lows and mids, and two Crown Micro 3600s for the highs and ultra-highs. I had all my speaker cabinets custom-made. On the low end we've got eight 18s, four each in two cabinets. For the mids it's eight 15s, four in each cabinet. Then I have four more cabinets, each with eight 10-inch speakers, two cabinets on the highs and two on the ultra-highs. You feel the power. Plus, with the effects, you've got to have a lot of speakers or else you'd be blowing them every night, which I was doing when I didn't have enough rig to carry everything. It all sounds like one big wall of sound, but when I kick on something, or kick out something, the bass is always there.

They haven't kicked you out of Cincinnati yet?

We intimidate the P.A. company so bad sometimes. One time they said they wouldn't even set up. They saw us pulling in and said, "What's this, another P.A. company? How are we going to compete with this?" It became a big joke, but I guess to them it wasn't too funny.

Are you constantly turning effects on and off while you're playing?

It depends on the song. Sometimes I'll play straight Mu-Tron or straight bass—actually, very seldom do I play straight bass, but I've been known to do that too. But when I kick on the effects, that's the gooey part—it's like, *Ooh, yeah!* I've got different things that come out of different

> **"Today you can make everything right. But our mistakes usually *were* the groove."**

sides of the speakers: Mu-Tron on the right speaker, and a wet whammy pedal coming out in another octave on the left. That's how I have it panned for live shows and recording.

How do you record?

Usually I go direct—or if the song is supposed to sound live, I'll do more of a live thing and mix a little of the direct with the live. I record four tracks at a time—one from each output.

You mentioned that Jimi Hendrix was an important inspiration. Who were some of your early bass influences?

The major one was James Jamerson. Before I knew anything about bass, we used to listen to all those Motown records when we'd go to house parties. He was so perfect in what he played; I always wanted to be like that. You didn't really know who bass players were then; they didn't put it on the 45 record. But when I found out who it was, I thought, "Wow, that's the cat."

Who turns your head now?

Victor Wooten. I want to do a record on him, because he is the cat. I don't think he's getting the recognition he deserves—he is *bad*, he is *awesome*. We did a session here about eight months ago, and he came in, getting on the floor, laying his hands out and stuff. I said, "Man, get up from there! Don't even try it!" And then that cat came in and played all the bass in the world. He's the one I'm definitely going to bank on. But it's not like there's nobody else. Armand Sabal-Lecco—that's another spankin' mug. Those two are the most incredible cats right now, doing all this new stuff. You know when I was talking about the "ands" and the "ifs"? Well, they go in between that. They've got their microglasses on. And *fast!* We look like we're standing still. It's good, because it gives hope for the future of players. I think young people are really going to be interested in playing again instead of just sampling stuff, because of young guys whose playing is really ripping heads off.

> "We are the DNA of what's to come, and the funk will always be encoded in that."

On your more recent work you seem to be backing off a bit on your playing to leave more room for the song.

That's exactly what we did, to try to be more commercial. I learned a lot from the other producers and artists. Working with other people really helps me clock in on what's happening. The way we came up is just doing things the way you feel. Today the groove is so perfect and you can fix everything, so I'm learning how to do that.

Don't you think that's less funky than playing with a live band?

Yeah, it is, but it's a new day. People are growing up a new way than when I came up. The closest thing you'd get to a sample in my day was the real James Brown or Parliament/Funkadelic. Today nothing has to be a mistake—you can make everything right. But our mistakes usually *were* the groove. The mistakes we made, rappers use for samples [*laughs*]!

In your song "Pinocchio Theory" you said, "If you fake the funk your nose will grow." Does today's way of making music fake the funk?

It depends upon the angle of the dangle. If you compare it to the stuff of today, it's the funky stuff. But if you compare it to the stuff we were used to—the real funk—definitely some noses would be growing. But it's two different worlds. I think what's happening today is best for today. However, the process changes with computers, and we are the DNA of what's to come, and the funk will always be encoded in that.

ANTHONY JACKSON

No Compromise

Interviewed by Chris Jisi,
Bass Player, Spring 1990, Summer 1990

Reclusive, intimidating, opinionated, intense—these were all terms I'd heard used to describe Anthony Jackson prior to our first sit-down. During a mammoth ten-hour interview, the real Anthony Jackson emerged: uncompromising and devoted, yes, but also highly intelligent, sharing, sensitive ... dare I say, a pussycat? But this is not kitten-on-the-keys when it comes to bass. Flea, Jaco, and Stanley may have risen to the level of household name, but among bassists few are more revered than AJ for his commitment to musical excellence. Even those who don't know his name have benefited from his sonic achievements—mainly, his invention and development of the six-string contrabass guitar. His sheer genius on seminal fusion and pop recordings aside, what stands out to me is that during a period when everyone was attempting to "revolutionize the electric bass"—usually by forgetting its primary function—Anthony focused his visionary skills on mastering the groove. In the process he elevated playing on a Chaka Khan single or a Budweiser jingle to a high art form.

—Chris Jisi

• • •

You were one of the original voices of the "bass revolution" of the early seventies. What atmosphere existed then?

There was more of a sense of adventure. Miles Davis's *Bitches Brew* was relatively new and had gotten a lot of people buzzing about new ideas and new avenues to try with rhythm sections. Even before that album came out, my best friend in high school [guitarist/producer] Reggie Lucas, myself, and many of our friends were experimenting with the concept of putting jazz ideas on top of funk rhythms. We'd all grown up on the Beatles, James Brown, and John Coltrane, and there were endless clubs and loft spaces to play and experiment in. In 1972 I joined Billy Paul's band, Stanley [Clarke] was playing with Chick Corea, Alphonso [Johnson] had left Billy Paul's band and was with Woody Herman en route to Weather Report, and Jaco [Pastorius] was down in Florida—a sensation, but not yet having attained international recognition.

When did you meet Stanley Clarke?

Reggie had told me about him, and I saw him play for the first time at Max's Kansas City with Return to Forever. Our second meeting took place at his West Side apartment in 1973. Reggie and I had finished a project and he had to stop by Stanley's to get something, so I went along. We had a mutual respect for each other's playing, and when we met it was really quite funny. I tried his upright bass, which had the lowest action I'd ever felt, enabling me to get around on it fairly well, to which he commented, "Man, you should play upright." I said, "If I had one with this action I probably would," although in retrospect, even though I've had the opportunities, I realize the instrument has never captivated me. Anyway, inevitably, he said, "Let me see your axe." I had my Gibson EB-2D with me, and I picked up his bass guitar, which was also a Gibson, I think. There was no amp in the apartment, so we sat opposite each other, one thing led to another, and we wound up dueling acoustically. It was good-natured, but because we were still young and mindful of our growing reputations, there was a serious undertone, rather like two big cats circling each other. I would lay down a *moderato* chordal passage and Stanley would play everything he knew as fast as he could, and then we would switch roles. This went on, back and forth, for fifteen or twenty minutes, after which we shook hands and had a real good laugh.

Some of your peers in the fusion world were critical of fellow players who became studio musicians. How did you enter the session scene, and how did you feel about the criticism?

I didn't set out to be a "studio," "stage," or any other "type" of musician. Understand that I was a child when I started playing, and my own motivation, reflecting a child's innocent idealism, was to find the greatest music to play and the greatest musicians to play it with. My first major recording experiences were very intense, beginning with Gamble and Huff in Philadelphia in 1972, and later as a freelancer in New York in 1974. One of the first people I came across in New York was L. Leon Pendarvis Jr., a great composer and arranger who managed to get me on a Roberta Flack recording project he was producing. That led me to one of his other sessions, which is where I first met the great Steve Gadd. As far as I'm concerned, there isn't anything that any fusion artist has done that exceeds the quality of work produced by what we can call the Pendarvis rhythm section, consisting of "The Darvis" [Pendarvis] on keyboards, Gadd on drums, Ralph McDonald or Crusher Bennett on percussion,

David Spinozza, Hugh McCracken, and Jeff Mironov—any two out of three—on guitars, and myself. We recorded hundreds of tracks, most of which were never released, but for sheer quality of composition and performance the music is as good as anything I or anyone else has experienced. Working with that unit was significant because it stimulated major personal growth. Steve Gadd decisively influenced the way I hear music and is really the only drummer I've ever worked with who has. He is one of the important talents of the twentieth century.

You also recorded three albums and did a thirteen-month stint with Buddy Rich's sextet at his East Side club around that time.

Yes. That was an equally rewarding, though totally different, situation. My first experience with Buddy was with the big band in 1973. I came in cold without a rehearsal and got sent home in shame after one show because I didn't read well enough. I boned up and about a year later I managed to get an audition with his sextet and was hired. I would say that Buddy is the only bona fide genius I've worked with. His importance to his instrument equals that of Heifetz and Horowitz to theirs. He's the ultimate example of an individual who allowed the warpage of his personality to occur in exchange for the development and expression of a transcendental gift. He took a lot of flak for his apparently dated style, four-on-the-floor bass drumming in particular, but let me tell you, it swung, and it swung hard.

How did you feel about Buddy's funk and rock conceptions?

> "My first experience with Buddy [Rich] was in 1973. I got sent home in shame after one show because I didn't read well enough."

Consider that when the various big bands began their flirtation with commercial music in the late sixties, the bass chair, formerly confined to the upright, became a doubler's chair. These people, often upright players of very high quality, generally possessed no redeeming qualities as bass guitarists other than good sight-reading skills. Their interpretations tended to be stiff, clichéd, and generally offensive, reflecting their disdain for the instrument that they usually played only out of economic necessity. On the other hand, genuine, committed bass guitarists capable of bringing good performance qualities to these bands could seldom read well—myself, at that time, included. Understand that big-band arrangers were generally a pretty pathetic lot as well, including some of the biggest names still active today. Their conception of the so-called "new music" can be judged by the typical style indications at the top of their charts, such as "Funky Boogaloo," "Get-Down Feel," or "Real Funky Here." These bigoted, stylistically limited—however well-trained—writers, working with bigoted and incompetent "Fender bassists," combined to make our instrument a laughingstock. This attitude, though slowly dying out, persists to the present.

By all accounts, it was one thing to play your part while he guided the band, but quite another to initiate something and have him react or follow. Were you able to do that?

Astonishingly, yes. I never got over my fear of him, because he was such an intimidating figure, but onstage I was soon able to communicate with him and persuade him to "dialogue" with me. By sheer coincidence, my emerging Jamerson-based funk conception fit very well with Buddy's busy, polyrhythmically based conception, which was only a modern variation on the way he'd always played. It often sounded cluttered, but I believe this was only because few risked trying to interact with him. I took a chance and tried, and his total mastery of all things musical allowed him to fit his style around mine like a glove. Of course, he didn't have to like it; I had heard endless warnings about how one could never presume to engage in a back-and-forth with Buddy Rich onstage. But I think Buddy realized that he finally had a genuine jazz player.

Who was your inspiration to play bass guitar?

I first became aware of it on an album called *Mr. Twelve String Guitar* by a then-unknown Glen Campbell and a studio band performing some generally awful pop hits. Let's just say that one particular instrument reached out of the stereo and bit me on the ass. The love affair with the bass guitar dates roughly from that moment in 1963. The jacket listed a credit for "Fender Bass," and while the player's name has long escaped me, the memory of how the sound of the instrument affected me is still strong. In June of 1965 my mother took me to Ben's Music on West 48th Street and bought my first bass guitar—a nameless, cherry sunburst, medium-scale, single-pickup instrument for $43. I continued playing standard as well as bass guitar until 1968, when I was forced to admit that my standard guitar playing should be quietly put to death.

When did you discover James Jamerson, and what kind of impact did he have on you?

I heard him with the Four Tops on "Baby, I Need Your Lovin'," on which he played upright. Much of Jamerson's earliest Motown output is on the upright, but his character was nevertheless distinctive enough to catch my ear. The beginning of a lifetime of being knocked to the floor and stomped on came in the summer of 1966, when "Road Runner" by Junior Walker and the All Stars was released. The song opens with a classic fill by [drummer] Benny Benjamin, followed by eight bars of Jamerson at his best. At that point, I knew I had my mentor, although I didn't know his name.

Was there something specific about his playing?

I could point to his tone or his rhythmic feel or his use of passing tones to redefine harmonic structures, but it was more the mentor relationship. He simply turned the key in the lock, in a very big way. A while later, in 1972, I discovered a 1968

Diana Ross and the Supremes album called *Love Child*, containing several major Jamerson performances and a consummate one, "How Long Has That Evening Train Been Gone?," and was in a position to spend virtually every waking hour for several months playing along with and studying them. It was probably then that one of the foundations of my style took root.

Having Jack Casady as your other main influence seems like such a striking contrast, much like the vast difference between your pick performances and the way you play when using your fingers.

> "Becker and Fagen made neurosis and obsession rewarding and uplifting."

I was fortunate in having two very individualistic and diverse bass guitar talents as mentors. Casady, whom I'd first heard on the Jefferson Airplane's *Surrealistic Pillow* album in late 1966, had a big, rich, metallic sound with a full bottom and a curious, guitaristic way that I was immediately drawn to. When I saw him perform live, I was struck by his dignity and serious mien. Both he and Jamerson were preoccupied with performance, not hype. I had doubled with a pick since the very beginning and had always been aware of the tendency for English players to use it, in particular John Entwistle—go back and listen to the Who's "Happy Jack" for a first-class pick outing, still very difficult to duplicate—but it was Casady's sound that kept me exploring the expressive possibilities of using the pick. To this day, when I use one and a flanger, Casady's influence emerges and can be clearly detected by an aficionado.

You've also cited contemporary composer/organist Olivier Messiaen as an important influence. Why?

In 1967 I came across an obscure [organ] recording that featured, along with works by Franck and Bach, a piece by Messiaen, a composer whose name and works were unknown to me. The piece was entitled "Dieu Parmi Nous" ("God Among Us"), described as part of a nine-piece suite. I found it curious, even compelling, but somewhat unsettling, which criticism I soon traced to problems I perceived in Virgil Fox's interpretation. I decided to look for another interpreter, and was stunned to quickly find an extensive collection of Messiaen organ works performed by the composer, including the complete *La Nativité du Signeur* (*The Birth of the Lord*), the suite from which "Dieu Parmi Nous" was drawn. I bought that album, and as I was on my way home I had a peculiar feeling that something spectacular was about to occur.

That night I listened to the album, and in the space of two hours my life changed completely and irrevocably. *La Nativité* totally and instantly changed the way I heard and played music. The effect was so shattering, so ecstatic, that all of my other sensual perceptions were subtly altered as well. Although there are many other composers whose music inspires in me sensations that can only be directly associated with the divine, Olivier Messiaen, alone among them, persists in having a voice, along with Jamerson and Casady, in every intuitively creative decision I make.

Was jazz also an influence?

Yes. I was very fortunate to discover jazz when I was about sixteen through the album *The John Coltrane Quartet Plays*, with McCoy Tyner, Elvin Jones, and Jimmy Garrison. Coltrane had died only a year before, and his influence was still fresh and dominant. Making the rounds of the New York jazz clubs, most of which are now gone, I slipped quickly and deliriously under the spell of the music, feeling at home with it alongside my other creative areas. The album *Ornette!* [by saxophonist Ornette Coleman], which was recorded shortly before Scott LaFaro's death in 1961, made a terrific impact on me as well. LaFaro had an uncanny ability to suggest key centers without elaborating them, forcing them to exist as what we could call subsidiary tonal islands in a larger sea of chromaticism. His approach differed from that of Ron Carter, who seemed to me a less angular inventor, no doubt due not only to his being a separate personality from Scott, but to the very different improvisational environment of the Miles Davis group compared to the Ornette Coleman ensemble. I am still astonished at how very different and unique LaFaro and Carter are, and how room remains for several more chromatically oriented upright players, including Garrison and Charlie Haden. Each is a master at supporting and pointing out directions to their respective ensembles without playing in a fixed key.

On Chaka Khan's Naughty, *you were able to express highly creative ideas while not only supporting the songs but kicking the hell out of the grooves. Is that the most freedom you've ever been allowed as a sideman?*

Certainly those recordings are among the best examples of blatant commerciality infused with high art that I've been involved with. The basic tracks went down quickly and easily. They probably could have been left untouched, ready for overdubs and sweetening, were it not for my inability to find anything good to say about my own performances.

> "These bigoted, stylistically limited big-band arrangers, working with bigoted and incompetent 'Fender bassists,' made our instrument a laughing-stock."

They were competent, but I was absolutely not thrilled, and this was unacceptable. I will probably never know what could have been going through the minds of Chaka and her producer, Arif Mardin, in allowing me to redo every single note of every single track I played on. To make a fascinating but long story short, *Naughty*, which was recorded in New York in 1979, went on without concern for the bass tracks. I was given absolute artistic license, with one exception, and an unheard-of amount of time—three months—to recompose the bass parts, whereupon I notified Arif of my readiness to record. I was then given all the studio time that I required. I never found out how much my indulgence cost Chaka, but the end result is as pure an example as exists, in my own case, of the ends justifying the means. The performances represent, with only scattered exceptions, the peak of my creative abilities at the time and in that genre. They are, hopefully, only elemental today, but I recall listening to the final mixes just before release and realizing that I was able, for the first time, to hear evidence of a defined, mature, and effective style coming through my playing. This was a revelation, a coming of age, and, I hoped, proof that my stubbornness in playing what I heard despite intense pressure to "conform or else" was paying off.

Compare that element of freedom to working with Walter Becker and Donald Fagen on Steely Dan sessions.

Becker and Fagen—and also Paul Simon—approach their goals a bit differently than Chaka, but all parties, at the end of the day, want all asses to have been thoroughly kicked. Fagen, in particular, is a stickler for detail, but no more so than I am, so the only important issue is whether my detailing as interpreter coincides with his as composer. Once a stylistic approach to a song has been decided—such approach, of course, having been determined almost entirely by Fagen—the actual recording of the performances begins, and this is where the legend of cruelty to musicians originates. It's true that Becker, Fagen, and Simon split more hairs than most and never hype players—no high-fives, no reverential cursing. You've played well? Good; next song. Or more likely: Not good; do it again. Still not good; again. Still not good; go home. Many did. This kind of ferocious performance-disciplining, far from intimidating me, sends adrenaline pouring into my bloodstream. Split hairs, will you? Split this!

Becker and Fagen made neurosis and obsession rewarding and uplifting. Endless hours were spent analyzing and refining the smallest performance details without noticeably improving the music. But I must say that the two tracks I did for Steely Dan's *Gaucho*, "Glamour Profession" and "My Rival," and the two on *The Nightfly* [Fagen's first solo album], "I.G.Y." and "Ruby Baby," did improve my ability to constructively analyze a performance. Becker and Fagen's constant prodding, combined with their willingness to let me prod myself—even allowing me to destroy a performance they loved because I insisted on redoing the entire part—helped put titanium in my spine.

By comparison, Chaka and Arif were more like political anarchists. Unsupervised creative license was the order of the day—well, almost—but somehow discipline always seemed to settle on top of the proceedings, and a need for order, or perhaps *consistency* is a better word, wound up governing the proceedings. If there is a lesson in this, perhaps it is that the final creative product is achieved by processes unique to the performer, and that external forces, whether highly regimented or equally intense but unrestricted, are no more than catalysts in the hands of a player determined to make a statement.

STING

A Frame for Silence

Interviewed by Karl Coryat,
Bass Player, March 2000

This **Sting cover story** was an editor's dream and nightmare. The former Police bassist's solo career was resurging with a carefully crafted album (*Brand New Day*), a world tour, and even a highly visible series of television commercials. Gaining access to that level of pop stardom can be difficult for a niche magazine like *Bass Player*, bringing us into competition with circulation powerhouses such as *Rolling Stone*. However, Sting's helpful PR folks had set up a live interview at a San Francisco–area performance. But it turned out to be the first of several meetings canceled for various reasons, and we found ourselves without a story a week before deadline. Our last chance came down to a phone interview scheduled for New Year's Day, 2000. So in addition to wondering whether Sting—if he answered our call—would overcome his usual reluctance to talk about bass in favor of such topics as tantric sex, we had to hope the Y2K bug didn't render electronic communications impossible. Fortunately, as he talked for 30 minutes by cell phone from the back of his airport-bound limousine, Mr. Gordon Sumner gave the indefatigable Karl Coryat a meaty cover story that turned into a top-selling issue.

—*Richard Johnston*

• • •

Why is it difficult for you to talk about playing bass?

It's become so second-nature for me that I rarely think about it anymore. I've carved this little niche for myself in playing the bass and singing. In many ways, as a teenager, that was a strategy. I was a guitarist, and I realized I wasn't going to be the greatest guitarist in the world. But if I could create a unique little niche—playing bass and singing—I'd have a better chance. My mentors were people like Jack Bruce, Phil Lynott [of Thin Lizzy], and Paul McCartney.

What about the bass grabbed you?

Well, my current band, for example, runs between my rails. I've got the bottom and the top, which is a great place to lead a band from. On the bass you lead the band dynamically, you lead it harmonically—after all, it's a *C* chord only if you play a *C* on the bottom. So I can have a lot of power without feeling like I'm dictating. It's not apparent to a lot of people what the bass does—if you listen superficially, you might not even hear it. But once you've played the bass in an ensemble, you realize exactly what it's doing.

How did you pick up on that so early?

I was pretty intuitive as a kid, and I figured this was what I could do. But it's not that easy to sing and play bass. It's easier to strum a guitar than play a line that goes against the melody. I learned to work out that little technical problem early on: I found I could learn to play and sing just about anything as long as I slowed it down to its constituent parts. You develop confidence when that works—and you can play something extremely complicated and sing against it as long as you start slowly and build up speed. Not that I play anything complicated now; I play very simply and leave a lot of holes. But that too was a strategy—a way of creating a signature, a musical identity.

How easy is it now to play something like "After the Rain Has Fallen," where the bass line is counterpoint to the melody?

I put the hours in practicing. I start at ten in the morning, break for lunch, and usually by then I've got what I'm working on down. *Brand New Day* was recorded in a different way—I'd play the bass, and later I'd sing. But for the tour I spent a good amount of hours getting my chops together so I could do both parts. "After the Rain" was actually the one I spent the most time on.

It's very satisfying too. I work with some of the best musicians in the world, and it always pleases me when they turn around and say, "I don't know how you do that!" They're so much better than I am—but this is my niche. It's what I do.

What instrument do you write most of your songs on?

I wrote most of *Brand New Day* on a Roland VG-8 [guitar-synth system] with synthesizer sounds. That gave me a shot in the arm about being creative on guitar. I created most songs by jamming with a drum machine and getting riffs—that sound is all over the album. The theme from "A Thousand Years," for instance, comes from the VG-8. I do sometimes write on the bass, though.

It isn't the easiest instrument to write on, is it?

If you've got the right riff, the song can just write itself. That's what happened with "Walking on the Moon" [from *Regatta de Blanc*]. I wish I could find another one of those every day: a simple, easy, three-note or four-note riff. The whole song is based around its cadence, and I'm very proud of that. But there are no rules with songwriting. I can write a song on piano, and I can write one walking down the street or at the computer. I try to explore as many different ways to write as I can.

Why did you play only guitar onstage for several years in the mid to late '80s?

I was kind of having a holiday, because I wanted to concentrate on singing. I wasn't really playing guitar; I was just kind of strumming along, being kind of Elvis. During that time period I used Darryl Jones and Tracy Wormworth, two of my favorite bass players, and it was educational to see how they interpreted the music. I also taught them a few things; they didn't have an affinity for reggae, for example, so it was a nice tradeoff. After two tours I decided to go back to basics. I said, "I'm the bass player, and I sing—this is what happens." It's been that way for ten years now.

> "I wasn't really playing guitar; I was just kind of strumming along, being kind of Elvis."

In your current live set you put down the bass for a couple songs.

I open with "A Thousand Years" and I play the theme on the synth guitar. I enjoy that; it kind of eases me into the set. Then I put on the bass, and I finish the set on acoustic guitar to calm down the audience a bit.

When people talk about your style, the concept of space always comes up. How conscious are you of putting space into a line?

It's an instinct with me. That partly has to do with singing in the gaps, and partly with the economy of music. For me, the sound is only half of music—the space between the notes is also vitally important. I gave a speech at Berklee College of Music a couple years ago and talked about silence. As musicians, all we do is create a frame for silence, because silence is the perfect music. You can argue this as a polemic, but music began as a religious practice, and it's in silence that we reach true spirituality. But I'm perfectly happy to play eight to the bar on the root, chorus after chorus. I just want to pump the band along, drive it, and give it a safe home.

A couple of years ago I went to see John Patitucci playing with Chick Corea, and John was playing a million demisemiquavers [32nd-notes] to the bar on his double bass. I went backstage and he said, "Oh, Sting, it's so great to meet you, man. You've really influenced my playing—all the space you leave." I said to him, "I never noticed that!" [*Laughs.*]

A lot of your bass lines aren't obvious. Do you try to write lines that are unconventional and unexpected?

Throughout my music you'll find a kind of perverted sense of fun: I like to twist things. I like expectations to be contradicted. It's just my sense of humor—my sense of fun and play. I'll indicate that things are going one way and then suddenly shift them in another direction. It just amuses the hell out of me. I've been accused of being capricious and pretentious, but I'm just amusing myself, in the hope that others will be amused in the same way.

Early on, how much work did you put into developing your playing?

I went through the Ron Carter school, and I spent years going through Ray Brown's double bass book, just playing his scales and arpeggios. So I've paid my dues. I also spent a lot of time picking apart the Beatles. I love Paul's bass line on "She's a Woman," for example. Plus a lot of Motown—Carol Kaye's playing influenced me, as did a lot of individual songs, like "Rescue Me" and "Knock on Wood." I learned by listening. I'd often turn the record player up to 78 rpm so I could hear the bass lines rather than just feel them.

How did your reggae style develop?

In reggae there's a power shift toward the bass and away from the guitar, which was very attractive to me as a bassist. The way bass is used in reggae, and particularly dub, is very radical. It's a revolutionary way of loading the rhythm of a bar, and it isn't easy to do. When a lot of people try to play reggae it ends up sounding like a cliché; you really have to get inside it.

> "All we do is create a frame for silence, because silence is the perfect music."

What was the first reggae recording that caught your ear?

In England we had reggae since its inception. Jamaica really wasn't the center of reggae—London was. Any reggae act that wanted to make it came to London, from [Millie Small's] "My Boy Lollipop" in the early '60s through ska, blue beat, up to Bob Marley. That's not to take anything away from Jamaican music—I respect it and love it—but London has a huge West Indian community, so we felt it around us.

I haven't mentioned Jaco [Pastorius] yet, but he was another huge influence. He also shifted the power away from the guitar toward the bass in a revolutionary, astounding way. Who would have thought to play a chromatic Charlie Parker tune, "Donna Lee," on bass?

Some of your bass lines, particularly "Rehumanize Yourself" [Ghost in the Machine], are uncharacteristically busy. What inspires you to write such a line?

It's mostly a matter of energy. When I feel you can play a lot of notes without taking away from the song's drive, I do it. I can play fast and furious if I want, and if I feel it's necessary. But I have no intention of showing off on the bass.

You change your plucking-hand technique from song to song.

Over the last ten years I've developed a classical guitar technique called *apo-yando*, where you play with the fingers underneath the thumb. I don't know many bassists who do that. Sometimes I use my thumb and dampen the strings with the side of my hand, and I use just my fingers for certain things too. I don't use a plec [pick] very often, except when I want to get an effect. I'll try just about anything, but I especially like to pump along on a dampened bass.

Do you play much fretless these days?

Not onstage—it's just a pain in the arse. But sometimes on a record I'll play a little fretless. I prefer the double bass to get that sound.

Are you still playing electric upright?

I haven't played my electric upright for years. But I play my double bass at home; if someone comes over to play piano, I'll join in on the upright. But playing upright is like an athletic pursuit: You have to play every day, otherwise the muscles go.

When did you start playing upright?

I picked it up in school. There was a double bass there, and nobody else was interested in it, so I started to play blues parts and a bit of jazz on it—and I became the bass player, even though I was a guitarist. So that put me in good stead to become a bona fide bass player later on. When you feel the power of the bass through your fingers, not to mention the effect it has on music—the width it gives a musical sound, and also the depth—it's an exciting revelation.

Later I bought my 100-year-old German bass—it was one of my first purchases as a wealthy young pop star. That's the same bass I played on "Perfect Love Gone Wrong" on the new record. I call it Guido, and I like to fantasize about all the music that's been played on it—I imagine classical music, cabaret, and who knows what else.

I also love my current main bass, a '54 Fender Precision. I rescued it from the orphanage about ten years ago and fell in love with its dilapidated appearance. There's no finish on it; it's just a wreck. Something about that really appeals to me. An old instrument is something to be cherished. I think instruments absorb and retain energy—it sounds mystical, but I really believe it. It could be only a baseball bat with strings on it, but somehow, if somebody plays it for many years, it just feels right. It develops a spiritual valence a new instrument doesn't have yet.

> "I've been accused of being capricious and pretentious, but I'm just amusing myself, in the hope that others will be amused in the same way."

What's become of the '62 Jazz Bass you used for many years?

It's still around, and it's still one of my favorites, with a place of honor at home. I look at it occasionally.

It must get jealous of the '54.

They don't know about each other; I keep them in separate rooms.

Do you ever take a liking to a new bass someone sends you?

Occasionally I see something interesting and unique. People have offered me 5-strings and 6-strings, but I don't need them. I'm not judging anyone who plays a 5—it's great to hear one played well—but I like to play the 4. When I was touring with Me'Shell NdegéOcello, we agreed: Four strings is where it's at.

When you're recording, do you still often double a bass line on upright or guitar?

Not much. We did that a lot with the Police; it was kind of a trademark. "Every Breath You Take" [*Synchronicity*] has electric bass plus double bass, as does "Perfect Love Gone Wrong" on *Brand New Day*. "Don't Stand So Close to Me" had electric plus electric upright. Sometimes playing guitar alongside a bass line adds a bit of depth to the line.

How much of a perfectionist are you, either in the studio or in rehearsal?

Probably not at all. I work with people whose job it is to rein me in. I'd make an album in an afternoon if I could, but it's a technical process that takes a lot of patience. I try to be as spontaneous as I can, and if an idea isn't working, I'll move on quickly and attack it another way. But I don't get too bogged down with getting a bass sound; I invariably go through the desk [direct into the board] and just EQ it at the end of the day. I'm also not a hi-fidelity freak, although I work with people who care about that.

You share a production credit on Brand New Day—*what's your role as co-producer?*

I arrange the music, I get people's energy up, and I know when something sounds good to my ears. "Producer" is a nebulous term, one that's usually defined by the limitations of the artist—so I have people around me who fill the gaps in my knowledge.

You sometimes use synth bass on your records—how often do you play a keyboard bass part yourself?

Sometimes. Whatever works—I'm not precious about roles in a recording situation. If somebody puts something down and I like it, that's it. If I think I can improve it, I'll try. That's the way you learn: Sometimes a keyboard player will have a totally different approach to a bass line, and you can learn by duplicating it. Other parts fall easily under your fingers on the bass but not so easily on the keyboard. So it's good to be open about who plays what.

I'm still willing to learn; even though I'm 48, I'm still a student. That's my only ambition, really: to remain a student of music. I never want to think I know everything—because the more I know, the less I'm sure about.

MARCUS MILLER

The Next Bass Genius

Interviewed by Chris Jisi,
Bass Player, October 1992, September 1995, April 1998

or someone who thrives on the pressure of doing five projects at once, Marcus Miller is a cool cat. Often when I interviewed him, Marcus was behind the board, flying in string parts or cueing vocals while fielding my questions. Yet he answered each with clarity, honesty, and insight. Once he told me about an early New York session he'd done with a Texas drummer who had one of those combination straight-and-shuffle feels. He said, "I learned things during that thirty-second jingle that I still use today." This level of perception helps explain the edge in his bass work—the grooves that sit just a little deeper in the pocket, the richness of his slap sound, the bebop-savvy flavor and phrasing of his solos—not to mention his vision as a composer, arranger, producer, multi-instrumentalist, and solo artist in the jazz, pop, and film worlds. As we gain perspective on the enormous impact made by Jaco Pastorius, one other fact has become clear: Marcus Miller is our next bass genius.

—Chris Jisi

• • •

Why was there an eight-year gap between The Sun Don't Lie *and your previous solo album?*

I wanted to make a bass album all along, but I didn't have the compositional skills early on. Soundwise, it's hard to put things under a bass, and the material has to be very strong to make the whole concept work. My first two albums were basically vocal-oriented R&B on which I got to co-produce and play all of the instruments myself. That was invaluable because it helped to launch my producing career. But after the second one I realized I hadn't found my own identity, so I decided to hold off for a while. Gradually, through working with Miles [Davis], Luther Vandross, and David Sanborn, I developed confidence. Finally, I started thinking of compositions for a bass project, and the ideas came pretty fast. Then it was a matter of finding some time and waiting for people to be available.

Your bass is prominent throughout the album, yet it doesn't overpower the material.

At first I was afraid of making a typical "bass album," with the bass being the loudest thing, so I brought it down in the mix. But after living with those tapes for a week, I decided to turn the bass back up so that everything I play is heard, because I knew that would be the focus. I used my '74 Jazz Bass and my fretted and fretless Sadowskys, and I recorded them direct into the board.

The melody on the opening cut, "Panther," reminds me of Stanley Clarke.

I tried playing it with my thumb, and when I switched to my fingers for a bit more articulation and speed, the sound paled in comparison. I knew the only way to combine both approaches was to move my fingers closer to the neck and pluck very hard to get that popping sound. I wasn't trying to sound like Stanley, but he was certainly an important influence. At the time, it was an inspiration to hear a young black musician come out of nowhere with such amazing technique and that aggressive bass-in-your-face sound.

What other bassists had an impact on you?

Robert "Kool" Bell, James Jamerson, Rocco Prestia, and all the Jacksons—Jermaine, Paul, and Anthony. I got into slapping through Larry Graham during his Graham Central Station period. In my neighborhood, if you couldn't play like Larry you might as well put the bass down. We used to have slap competitions on a little cafeteria stage in high school to attract girls. When fusion hit and piqued my interest, I was fortunate to have a friend, [drummer] Kenny Washington, who sat me down and played me the history of jazz, which put things into perspective. That got me into upright players like Paul Chambers, Sam Jones, Ron Carter, and Eddie Gomez. Then Jaco came out and blew my mind. He had it all covered. I left his first album [*Jaco Pastorius*] on my turntable for two years and learned every solo note-for-note. But without a true knowledge of harmony, I had no idea what the notes meant. Jaco's playing and writing were like a wake-up call; it led me to study bebop, which really got my harmony together.

You used to play Jaco's "Teen Town" slap-style as a lead-in to the commercial breaks on David Sanborn's Night Music *show. Were you aware of the buzz you were creating among bassists?*

Yes, and that's why I included "Teen Town" on *The Sun Don't Lie*. I wanted to cut it live, since the focus is on the energy and musicianship. You should have seen the studio that day: There were drums everywhere for Omar Hakim, Steve Ferrone, Andy Narell, Don Alias, and Paulinho Da Costa. We stuck to the original arrangement, except we opened it up in the middle for Hiram Bullock's guitar solo, which is where I switched to fingers.

As a slapper, you've developed a reputation for having a clear sound and for using mostly your thumb with only the occasional pop.

I strike the strings right in front of the chrome neck-pickup cover, not at the bottom of the neck where you get all the overtones. A lot of times I don't pluck [pop] at all. That developed during my jingle days, because I found that using my thumb was the best way to hear the bass coming out of a tiny TV speaker. Plus, if you use two alternating fingers, as I do when I play fingerstyle, there's always a strong note followed by a weak one; with the thumb, every note is strong. That became really important when I started doubling sequenced keyboard-bass parts. Then I began challenging myself to see if I could develop the speed to play entire charts using only my thumb. I still add plucks whenever they're necessary, as they were on "Teen Town." But I think a lot of players tend to overuse them. The plucks are just accents, afterthoughts; the funk is in the thumb.

When did you start doing overhand slaps?

That started back when I was playing R&B clubs in the seventies. The people there weren't really into the music, so I figured I'd give them something to look at. When I got my band together I started finding musical ways to apply it. My original concept was to use both thumbs, but the left thumb is just too far from the pickups. To compensate I brought my left hand over the top of the neck; I found I could get more power and create a sound that's more balanced with my right-hand attack. Now when I use it, either I'll bring both arms over the neck and pat the strings like a drum, or I'll use my left fingers overhand in conjunction with right-hand slaps. In both cases the bottom knuckles of my left-hand fingers are striking the *E* string, while the rest of my fingers hit and mute the top three strings.

Describe how you use your left hand, especially with regard to intonation on the fretless.

Playing a four-string requires a lot of hand-position changes. Fortunately, studying bebop helped me to get up and down the neck. I'm basically a one-finger-per-fret guy. As far as the fretless goes, it's important to stick with one instrument and find where the pressure points on your fingers are in relation to the notes on the neck. Beyond that, you just have to keep

> "In my neighborhood, if you couldn't play like Larry Graham you might as well put the bass down."

putting in time, really using your ears. I'll check myself with open strings, but it's always a battle—especially when you play with other instruments that use tempered tunings, like keyboards.

What about your muting technique?

That started when I was 21 and playing in Ralph McDonald's rhythm section with Steve Gadd, Richard Tee, and Eric Gale, doing jingles and backing people like Grover Washington Jr. and Sadao Watanabe. They wanted my bass to sound more like James Jamerson and Chuck Rainey. Eric doubled on electric bass before me, and one day Ralph put on a track they'd done and said, "C'mere, kid. Here's what a bass should sound like." I imitated it, and he was thrilled. The way I do it is by muting the strings with my right palm near the bridge and plucking with my thumb. Sometimes I'll use a pick if I want more speed. You can also get a decent upright sound with muting.

> "Young bass players are constantly asking me, 'Should I concentrate on grooving or soloing?' And I always tell them, 'Who said you can choose?'"

How do you do that?

I mute the strings with my palm and pluck with my thumb. Over the years I've been able to incorporate my first two fingers in order to play faster, but I like muting because it prevents you from moving too quickly. You have to play more simple and solid and choose better notes.

Your muting approach differs slightly when you use it in acoustic jazz, R&B, or hip-hop. Is that intentional?

I never really think about varying my technique, but subconsciously I do play the notes differently. Essentially, a note on the electric bass lasts too long, so it doesn't have any thump. If you can get it to die out, either by slapping or muting, you give it a whole new character.

You dedicated "Eric," on Tales, *to Eric Gale. He must have had a tremendous effect on you.*

Eric was the first guy I met whose every musical phrase meant something to me. There was never a wasted note. Someone once told me a story about his first big gig with Aretha Franklin. King Curtis was the musical director, and during a song he pointed to Eric to take a solo. After he finished, Curtis reached into the bandstand, grabbed Eric by the collar, brought him face to face, and said, "Look, motherfucker—don't you ever play a solo you don't mean!" And then he threw him back into his seat.

Talk about your relationship with Miles Davis.

Miles was like a musical father to me. In 1980 I was booked to play on a session for him, but he never showed up. A year later, during a country date, I got a note saying, "Call Miles." He answered the phone and asked me to meet him at CBS Studios in an hour. I went in and introduced myself and played with everyone for a while without much being said. When we were finished, he asked me to join his band. Early on, he occasionally gave me a hard time, but he was always very supportive and proud of my session career. He used to tell his girlfriend, "This is Marcus Miller. He drives a BMW." Eventually, as we grew together musically, he placed entire projects in my hands, which was incredibly scary yet extremely encouraging. In retrospect, I would say that my bass style solidified on *The Man with the Horn*, and my composing took giant strides beginning with *Tutu*.

On the bebop middle section of your tribute to Miles, "The King Is Gone" [from The Sun Don't Lie*], you play the first chorus of your fretless solo muted, almost as if you're paying tribute to Paul Chambers as well.*

That's right. For me, *the* bass player with Miles was Paul Chambers, especially at a tempo like the one on this tune. People think of him mainly as a groovemaster, but check out his bowed solo on "Moment's Notice" [on John Coltrane's *Blue Train*]. Coltrane handed him the changes, and they recorded it! He's *the* cat, as far as I'm concerned. He doesn't get his due. He had great time, he was a superb soloist, and he was very skilled with the bow. Young bass players are constantly asking me, "Should I concentrate on grooving or soloing?" And I always tell them, "Who said you can choose?" You've got to be able to do both. Would you ever ask a pianist or a guitarist if they comp *and* solo? If you play the instrument, you should be a complete bassist.

> "[Miles Davis] used to tell his girlfriend, 'This is Marcus Miller. He drives a BMW.'"

You don't advise young bassists on the importance of locking onto a groove?

No. Telling young players they have to play grooves is like telling painters they have to use blue. You have to encourage beginners to do whatever turns them on, because that's what they're going to do best. When they get a bit older, you can tell them the realities of the music business—that there are more opportunities to work if they learn to function as a bass player. The important thing is to listen to as much music as possible. The young ear is naturally drawn to the high frequencies played by solo bassists, but if you listen to a lot of groove players you'll get caught up in that as well. Ultimately, you should be able to lay down the baddest groove *and* blow the hottest solo.

Who are your favorite bassists today?

I don't get to hear that many players, but the guy I really like is Pino Palladino. Doug Wimbish is wicked. John Patitucci is bad, and so is Victor Wooten. And Anthony Jackson, of course.

How did you get started as a composer?

I used to watch my cousin, Denzil Miller, write for a local band we were in, Harlem River Drive, and I just assumed you weren't a complete musician unless you wrote your own material. Later, when I met Sanborn in the *Saturday Night Live* band, I gave him a demo of some fusion tunes I'd written, and he asked to record them. Shortly afterward, I began writing vocal demos with Luther Vandross; he's so talented that I was able to gain a lot of insight. What I always try to do when I write for another artist is to see his face in my mind. If I can envision him moving to the music, then I know it's appropriate.

You've said that Herbie Hancock's Speak Like a Child *had a strong impact on your writing.*

Yes—that one and his other sixties albums, as well as *Head Hunters* from the seventies. They all have intriguing harmonies and colors, with intangible chords you can't really name. For me, harmony is the most interesting part of composing because of the many different ways you can make people feel with it. It gives music dimension.

How has your career as a solo artist affected your work on other projects?

For me, it's all about balance. I'm one of those people who have to have five things going at once. I need to feel like I'm pushing my limits. I love being in the studio making records, but that wouldn't be enough. I love being onstage playing, but that wouldn't be enough. I love scoring movies, but *that* wouldn't be enough. I try to maintain a balance, because each situation helps all the others. The precision of the studio helps me when I play live; then I'll come off the road with a lot of inspiration to take into the studio—or I'll come out of a movie score with new colors I otherwise wouldn't have found. The cool thing about having a solo career is that now I have a place to experiment and apply everything.

Do you worry about spreading yourself too thin?

Never. For me, the main purpose of any art is to reflect what's going on in the artist's life. If it's done honestly, people are able to contrast their own lives with it, sort of like a mirror. I believe music should capture the world in which it was created. Years from now, I want my music to reflect what's happening now, while also capturing the history that came before it. A lot of people worry about their creativity running dry, but to me, as long as you're living and observing and experiencing life, you'll always have music coming out of you.

MIKE GORDON

Flying with Phish

Interviewed by Karl Coryat,
Bass Player, December 1996

Mike Gordon has it made. What bass player wouldn't want to be in a jam band with complete artistic freedom—one that could sell out a venue like Madison Square Garden in hours, even though Phish gets almost no commercial airplay? But unlike some arena-rocking bassists, Gordon didn't get to the top just by being lucky. He's the ideal jam-band bass player, able to hold down the bottom and riff and swing ferociously, yet ready to take the controls in an instant and drive the band in new directions. He's as multi-dimensional in non-musical life too, as a budding filmmaker and writer. When he told me about his childhood experiences filing file cabinets with pretend "bureaucracy beyond belief," I felt an instant bond: I had invented numerous sports and games as a youngster myself, complete with rigorous rulebooks and stadium plans. When that kind of connection happens—I call it a "Barbara Walters moment"—you begin to get a clear picture of a musician's developmental roots: who exactly they are and how they got that way.

—Karl Coryat

• • •

What first attracted you to music?

I was a very strange kid. I never played any sports, ever, and I spent much of my time alone. I didn't want to be a kid; I wanted to be an adult. I spent a lot of time planning projects: When I was nine I planned a full-length feature film, and I also put together these clubs that never existed, with a hierarchy of president, treasurer, and everything. I typed everything, probably from the age of six, and I generated file cabinets full of these typed plans for clubs and clubhouses and inventions—bureaucracy beyond belief, like something out of the movie *Brazil*. I was completely introverted; even when I was one or two, I'm told, I never played with toys. I preferred things from the real world, like going through the stuff in my mom's purse. I always needed to be building something, like a little-kid mad scientist. Finally, in high school, I came out of my shell, and music started to become this thing I cared about more and more. I had always enjoyed music; I probably listened to *Abbey Road* a thousand times when I was a kid. Music started to slowly develop as my way of soul-searching. Certain songs would take over and represent the struggles I'd been going through.

When did you actually begin playing?

I had played piano since about age six, and I really liked to sit down and play things by ear; I didn't like taking lessons very much. Later I decided I wanted to play guitar, and I took a guitar course at the local music store when I was twelve or thirteen.

When did the bass enter the picture?

I was in the Bahamas with my family, and at the hotel there was this calypso band that played all day long at the poolside. It sounded so good, much better than any music I had heard, and I was completely into it. I was in the pool, I could feel the bass vibrating me, and I told my dad, "If I'm ever in a band, I want to play *that* instrument!" Shortly afterwards I rented a Beatle Bass copy and an old tube amp and took some bass lessons at the music store.

> "I often try to make myself as naïve as possible so I lose a sense of the *one*. I love not knowing where the beat is."

Who were your first teachers, and what did you learn from them?

In my last year of high school I joined the jazz band, and the guest conductor, Diego Poprokovich, hooked me up with Jim Stinnette, who later became my bass mentor. One day in jazz band Diego said, "Mike, you've got to keep time. It almost doesn't matter what notes you play; you can crumple up the piece of paper and throw it on the floor—all I want you to do is keep time. That's ninety-nine percent of what matters." I have this problem of hearing things a half a beat off at fast tempos, so Diego would always be looking at me and clapping on the *two* and *four*, because after a minute I'd turn the beat around. It's funny, because now I love it when that happens. When Phish goes on these musical journeys, I often try to make myself as naïve as possible so I lose a sense of the *one*. I love not knowing where the beat is.

Phish is constantly being compared to the Grateful Dead, so was Phil Lesh a major influence on you in those days?

I've never spent a lot of time studying any one bass player, so it's hard to say, but I definitely love his playing. To me, it feels as if he has a sense of the kinetics of

Mike Gordon, 1999. Weaving a line past a guy in the tenth row.

sound. There's a sense the notes are resonating through your whole body, and he seems to know how to give a bass line a lot of gravity in its interaction with the other instruments. To achieve that, I think it takes a certain sensitivity to what's going on. You can pick up the bass and just start thrashing on it, which is fine if you're an aggressive person and that's what you want to get out of the instrument. But if you're sensitive to what the notes are doing to you, things can blossom unexpectedly. I also like Phil's tone. I used to play with my fingers a lot, but now I use a pick ninety percent of the time. The picks are graphite, custom-made by Ken Smith. Actually, it was Phil's tech who gave me the graphite picks to begin with.

How did you make the move toward playing professionally?

As high school went along, suddenly I had a social life, and I didn't want to work on projects in my basement anymore; I just wanted to play music and be with other people. I went to college and studied electrical engineering, but I quickly learned my professors didn't want me to be a mad scientist—they basically wanted me to build a small, secret part of a missile that would kill Russians. So I eventually switched to film-making. When I was a freshman I saw a sign that read "Bass player needed." The first Phish jam was in a dorm lounge, and there were actually twenty-five people dancing. When it was all over I asked, "So, do I get the job?" And I got the job.

Did you sense from the beginning that there was something special in this combination of players?

It's funny, because the first time we jammed together, it didn't really click. There were other people I had jammed with where I felt it had clicked better. Now, in retrospect, I think that was a good thing, because it made us work at it. We still practice a lot when we're not on the road, but we used to do it all the time—after school, every day. For hours and hours we would jam, write music, and experiment. We tried to zero in on things and push them—rhythms we weren't good at, or grooves, or styles. The listening exercises were the culmination of all that. [*In this exercise, members of Phish stand in a circle and take turns altering a prearranged riff, while the others react and follow. The purpose was to heighten each musician's improvisational sensitivity and fuse the band into a cohesive, communicative unit.*] Our favorite thing to do was just throw caution to the wind and jam without expectations. But we also realized how easy it is for the four of us to lapse into our own little worlds, playing up and down scales or whatever, not necessarily in the group mind. By getting together and just allowing this group mind to exist, we grew together.

> "By playing a high note, I can take the band higher, almost like a hang glider on an updraft."

Did these sorts of exercises affect the band in personal as well as musical ways?

Well, we found that when we weren't playing our relationships developed the same way. When we're jamming we're communicating, but if we're just having a meeting we're also communicating; it's sort of the same dynamic. We recently did this photo shoot that lasted for eight hours, and the whole time we were trying to make each other laugh by going in a circle and saying stupid things, which felt a little like jamming. The other guys in the band would say that music is communication; I'd rather say that communication is the vehicle, and music is the motion. Either way, communication is the first step, and if one person is thinking "How do I look?" or "Is this a cool bass line?" or "Are we having food on the bus later?" it throws the whole thing off. What happens in that case is it feels as if we're mocking ourselves—pretending to be Phish.

Phish is one of the few bands that tackles such disparate styles as jazz and bluegrass. How did you learn to play over such a wide range?

We spent one year playing jazz gigs every Monday night with local horn players. We did the same thing with bluegrass: We bought a bunch of bluegrass instruments while we were in Kentucky, and we learned how to play them on the bus. But we don't pull it off the way a real jazz band, for instance, would; we're just trying to learn something from music that inspires us.

How do you see your role in the band?

We were discussing this the other day. All of us in Phish have very specific roles, and my opinion is we'll always have those roles. Trey [Anastasio] is very much the leader, and at meetings I'm the person who usually doesn't say anything—again, the quiet one, the outcast. But if I do care to say something, I'll talk and argue forever. I'm not cut out to be a leader; being a leader requires you to be diplomatic, encouraging the others to be their best and making everyone feel together.

But isn't that the function of the bass?

Right, and I'd say I'm much more a leader musically than verbally. It's funny, though, because sometimes I don't play like a bassist. I might jump up the neck and harmonize a riff Trey is doing for two minutes. At other times I play like a bassist but don't play the chord progression that's been bestowed upon me. That way I can harmonically lead the band in different directions. Our listening exercises are a good way for each of us to practice being the leader, and when we're jamming I'm definitely the leader at least a quarter of the time. I guess musically we don't really have a specific leader. Any group of people has to let individuals flourish; individuality is a very right-wing theme, but even in pure socialism there are individuals with ideas that must be recognized. If we're jamming and I start leading, though, it usually isn't an ego thing where I think, "Oh, I'm finally in charge." It's more about everyone being excited that we got to a new place where it's fun to be.

Taking the lead doesn't necessarily mean taking a solo.

Right. I'm not interested in playing solos. I love to see incredible bassists play solos, but even with a great soloist such as Oteil Burbridge, I prefer what he plays in the *middle* of a groove. He might go up the neck and play some wild, five-note chord and make it fit in. Weaving into the network of the motion—that's what I like about bass and music in general. By playing a high note, I can take the band higher, almost like a hang glider on an updraft. Rather than having to create a solo the music world will think is cool, I can be in the gears of the motion, in the engine room. The notes vibrate different parts of my body, and on the best nights it feels three-dimensional, where it's way inside but also way outside. I might see someone in the tenth row, and I'll weave the bass line past his head. At that point I'm not the introvert I was when I was younger; I'm completely opened up to the point where I'm not even the musician—God is the musician coming through. The bass seems to lend itself really well to that.

> "Individuality is a very right-wing theme, but even in pure socialism there are individuals with ideas that must be recognized."

That's an extraordinarily tactile way of thinking about performance.

I keep wanting to come back to the analogy of flight. If you were actually flying, your inner ear would be giving you information about balance, there'd be wind rushing past your face, and there'd be pressure from the altitude. All of those senses come into your brain, which perceives that you're flying. My theory is that by standing completely still, you can create not only a feeling similar to flight but the *exact* feeling of flight. When music is great, that's how it is for me, and the bass is the vehicle for that to happen. Sometimes it feels like the battle between God and the Devil, or entropy and order, just carrying itself out in its own way.

If it was easier, the payoff wouldn't be as great.

You might be right. When I was in college taking four or five engineering classes, we played a gig one night when I had three weeks off before finals—and that was the peak experience I still chalk up as being my best ever. It makes me think that if I ever wanted to get to a peak like that again, I'd probably have to re-enroll as an engineering student!

Do you ever get lost during jams?

All the time. These great journeys are the ideal, but there's another side. Sometimes we get off the stage and fight with each other about who wasn't concentrating. It always comes down to hooking up and communicating. Jamming is definitely the most important thing for me. There are other important parts, like songwriting and arranging, but all I really care about is going on these journeys. It's impossible for people … Let me rephrase that: It's impossible for *me* when I'm not on one of these journeys to remember how ecstatic it feels and how much of a celebration life becomes. On the other hand, it's the worst feeling to get together and play bad music, and we definitely do that sometimes. The good side, though, makes it all worth it.

Jerry Garcia often complained that Deadheads adored the band's music no matter how horribly they played. Are Phish fans similar?

A lot of our fans are that way, but at the same time they're critical even when we're playing well. They pay attention, and they're aware of what's going on. If we have a bad gig, people backstage say, "You guys were great," but we know that means it was a bad show. If we have a good show, the fans might say, "This was the best day of my whole life." Like the Grateful Dead, we have a certain percentage of fans who have left mainstream society for a while to go on tour with us. For them, our music is just the theme of their lives—the background music. Our fans are great; we really do weird stuff onstage sometimes, and we have a group of people listening who'd rather we did that than play the same thing each night. It's so much fun to know we can take chances and that there are people willing to come along and listen and dance.

Do you warm up before shows?

Not these days, usually. When we were playing clubs I had a list of things to practice backstage, like running scales with a metronome. Now we have a room backstage specifically for practicing, with instruments and amps, a metronome, and even music stands—and I don't use it. But I've found practicing daily really does help. It puts me in a learning frame of mind, and then when I'm onstage jamming, I'm in the same mode, eager to learn more.

Do you keep your chops up during your off time?

I go through two-octave scales and arpeggios and other dexterity exercises, like playing certain riffs or patterns over and over again. Considering the kind of music we play, with all our different rhythms and atonal fugues and things, I don't think I have great chops. What I do have is a sense of vision—being able to play two great notes rather than ten mediocre notes. There are times when I wish I could do a fast sixteenth-note run, but I'm so much happier *not* to try to do it, because there's an absolute infinite number of things I can do without it. Sometimes I don't even play the bass for a couple of months because I'm working on something else. Oteil once said the more you practice, the more you'll sound as if you're practicing when you're playing—so if you feel you need to practice, you should at least practice playing.

Your hands are somewhat small. Does that ever present problems?

At one point I thought they'd keep me from becoming a great bassist. But Jim Stinnette had me doing these unnatural stretches up and down the neck, which felt like more stretching than I'd need—but after that, the size of my hands didn't matter. Plus, with my philosophy of playing as few as two notes, I can put those two notes right next to each other. These days, I'm into stretching other limits; if there isn't a limit you're stretching, you can probably imagine one. It could be how fast you can play over a song, but it could also be how slowly, or how softly. You can always find new limits to stretch.

4

DRUMS &
DRUMMING

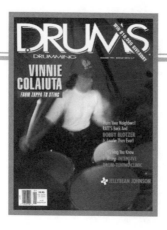

Drums & Drumming **was an exciting** experiment that failed. Yet during its five-year existence, our staff had a load of fun doing everything we could imagine to create a publication for drummers that was significantly different from its competitors. Specifically, we recognized a need for a drumming magazine with a rock & roll edge and splashy design that didn't skimp on educational material and honest consumer reporting.

We accomplished those editorial goals, although our timing was flawed. The first issue of *D&D* was published by the GPI Books division in the summer of 1987 as a one-shot, and was used to measure the interest of potential readers and advertisers. Fortunately, the response was strong enough for us to publish four more issues as one-shots until spring 1989, when Miller Freeman Publications purchased the company and *D&D* was transformed into a full-fledged subscription- and newsstand-based magazine.

D&D accomplished a lot in a very short time. It was the first drumming magazine to include drum-set diagrams with every artist feature. It anticipated the drum circle movement long before any other publication. It also was the first drumming magazine to feature concept covers on topics such as double-bass drumming and soloing. But it also became one of many victims of the recession that hit in the early nineties; its doors were finally closed in '91.

In that brief period *D&D* made a big impression on the drummers who read it. Everyone involved should be proud to have been involved with it. It seems so long ago since we published the final issue, yet I continue to be amazed to hear from former readers who still regret its closure. I guess we did something right.

> —*Andy Doerschuk,*
> *Editor,* Drums & Drumming, *1987–1991*

GINGER BAKER

The Tao of Me

Interviewed by Andy Doerschuk,
Drums & Drumming, January/February 1989

When *Drums & Drumming* **tackled** its first special issue, we decided to cover the topic of double-bass drumming, which was particularly hot due to the prevalence of heavy metal at the time. We chose to interview Ginger Baker, whose groundbreaking work with Cream helped popularize the idea in the late sixties that you could pump bass drums with both feet. We had heard that Baker could be a peppery interview, but we were unprepared for the level of animosity he maintained throughout our dialogue. A pregnant pause, a cackle, and comments about the idiocy of our inquiry followed practically every question. I was certain that he would hang up on me prematurely, but he didn't. And despite his apparent disgust, he answered every question we asked. To this day, it is one of the strangest interviews I've ever conducted.

—*Andy Doerschuk*

•   •   •

Did you originally play single bass drums?
Yeah. I didn't get a double-bass-drum kit until 1966.

What interested you in playing double bass?
It was a Duke Ellington concert I went to, with Sam Woodyard on drums. I was very impressed by his sound, so that's why I got a double-bass-drum kit. In fact, every drummer who ever played with Duke Ellington played two bass drums, like Dave Black, Louie Bellson, Sam Woodyard—they all played two bass drums. It was part of the thing to play two bass drums with Duke Ellington.

What was it about that performance that made you decide to make the switch?

It was a whole new field. I've always had very fast feet. It was just another area for me to explore.

Was it an easy transition?

I found it to be no problem at all, actually. The only real problem I found was getting the hi-hat in the right place as well, because even when you're using two bass drums the hi-hat is very important.

Did you start doing gigs with two bass drums right away?

Yeah, straight away. I was playing with Cream at the time.

It really was impressive back then to see your setup—few people in the rock world had been exposed to such a large drum kit up to that time.

Well, they obviously hadn't heard of Duke Ellington. But when you talk about the rock world, I don't know quite what you mean. This really bugs me when people talk about Cream playing rock & roll. It never was rock & roll. Never *ever*. It was sort of jazz/blues, and that's about as close to rock & roll as it was.

> "This really bugs me when people talk about Cream playing rock & roll. It never was rock & roll. Never *ever*."

Even in blues bands, though, it didn't seem that very many drummers were using two bass drums.

Well, in actual fact Keith Moon got a two-bass-drum kit before I did. He got the idea from me, of course. I told him I was getting a new two-bass-drum kit; the only thing was that mine was coming from the States and was being made there, and he got a Premier kit, which is an English drum kit. So he got his, in fact, before me.

Did you design your own kit?

Well, the sizes were a bit strange. That's why it took a little while to arrive. I had 11-inch shells on the bass drums instead of 14-inch shells. So they had to be cut down.

Did you prefer 11-inch shells for tonal reasons?

Yeah. The kit I had before that was a kit I made myself, and that had an 11-inch shell on the bass drum.

Was that your first kit?

No. I started playing the drums in 1955 or '56. I got a two-bass-drum kit in 1966. The kit I had before that was a kit I made for myself in 1962. I had another kit before that, and another kit before that. Everything didn't begin with Cream, you know.

Have you ever gone back to playing one bass drum for any particular gigs?

I did thousands of them before Cream.

But how about since then?

I scrubbed one of the bass drums for a little while in 1979 or something, I think. But everybody kept going mad, saying, "Why aren't you playing two bass drums?" Also, I missed it, actually.

Who were your influences on double bass?

I've always dug Duke Ellington—I'm a jazz player. I'm not a rock player, I'm a jazz player—always have been, always will be. The Ellington band was my favorite band, so I listened to people like Louie Bellson, Dave Black, Sam Woodyard, those sorts of drummers. But there was no real influence on me about how to play the drums. I got my influences, drum-wise, from people like Baby Dodds, Big Sid Catlett, Max Roach, and several African drummers. I've had several drummers that I like, but I play *me*, I've always played *me*, and will never play anything else but *me*. I don't copy people. I don't listen to somebody playing something and go back home and practice for days to get that lick together, because that's not where it's at. You have to play yourself; that's something I've got. That's why I'm a great drummer—because I play *me*. You hear Art Blakey playing, and you know it's Art Blakey playing. You hear Max Roach, and you know it's Max. You hear me playing, and you know it's me. Exactly.

You've always been a really hard-hitting drummer. Do you use any extra padding on your bass-drum heads?

No. I used to, in those days, put a calf pad on, calfskin with Evostick.

Were you using calf heads as well?

No. I put a calf pad on the plastic skin, but now the heads are a lot more advanced. I was only a hard-hitting drummer with Cream, because the other two shits were playing so fucking loud that you *had* to hit the drums hard, because otherwise you couldn't hear them.

They didn't have very sophisticated monitor systems back then.

Yeah, but I'm totally anti-volume. It was only in the days of Cream that they started miking drums up, which to me was totally fucking insane. The drums were the last things you ever miked up. It's only when they started getting these huge amplifiers and going into the rooms with total lunacy on the volume that they started miking drums up. I'd have to go back to the hotel room with my ears ringing with noises that would go on half the night. I can't stand volume, man. I think it's madness.

Has your double-bass style evolved over the years?

Evolved? Yeah, it's gone into the realms of lunacy at the moment. I'm doing things now where my hi-hat's going all the time as well. My left foot's become very fast.

Are you playing more hi-hat parts with your left foot?

No, but I've now got it together where I use the left bass drum but keep the hi-hat going as well.

So are you keeping your left foot on both the bass pedal and the hi-hat pedal at the same time?

No. The same part of my foot goes from the hi-hat to the bass drum and back again. It's something that came about pretty recently, really.

Do you undo your hi-hat clutch while playing two bass drums, so you can ride on the hi-hat closed?

I just left it as it was.

Would you ride on the open hi-hat then?

I dunno. I might have once in a while. I have no idea, really. I'm not a thinker. I don't think about what I'm doing. I have enough technique to just do things without thinking about it. That's something you have to work at.

Do you play double-bass parts with your heels up or down?

I play with my toes—heels up. If you've got just your toe on the pedal, you have several pivot points: your ankle joint, your knee joint, and your thigh joint all moving. If you've got your heel on the floor, the only thing that's moving is your ankle joint. If you sit and try it, you figure it out. You've got three pivots if you use your toe, which gives you three times more control. The whole system is obviously a matter of science.

Are your feet and hands equal in agility and quickness?

Yeah, I'm pretty ambidextrous in all directions. It's something I've worked at. It's very helpful in all forms of life. For instance, if you're pruning an olive tree and you've got to saw a branch off, sometimes the only way you can do it is with your left hand, depending on where it's got to come off or something. Also, when you're building, if you're in an awkward spot, the only way you can bang a nail in is to use your left hand. If you can do it, then you can do a much better job. I can do anything with my left hand. I can write with my left hand if I have to. I'm basically right-handed, but I've really worked very hard at something Phil Seaman told me years ago, "You should do things like eat your dinner left-handed, if you go for a piss get your dick out with your left hand," things like this. For everything you do with your right hand, do it with your left hand. It's better than practicing.

It's a mental exercise.

Yeah, your brain's got a right side and a left side. It's quite simple. All you do is just imagine your left hand's your right hand, and it's quite easy.

When you've written songs that include drum solos, such as "Toad," do you write the solo to fit the song, or vice versa?

A drum solo's a drum solo. I've never played a drum solo the same two nights running. That's what it's all about. How can you play a solo the same one night following the other? You feel differently; maybe something different has happened. You can't do that. A drum solo is a drum solo is a drum solo is a drum solo, and that's it. Solo means improvised. Improvisation is improvisation.

Is there a particular time signature that you enjoy for soloing?

Well, I go through the time changes. I mean, I don't like things like fives and sevens, because it's a very unnatural time signature. But if you've got four beats to a bar, you can go into all sorts of times with the four still going on underneath it, through it. You can go into three over the four, you can go into twelve over the four. In fact, there's a thing that I do now where I can get four different patterns going at once, playing eight with one foot, four with the other one, and playing in twenty-fours and threes and twelves with my hands.

That sounds like one of those situations you were talking about where you have to feel it rather than think it.

Yeah, you have to feel it. But in Africa you get the four drummers who play the four times, you see. This is why I get on very well in Africa, because I play four drummers' parts myself.

Has double-bass drumming progressed very far since the time you started playing in that style?

Quite honestly, there aren't many that can play them. There's a lot of guys with two bass drums up, but they don't really say anything. There aren't many drummers—period—that I like to listen to. Really, not a lot. It's quite difficult to pick out any. The guy with Peter Gabriel, Manu Katche, is a nice player, but he doesn't play two bass drums. I don't think I've heard anybody with two bass drums that has impressed me at all.

> "I don't copy people. That's why I'm a great drummer — because I play *me*, I've always played *me*, and will never play anything else but *me*."

Should drummers at least experiment with playing double bass drums?

It depends on the individual. My son Kofi plays drums. He's playing with a single-bass-drum kit, and he's playing fucking good too. He's playing in a band with one of Jack Bruce's kids at the moment, funny enough. But I think it depends on how your technique is, and how you are, and what happens. I'd been playing over ten years before I got a two-bass-drum kit.

Would double-bass drumming be appropriate in a wider range of pop styles?

I have no idea. I absolutely don't have the slightest idea. Nowadays, you've got computer drums that play really fast bass-drum things better than any drummer.

Has that taken away some of the impact of double-bass drumming?

I've no idea. I really enjoy working with computers, actually. I've done some stuff with Jonas Hellborg where we use computers. If you program a computer to play an answer to a pattern that you're actually going to play, it can be quite fun. You can program a computer so that the beats are never arriving with you, right? I do question-and-answer things; this is really quite fun.

Do you normally lay down the drum machine track before you play the drum part?

What we've been doing is putting the computer track down first. We've done several things where we write the whole arrangement on the computer, which takes several hours. But then the drum track is so easy, because there's no musicians. It's perfect every time. Then you can do a drum track in five minutes, if it's a five-minute number. I find it incredibly easy to play with computers, because they keep time. The problem for a lot of people is that you get the other musicians fucking up with the time, and it's very difficult.

> "I was only a hard-hitting drummer with Cream because the other two shits were playing so fucking loud that you *had* to hit the drums hard."

Do you practice very much?

No, I haven't had my drums out of their boxes for a couple of months. I haven't finished work; in fact, I've still got some stuff to do now in the dark. After a day's work all you want to do is have a bath and go to bed. I'm hoping I shall finish most of the hard work this week.

Do you have a studio in your house?

A studio? I'm a farmer—why the fuck would I have a studio in my house? [*At the time of this interview, Baker was working as a solitary olive farmer in a remote corner of Italy.*]

Is this a particularly busy season on your farm?

No, harvest is November. It's tidying-up time. I'm very nearly finished. But it's very difficult, physical work, which I find a very good thing for a drummer. You have to be very fit to play the drums. You certainly keep fit farming olives on a mountainside.

What are your most recent musical projects?

I'm not sure exactly what I'm doing at the moment. I'm finishing my work on the farm. At the moment I'm not able to do anything, because I'm totally on my own and I've got lots of animals and lots of work to do. Therefore I can't even think about touring. I'm on my own; therefore I can't go away.

You don't have anybody else working with you?

Nobody at all, just me. I'm not one of these gentleman farmers who say they're a farmer and have people out there that they're paying to do the work. I do everything myself. I keep the house clean and I cook my own food, as well.

Still, if you could take a minute to offer advice to drummers who are exploring double-bass setups for the first time, what would you say?

I dunno. I was teaching, but I had to give it up. You get twenty students, and one of them may become a drummer one time if a miracle happens. There are very few drummers about. A drummer is born. If you haven't got it, really and truly, then you shouldn't bother.

MAX ROACH

Form and Freedom

Interviewed by Robin Tolleson,
Drums & Drumming, June/July 1990

onsidering that *Drums & Drumming* was positioned against its competitors as a rock drumming magazine, it might have seemed odd to our readers when we published a cover story on jazz innovator Max Roach. Believe it or not, the idea came to us as a dare while we were planning the second issue of *D&D.* We had scheduled Max Weinberg as the cover story, and we wanted to commission a well-known drum journalist to compose the story. Our search led us to a New York–based writer, who upon hearing our query responded, "Max Weinberg? He's a hack! Why don't you put a real drummer on the cover—like Max Roach? If you do that, I'll write the story." Well, we never called that particular writer back, but we also never forgot his suggestion. Our June/July 1990 issue turned out to be one of the last cover-story interviews that Roach ever granted.

—*Andy Doerschuk*

• • •

You've spoken frequently about the freedom involved in playing jazz.

Yeah, it's freedom, but it's not without road maps and form. And it's not without certain disciplines that the performer has to be aware of. It's not by chance when someone plays in a certain key and they have certain harmonic changes, and they have the attitude whether it's fast or slow. For example, if you are playing "Sophisticated Lady" you have freedom to speak, but you have to preserve the subject matter. You wouldn't be playing a solo on a ballad and all of a sudden play John Coltrane's "Giant Steps." So when I talk about freedom, it has freed musicians to do something collectively; as long as everybody's on the same musical wavelength, they know the subject matter and understand the language. It takes years to do that. People often say, "When you guys are up there playing, how do you know when to stop, and how do you know when the next person comes in to play?" Well, it's very simple. We're all playing whatever harmonic and musical design that we follow—a twelve-bar blues, eight-bar blues, or sixteen-bar blues. The art of that kind of improvisation is how much you can do with just that small a time frame, with the same kind of progressions in that time frame, and how many new melodies you can create. That's not easy. Everybody has an idea of what the blues is all about, and they perform that. They have the freedom to express themselves within the confines of the structure. It's very logical.

So the discipline frees you to do whatever you want.

Yeah, but you've still got to master the instrument as much as you possibly can, and be a part of the whole thing. It takes more than one person to really make it fit. It's a very democratic spirit. I think this music is revolutionary because it tells people to think for themselves and it tells people to think collectively. And that's dangerous if everybody started really thinking together like that. When jazz came on the scene, it democratized the music because the music is now collectively created. You take a theme written by Duke Ellington, like "Perdido," and that's all you need. You don't need any written music. The great music can be improvised by the pianist, bassist, and others on a collective level. In truth, the jazz musician is unique in that he's not only a composer but an improviser. The great jazz musician must be able to compose and also perform to a very high level, to be a great instrumentalist and to be well versed in theory and harmony, and to listen to the vast world of sound out there. Contemporary music is about true freedom for the people. I get emotional when I think about what has happened, because, coming from a group of people who have been oppressed in the United States for a long time, freedom means a great deal.

In the discipline of mastering the drums, how important is learning the rudiments?

I grew up in marching bands and played with the local symphony orchestras. Of course, the drum set requires additional techniques because you have to use both feet and both hands. The rudiments are good for building up your hands. Then you can do the same thing with your feet—build the strength up. But the art of the instrument is how to use all these things, separately and equally, and have them make sense as a unit. With the cymbals and other things, you can get a great deal of variety out of the drum set. Since you're dealing with both hands and both feet and all the different things that go along with it, what you can do with the kit is endless. I don't think we've really scratched the surface yet. It's exciting, because it's still uncharted sound territory. Drummers, if I can say it, are the new voice, because heretofore it wasn't really listened to or looked at, and what was it? People tuned in to the melody and harmony. The drum set is an instrument of undetermined pitch. You

Max Roach, 1973: Not confined to keeping time.

don't listen to it for melodies and harmonies. You listen to the kit for the *sounds*, and the architecture and nuances that are so peculiar to that instrument. That's why it's a discipline. If you can't hear all the drums and cymbals equally well, then you don't have a real good sound. The sound should be transparent, meaning that when you listen you hear everything your hands and feet are doing.

Is there a way to learn to listen?

I think so. Your bass drum and the bass violin are about the same octave, even though one is "pitchless." The hi-hat is independent, because that's got its own sound—that *chick*. With the cymbals, you can't override what's going on around you. When we test sound with our quartet I usually play first without the monitors and the mics, so the engineer can hear it naturally. Then he can mic it as close to that sound as possible. I want to hear the trumpet and saxophone and bass, but not at the expense of the drums. Some engineers assume during a solo that nobody else means anything, but this music isn't like that. In order for the soloist to improvise on progressions that move and change so rapidly, he's got to listen to all of it and play at the same time. So does everybody else.

You frequently play in a quartet setting, but without piano or guitar. Most groups have a chordal instrument of some sort.

Yeah, but the harmony is implied in the line that you play. [*Roach sings a melody line.*] You can hear the II–V, II–V, II–V, II–I. The guy who plays that line does it, and you can hear his harmony. So harmony is not just block chords; it's also linear. You can hear where the song is going through the line the player creates.

That also gives the audience a chance to hear it in a different way.

Yeah. When the piano is added to my group, all of us have to play differently. Because he's making all the fills now, the best thing for me is to play it straight. Once in a while I can use sounds to do certain other things, but basically I'm content with playing it as straight as possible.

Is time a problem for young drummers?

That's one big problem, and there are many factors that create that. One thing about keeping good time is that you cannot get distracted. You've got to lean into that quarter-note, no matter how much you dance around or above or underneath it. You've got to know that this is there, in the same place you start, even though you might be all over the place.

Is that the drummer's most important job?

No, no. It's essential to all musicians to keep time. The instrumentalists that I've really loved accompanying are those horn players or pianists who have what we call "a built-in rhythm section." If they play a Charlie Parker line, you can hear the pulse; you can hear the beat. When you run into a player who's that good, it's ice cream and cake, because you're not confined to keep the time. Why should I keep time for somebody? I have an instrument that can color, that can build and do anything in the world to enhance the performance. So am I going to be restricted to just saying "ding ding-a-ding" for you? If you can't keep time, then you should not be involved in this music. If the horns can't keep time and are racing and just playing chorus after chorus and repeating themselves, I subconsciously play faster and faster because I'm bored and I want to take the song out, psychologically. It took me a long time to figure that out. Guys would say, "Man, you're really rushing the time." I'd say, "I know I'm rushing, because nothing is happening up on the front line. What you're doing up there is boring to me, so I want to get the song over with. And when the song is over, I'm going to get up off the drums and get somebody else to do this for you."

> "Contemporary music is about true freedom for the people. I get emotional when I think about what has happened."

Is better time something you can learn?

Yeah, you can work with a metronome, but time is elastic. It gets fast and slow. Don't try to keep time like a metronome; it's inhuman. Time breathes. It's human, because we're human. We breathe. After the metronome starts, cut it off and practice your time exercises for a while, and keep it in your head. Then push the button and get it started again and see how far off you are. I'd advise everybody to practice time with all four limbs playing quarter-notes. Snare drum, cymbal—everything on the quarter-notes. And make sure you're listening to yourself so that you can hear everything equally well and balanced. You're always listening, and you're always a little off. It's interesting. Everybody can keep time. If you can walk, you can keep time, or else you'd be stumbling all over the place. Walking is an even gait, and you do that automatically.

How do you compare studying drums with the experience of getting a gig and just doing it?

I think just doing it is perfect. If you can get a gig and learn on the job, that's the best experience. I've been a very fortunate musician. At sixteen I worked with Duke Ellington. After that I had the good fortune to work with people like Coleman Hawkins and Dizzy Gillespie in studios, speakeasies, nightclubs, after hours. I have a very high standard of musicians that I want to work with. But I would continue studying as well, even though I'm learning on the job. You can get there faster if you're working with someone who'll tolerate your little mistakes. Because any time you make a mistake, if you know it's a mistake, it's a lesson. When I was growing up, I was like, "Have Drumsticks, Will Travel." I'd play in any kind of situation, whether it was rhythm and blues, big band, marching band, symphony orchestra—anything to do with percussion. All I wanted to do was to get to know the sound of that instrument. I just wanted to learn how to touch the instrument and make certain things sound a certain way. And the only way to do that was to hear it constantly, touching it and feeling it and working with it.

> "I have an instrument that can color, that can build and do anything in the world to enhance the performance. So am I going to be restricted to just saying 'ding ding-a-ding' for you?"

Is playing with brushes a lost art?

No, I don't think so. It's coming back now in the recording studios. When we started recording in 1943, I noticed that brushes were taboo, because if you really swept, the engineer would come in and say it sounded like surface noise. You could play the brushes like sticks and it would work. But if you played that *shhh-shhh-shhh* sound, the engineer would say, "What the hell is going on in there? What am I hearing?" Sweeping is a very pleasant sound, especially on some ballads. I worked with Dizzy Gillespie recently, and when he plays a ballad, that's the way he likes to hear the drummer play—he likes to hear him sweep.

Do you encourage your students to study brush playing?

Of course. They should learn it because out in the world they might ask you for a lot of things. I encourage them to play with big bands. They may get a job at a studio and have to read real well, or they may get a job with a rock group, or a group like Basie's, which is another way to approach the instrument. What all of these things have in common is that you have to have technique. So I advocate students to practice, practice, practice, and you can use it sometime.

What do you think of rap music?

I love it. That's an extension of Louis Armstrong and all the rest of us. These people came like a Phoenix from the ashes, from nothing, and they became something. Louis Armstrong, Charlie Parker, all of these great people came from the same place, and nobody taught them anything about music. Charlie Parker went to school to be an automobile mechanic, and Dizzy Gillespie and a lot of other great musicians were the same. The rap people have come from the same sociopolitical environment, and nobody ever gave them anything, nobody ever showed them how to do anything. In the inner-city schools of New York like Harlem and South Bronx, there's no music, no instruments. There's no rhetoric to teach them how to write poetry, either. But nevertheless they invented something that's very pure, and they created their own poetry. They created their own world of sound, with turntables and sampling, that resembles nothing else. It's an amazing phenomenon, and I think it proves to us all that you can take the least and get the most. From a revolutionary point of view, they created a world of sound without using harmony and melody—only rhythm. It's amazing.

> "The basis of contemporary music is to stimulate creativity in people to be themselves. If someone masters the language that Bach created, he's not being creative."

You've learned from some of the greatest musicians of an earlier era. Do you see yourself as part of that process, bringing young musicians along through your own teaching?

Well, you can teach what *has* happened. But the new music of the twentieth century, all over the world, allows the young artists to be themselves. You can only teach what Charlie Parker did. For them to really be like a Charlie Parker or a Kenny Clarke or an Art Blakey, it's not to imitate them, it's to be creative *like* them, and that is difficult to teach. You can show them the way Art Blakey did this, or Elvin Jones or Chick Webb. But the basis of contemporary music is to stimulate creativity in people to be themselves. If someone masters the language that Bach created, he's not being creative. I think Anthony Braxton is closer to Charlie Parker, because he does something totally different with the instrument than Parker did. That kind of creativity is what I look for in young people. It's like, Cecil Taylor is an extension of Bud Powell. John Coltrane was an extension of Lester Young. They sound totally different, and that's fine. They are extensions because what they have done has made such a strong and individual impression on the world.

Where did you get the inspiration to do an entire solo on the hi-hat?

Oh, from a gentleman by the name of Jonathan Samuel David Jones—Papa Jo, with the Count Basie band. Gene Krupa was very sick, and the Newport Festival decided to give a testimonial to him in Central Park. We were all there, from Elvin Jones to Buddy Rich to Art Blakey to Louie Bellson to Tony Williams. Drummers came from far and wide just to celebrate and perform that July in Central Park. Krupa sat onstage and listened and thanked everybody. He was really polite. He'd stand up and come to you, put his arms around you. It was a very moving event. But the guy who closed the show was Papa Jo Jones of the Count Basie band, and he's a peer of Krupa's. Mr. Jones came onstage and stopped the show and ended the whole concert when he did this hi-hat piece. It was the first time I heard it done. He just came onstage with a hi-hat, a pair of sticks, and a stool, and it was beautiful. It just gave us all an idea that you can get the most out of the least. That was the perfect lesson.

PHIL COLLINS
& CHESTER THOMPSON
Two for the Road

Interviewed by Robin Tolleson,
Drums & Drumming, Summer 1987

Aﬁer **Peter Gabriel quit as** the lead singer with Genesis in 1974, the remaining band members searched for his replacement. In the end they promoted sometime background singer and full-time drummer Phil Collins to the position of front man—and defied all expectations by enjoying even greater success. But Collins loved drumming and was never willing to forsake his role as Genesis's drummer entirely, so the band settled for a compromise: Collins would record all the drum parts in the studio, and the band would use studio whiz Chester Thompson onstage, with occasional percussive contributions from Collins. The premiere issue of *Drums & Drumming* featured both drummers on the cover, which was quite a coup since it was published on the heels of the band's top-selling album *Invisible Touch* and would mark the only time these two drummers ever graced the cover of a drumming magazine together.

—*Andy Doerschuk*

• • •

You got your drum gig with Genesis after auditioning at a farm owned by Peter Gabriel's parents in Surrey, England. It sounds like a rather bucolic setting.

Collins: It was a lovely day. The grand piano was pushed out onto the patio, and there was a big umbrella for the drum kit to set up underneath. I was a little early, as always, and they said, "Go have a swim while we've got a couple of guys in front of you." So while I was swimming I heard the other guys auditioning, and by the time I got to play I kind of knew everything. I didn't know the songs when I started swimming, but I did by the time I finished. I went in there and made it look a little hard, so it looked like I hadn't been cheating. Any fool ought to know the part after hearing six drummers playing in front of him.

What did you bring to Genesis that was different from the drummers who preceded you in the band?

Collins: Genesis was a little unfunky when I joined the band. I tried to change that because of my love for R&B and jazz. In comparison to drummers like [Bill] Bruford, I'm not very well versed in that. I like big bands, and some Coltrane and Miles Davis stuff, but past that there are a lot of names and music that I've never heard of. But I was listening to a lot of jazz at that time, and that was the kind of thing that came out on *Foxtrot* and *Nursery Cryme* and I guess on *Selling England.*

Chester, has your jazz background helped you in Genesis?

Thompson: Possibly. You've got to be a lot more musical in Genesis than if you're only playing rock. There is some basic musicianship that you stand a better chance of learning through jazz. At the same time, I think the idea is just to give it your best shot every time you hit the stage, whether you feel like it or not. If more people did that, a lot of guys wouldn't be as frustrated in their local situations.

> "In the early days I wanted to *tell* everybody it was a complicated time signature, so that everyone would see how clever I was."
> — Phil Collins

What elements of musicianship do you learn from playing jazz?

Thompson: The basic one is how to listen, how to feed off of other players, as opposed to sort of being wound up like a clock, like you go and I'll meet you at the end. Rock isn't like that all the time, but very often it feels that way—first one to the end wins, or something. There's a lot of great rock players out there now, but I find, more and more, guys that really impress me usually are pretty good jazz or fusion players as well.

Has your playing evolved much since the days when you were playing with Frank Zappa in the early seventies?

Thompson: A lot of it depends on what I'm playing at the moment. I went from Zappa immediately into Weather Report, and the way I look at that period of time is that with Zappa it was like learning how to pretty much read and play anything. And with Weather Report it's like learning what to leave out. So hopefully somewhere along the line the balance continues to grow as far as knowing when to play and when not to.

Has your approach to playing odd time signatures changed?

Thompson: Well, the stuff I do now doesn't call for as much odd time as with somebody like Frank. Not only the drum parts, but the music itself is not quite as complicated. Groove is incredibly important with the stuff we're doing with Genesis. It's odd time, but it's very much about how it feels. With Zappa the feeling was kind of written in. Once you played it right, the feel was established, because Frank was so specific about what had to be played.

With Genesis, do you almost try to disguise the odd times to make them feel straight?

Thompson: In some cases, yeah. Things tend to not feel like odd times. I know as I listen to old stuff, some of that disguise seems to go back for years. Gabriel still seems to do quite a bit of that, where it's an odd time but it has a consistent pulse to the point where it doesn't feel like an odd time.

Collins: Something like "Turn It On Again" [from *Duke*], for instance. A lot of people don't realize that song is actually in 13/8. It's a rock song, and it doesn't really feel like it's in any complicated time signature. What I try to do is make the time signature as simple as possible so that they don't really know it's a complicated thing. Obviously I'm better at doing that now, because in the early days I wanted to *tell* everybody it was a complicated time signature, so that everyone would see how clever I was. Attitudes change.

Thompson: It comes naturally, after you've done it for a while. You don't really think about it; you just feel it and play it, maybe count in your head the first couple of bars or, if it's real ridiculous, the first four or five bars. Then it tends to lock in. And if you get in trouble, you count again.

Collins: On something like "And So to F" [from *Product*], which was a Brand X song we did on my tour, I still have to sing the bass line to keep myself in time. A lot of the time I hitch up with a bass on something like "Nuclear Burn," which is in 11 on the Brand X album *Unorthodox Behaviour*. I usually just hitch up with that, and apart from the odd bits of dancing around in it, I end up staying with it.

You sound a little like Billy Cobham on some of the Brand X stuff.

Collins: He was a huge influence. *Inner Mounting Flame* [Mahavishnu Orchestra] was the best example of rock/jazz drumming that I'd ever heard. I probably still haven't heard any better than that album. His playing on that album was phenomenal, and he only played one bass drum as well, which was fantastic. That was one of the reasons why I haven't really played two bass drums since my school days, when Ginger Baker and Keith Moon were in fashion. I wasn't bad, but I always liked the hi-hat. I found that the hi-hat was too important to just sort of have as a secondary thing. Keith Moon was a big influence on me. His drumming on some of the Who records was very original and very unique. Completely original.

Chester, what records influenced you when you were young?

Thompson: The first thing that got me was an old instrumental called "Last Night" [by the Mar-Keys], because it had the first sort of blatant drum fill in the middle of it, which was kind of nice. I liked a lot of the Meters stuff; I was playing a very similar kind of thing already—the stuff that was happening on the early Meters records, like *Cissy Strut.* And a lot of James Brown stuff. James Brown was usually the freshest thing out, rhythm-section-wise. Curtis Mayfield would always get these incredible drummers on his records who were mainly jazz players; they would play with a whole different kind of aggressiveness on the rock stuff. That was kind of nice.

Who were the first drummers who really knocked you out?

Thompson: The first people I was actually impressed by were Max Roach, Elvin Jones, and Art Blakey.

Phil, how did you know that Chester would work out so well with Genesis?

Collins: The thing that clinched me with Chester was a song called "More Trouble Every Day" [by Frank Zappa, from *Roxy & Elsewhere*], which he and Ralph Humphrey play, and I heard that drum fill, which we actually do at the end of "Afterglow" [from *Wind and Wuthering*]. It floored me completely. I saw what two drummers could do. It could be like a machine. I play flams quite a lot, and with my flams and another drummer you get this huge, solid, thick backbeat. So one of the first things we did when I met Chester was get him to teach me that lick, and we always put it in the show somewhere. But that was really just listening to him. I had never met him. I rang him up and said, "Hi, Chester. I've heard your stuff. Would you like to play with Genesis?" He came over as a member. He didn't even audition. He just came over and set up his drums, and we started rehearsing. We never had any doubt that it would work.

Did you have to compromise your style to fit into Genesis?

Thompson: Quite a bit—an awful lot in the beginning. I did have to make some pretty dramatic changes in concepts as far as playing with Phil, but that's the whole point anyway. Diversity is what I love most about music. Genesis has become a lot more Americanized over the years. Obviously we've been together long enough to where I've gotten used to playing with them, so now it feels pretty natural. But in the beginning it was almost opposite everything that I was used to doing, just because in those days everything sounded real English.

What do you mean by "real English"?

Thompson: Just without the sort of extra bits of swing. I mean if things are on the beat, they are *on* the beat. The whole band tends to play a little on top of the beat, but very even, very understated in parts—especially drum parts. Americans, on the other hand, tend to embellish things a little more, especially the simpler parts. It's very seldom you would play many American beats where you're only playing, like, *one* and *two* on the bass drum and *three* and *four* on the snare, and that being the dominant feeling. But most English groups don't play like that anymore. It's all actually reaching a point where there are less boundaries in music, as far as distinguishing one style from the other.

What's the most essential skill a drummer needs in order to play with another drummer?

Thompson: Listening.

Collins: If you've got a strong groove going with two drummers, you've got to listen to the other guy. You've got to get rid of ego. Obviously on one's own you can play faster and more complicated stuff, and go out of time and go free for a while. Whereas if you've got a strong groove going with two drummers, you've got to listen to the other guy.

What makes Chester such a good partner for you?

Collins: Chester is the easiest person for me to play with. We read each other like a book. We can solo and stretch out a little bit and actually improvise, but at the same time we keep out of each other's way, which for two drummers is a rare thing. Bruford was a little busy, and probably because of my inexperience at playing with two drummers I was a little busy too in those days, so we never locked in as well as Chester and I do. Bill would always play as an individual, and it just wasn't as solid. Then I did two dates with Clapton in London, where I played with Steve Ferrone. He's a very solid drummer and was very easy to play with. Occasionally we'd get tangled up, but very rarely. At Live Aid, me and Tony Thompson were a disaster. Some guys are easier to play with than others. Some guys are prepared to make sacrifices in their attitude and they listen.

> **"[Jazz teaches] how to feed off of other players, as opposed to sort of being wound up like a clock. Rock very often feels that way —first one to the end wins."**
> —Chester Thompson

How do you coordinate parts during solos?

Collins: In the early days of the drum solo that prefaces "Los Endos" [from *Trick of the Tail*] we would get a groove going, then I'd play a bit, he'd play a bit, I'd play, he'd play—almost like a duel. But we decided that the stronger thing is to actually get two guys to play the same thing. That's almost stronger than someone saying one guy's better than another guy. So we sat down in a hotel room in Dallas, put a tape recorder on the table, and sat opposite each other, playing with sticks on a chair, and taped it all. We listened back to it and would point out what sounded good. We'd say, "Right, remember that," and then we'd listen to another bit. We'd piece this jigsaw together and we'd learn it. We had reference points—like Part A was something, and then we'd improvise for X amount of bars until someone gave his cue, and then to Part B. It's something that's developed, and for me it's one of the highlights of the show.

What about arranging drum parts in the studio?

Thompson: I get a tape long before the record is released, so by the time it comes out I pretty much know the part, other than the fine-tuning of it. A lot of times with Phil, though, with the kind of recording techniques they get into, I don't put too much time into trying to figure out what it is because the final result is never what the basic tracks sound like anyway. If there are any tricks to the trade of recording, they've got 'em down, believe me. You think you hear rolls, and you find out it's the reverb feeding back. Plus, very often he tracks with a drum machine, then goes back and puts in the drum part to replace or add to it.

Collins: That's because the drum machine patterns that the songs are written to are usually too important to replace. Sometimes you get the real drums coming in halfway through a song, like a guitarist might switch on a fuzz box. On "Don't Lose My Number" [from *No Jacket Required*] we had a Linn [electronic] bass drum and snare drum, and real tom-toms. I just played some tom-tom fills over the Linn bass and snare drum, and added some cymbals.

You've followed that approach for quite some time.

Collins: Well, the whole thing behind my first album was that I wasn't really making a record. I was just learning how to operate my eight-track equipment at home. When Tony [Banks, keyboardist] and Mike [Rutherford, guitarist] and I were in Japan in 1978, we got the first three Roland CR-78s off the production line, and I said, "I don't want a drum machine. Why do I want a drum machine?" So then my divorce thing happened, and I found myself with a lot of time, and I asked for my CR-78 back, just so I could fool around and write some songs. And it opened up a whole lot of space. Suddenly you didn't have to supply the rhythm on the piano, because you had a rhythm machine. People might have been doing this for years, but I had never done anything like it. So on "In the Air" [from *Face Value*] I just set up an interesting pattern and got a nice sound out of my [Sequential] Prophet-5 synthesizer. I played a few chords and then overdubbed another synthesizer and sang a few words. All the "In the Air" words were improvised. They came out of the top of my head, and I kept them all. Then because I didn't want to redo those demos in the studio, I took my eight-track tape into the studio at Townhouse and copied it to 24-track. I tidied it up and got rid of some hiss, then carried on overdubbing, like the real drums and the horns and strings and everything. That's the way I work now. I just work from home, using my demos.

> "You've got to get rid of ego.... With two drummers, you've got to listen to the other guy."
> — Phil Collins

Does it bother you not to be playing drums as much as you used to do?

Collins: Well, I play on every album, every Genesis album and obviously my own albums. I'm more likely to surface as a drummer on anybody's album than anything else, because people tend to ring me up and say, "Are you free for this?" And I can go down there and do something in three hours, and it's a great pleasure just to play for somebody else. I still get excited about doing that. I just did half a dozen dates with Clapton in Europe, and people actually said to me, "I didn't realize that you played the drums!" Even Clapton's tour manager thought that I did it as a secondary instrument. He came up after two or three gigs and said, "I didn't realize you were that good. I thought you just sang and played the piano a bit, and played drums when you weren't singing." It amazes me. I forget that people think that.

How would you hope that people think of you as a drummer?

Collins: Someone who plays with musicality, plays what's right for the music. My tastes go completely across the board, from Weather Report to R&B, to what would apparently be middle-of-the-road music from what people think of Stephen Bishop's writing. I'd be quite happy playing any of that stuff, because I'd be quite happy to add something to the song that was being played. It's really being a musician/drummer rather than just a drummer.

STEVE SMITH

Drum Circle

Interviewed by Robin Tolleson,
Drums & Drumming, April 1991

Steve Smith is one of the greatest chameleons in drumming. He first gained notoriety as a flashy double-bass fusion player in the mid-seventies with Jean-Luc Ponty, then evolved into a full-fledged rock star in 1979 after replacing Aynsley Dunbar in Journey. After recording five of the pop band's chart-busting records, Smith departed in the early eighties to pursue jazz drumming, in particular with his own band, Vital Information. When *Drums & Drumming* featured Smith on the cover of the April 1991 issue, it had been eight years since he had released *Frontiers,* his last album with Journey in the eighties. When the *D&D* staff sat down to brainstorm cover lines for the issue, we came up with "Forget Journey. Steve Smith Has." He later chewed us out for publishing that headline, accusing us of resorting to tabloid journalism. In retrospect, he was probably right.

—Andy Doerschuk

• • •

Your first gig coming out of college was with Jean-Luc Ponty. Were you prepared for it?

That was difficult to play night after night and be consistent. I attribute a lot of getting the gig to being able to read well, because I had to read at the audition. I did play some fusion at Berklee, but I didn't have my chops developed for it. I realized while doing the gig that I needed more rock & roll experience to be better suited to this kind of fusion music. So when I left Jean-Luc I sought out rock rather than more jazz playing. I moved to Los Angeles and auditioned around, and got gigs with Freddie Hubbard and Ronnie Montrose in the same week. I chose the Montrose gig, and that led to Journey, and that's exactly what I wanted to do at the time—experience what that was like and add that to my playing.

Did you study with Alan Dawson at Berklee?

For a year. He helped me a lot with independence, technique, and form. It's only recently that I realized what a great musical awareness he put into his teaching. He would give you very technical exercises, out of the Ted Reed *Syncopation* book. You'd play the different lessons, substituting your right foot and left foot for different hands, while playing a ride cymbal. But then you had to sing a jazz standard tune at the same time, so you were becoming aware of form. That's a great teaching tool. For a drummer, the next best thing to be aware of after time and feel is the form. It's especially important in a small jazz group, where you're playing chorus after chorus of a tune, to know the form without having to rely on hearing a familiar chord pattern. You can't let the concentration go, unless it's something like a twelve-bar blues that you can feel very easily, or a real predictable A–A–B–A standard type of form where it's easy to hear or feel the chord sequence. When the form isn't so obvious to the ear, it's really important to do whatever you have to do—concentrate, follow the chart, or whatever—to always mark and know the form. It's that internal thing of just knowing where you are all the time.

Things have come full circle, and you've gotten seriously into teaching.

I really enjoy it. I get to go out and do my thing, kind of create my own gig.

What makes for a good drum teacher?

It should be someone who has a good understanding of the application of drums in music, versus a teacher who is really out of the playing mainstream. There are some teachers who are strictly isolated to teaching, and I think that can sometimes steer students in the wrong direction. So I think a good teacher is someone who is really aware of the end result of whatever the student is trying to accomplish. And I think it's really important to have a balance between the reading, technique, time, feel—all the aspects. At different times in each student's development, they're going to have to focus more on one aspect rather than the big picture. So I think it's up to the teacher to help the student decide what that person needs at that moment in time. Then the practical experience of being involved in playing music will help you to guide yourself to what you need. Ultimately, the student has to become his own teacher. It's such a balance between all of the elements.

> "From playing rock & roll I notice that time is generated from underneath, so I concentrate on building time from the bottom up."

Steve Smith, 2002: Giving each note its due.

What do young drummers need to work on?

One of the most common things is not having the awareness of how important it is to be a good time and feel player. It's been said a million times before, but I still see people practicing and working on all kinds of intricate ideas and concepts without first getting a good groove and good time thing going.

Has time gotten any better since the appearance of drum machines?

Well, people who play along with a click track or sequencer will develop their time better. I never had to play gigs with a click track when I was young, but a lot of people do that now. But I also see a lack of touch and finesse on the instrument. I'd say in the forties, fifties, and early sixties the working musician had to read music most of the time—to read and play that music required a lot of work, and more years, before you were a professional player. Now the music you play in a club is actually easier. You don't have to be able to read, and the drumming is less sophisticated and takes less technique. By lack of technique I mean finesse—the touch, and not having the control to play things soft. So you get a lot of heads, sticks, and cymbals breaking, and that isn't a result of anything but undeveloped technique. A lot of people play louder than they have to play—too hard, without control.

What else has changed?

The left hand nowadays is *two* and *four*, and then a few fills around the drum set. In the past, jazz drummers weren't playing just *two* and *four* with the left. The older music was based on triplets. If you ever sit down and practice triplets, you go from one hand to the other hand because it's an odd number of notes—left-right-left, right-left-right, left-right-left, right-left-right—so you're working each side equally. When you play sixteenth-notes everything comes out with the right hand, and it gets real right-heavy, not so balanced. That contributes to uneven technique. There's some swing feel going on now, especially with hip-hop. Practicing that style gets you more even-handed because it naturally alternates.

How did you become aware of the positive attributes that playing jazz could develop in a drummer?

I was lucky enough to grow up at a time when I could catch the very end of some big bands on the road. I saw Buddy Rich a lot, [Stan] Kenton's band a lot, Woody Herman, Count Basie, Maynard Ferguson. I got to play that type of music. Now that's almost extinct, you know. But I saw Randy Jones with Maynard Ferguson, and Peter Erskine with Stan. I even studied with Peter at a Stan Kenton camp. I was eighteen, and he was eighteen [*laughs*]. He got me to really concentrate on playing swing time, to focus on the ride cymbal, how to play four quarter-notes in a row that feel good. It was that basic, that simple, but it was what I needed. It really got me focused into the priority of playing everything so it swung and felt good. Taking charge of the band. Laying down the time and feel so the other guys are much more comfortable at what they're doing.

Even when you're wailing on something, you give each note its due.

I guess that's the result of the "coliseum" kind of drumming. In the coliseums only big notes are heard. I had to develop that when I joined Journey, and I've applied it to my jazz playing, which makes it feel much more relaxed and centered and controlled than ever before. Lately, though, I'm playing a lot more notes than I used to play—a lot more little notes too. I've developed in a different direction, but I still try to give each note its due, and be very clear and relaxed.

> "Ultimately, the student has to become his own teacher."

Being relaxed?

When people play simply and slowly, it still has to have some tension holding it together so there's a forward motion. It has to have the illusion of being relaxed and comfortable, but it also has to have forward motion. On the other hand, when you play something really fast it has to be completely relaxed, so it doesn't have a tense feeling. I've had to work hard on the samba; that's difficult to play. And the real fast swing stuff is hard to maintain. I work on it and get it together now, and then play it faster and faster until it gets there.

Although you're a pretty flashy player, your priority doesn't ever seem to be the licks.

Right. What turned me around on that was the Stan Kenton clinic with Peter Erskine. I was eighteen, but I wish I had learned that the first day I started playing. You can analyze music by breaking it down into melody, harmony, and rhythm—and the one connecting factor that makes it possible for all musicians to communicate is rhythm. It's the thread among musicians, and it's every musician's responsibility to work on their time. If the players are mature and proficient rhythmically and in control, then the likelihood of a great musical experience is high. It's important for every musician to make that their first priority.

> "The drummer does have more responsibility because the instrument is so powerful that you can't fight it: If the drummer slows down or speeds up, everyone has to follow."

But if the time gets off in a band, everybody always turns around and looks at the drummer.

Ultimately, the drummer does have more responsibility because the instrument is so powerful that you can't fight it: If the drummer slows down or speeds up, everyone has to follow. If it's happening the other way, the time's gonna feel uneven because the drummer's going to be searching. When it's an ideal situation with great jazz musicians, everybody can just *play*. I saw Peter Erskine, Marc Johnson, and Eliane Elias, and I can't say Peter was really playing time for them. Keith Jarrett and Jack DeJohnette are very much like that as well. It's sort of the highest level of playing.

How do you develop your time?

I tape myself a lot, then listen for problems. When I'm playing in time along with a click track, and it feels great and everything's flowing, it creates a certain body sensation. It's important to be aware and in control over that, so it can be re-created. You can create that the moment a tune starts and never let it go from the beginning to the end of the tune. It's usually a very comfortable, relaxed sensation. But it's a self-taught process of training your body to feel time and then play everything without losing that sensation.

What about playing fills? You give the impression in your playing that it's not just about the fill; you're looking down the road to see what's coming.

Right. Fills are there not so much to showcase what the drummer can do, but to make the hits real obvious and easy for the other musicians to play.

What do you mean by hits?

Downbeats in rock or a horn figure in jazz. Fills complement the music and help the other players' parts come out real strong.

Is being a solo artist—leading your own band—more work than being a sideman?

It's a lot more work. Being the bandleader is a lot of work, and a lot of headaches. Peter Erskine once told me that in jazz the bandleader makes no money; only the sidemen make money. It's really true. But in rock & roll the bandleader makes a fortune, and the sidemen comparatively don't make that much. When I go on the road I have to pay the other musicians, and hopefully I come home breaking even, if it works out. I still want to make my own records, because I enjoy it and there are people that like to hear it. But I have to do a lot of other stuff to make a living. I've had my most success in a situation where I pooled my talents with other people, like with Journey: We pooled our talents and in a collective voice created a sound and a type of music that was appreciated.

What were the differences between playing for jazz or fusion audiences one night, and for rock fans with Journey the next?

They're really different audiences. I feel that the people who hear me play in the jazz/fusion setting have more insight into what it is that I'm doing. But the reaction I get from the rock & roll crowd is an appreciation of the overall sound of the band, the songs, the lead singer. They respond to the excitement of the drum solo in a more innocent sense.

When playing with Journey you tended to set your drum stool pretty low.

Sitting at that height, I feel that my legs have more strength. From playing rock & roll I notice that time is generated from underneath, so I concentrate on building time from the bottom up. I don't usually crash the cymbals real hard, but I hit the bass drum hard and the snare medium hard so it feels bottom-heavy and relaxed. With Journey I had to develop a more relaxed sense of time. Before, I played very cymbal-oriented, driving on top, which is a holdover from bebop drumming, where all the time is generated from the cymbal.

Looking back, what does the experience of playing with Journey mean to you?

One of the things that satisfied me musically in that situation was taking care of the needs of the other musicians, playing things that they liked to hear. I also tried to take care of my own needs, which were the physical chops kind of things, and the intellectual things—the sophistication of what I was doing. In doing that, hopefully, I created some good music.

MAX WEINBERG

Born to Drum

Interviewed by Andy Doerschuk,
Drums & Drumming, January/February 1988

I felt like the proverbial kid in a candy store when I began planning my first issue as the editor of *Drums & Drumming* in 1987. While I can't recall the number of names on my wish list of drummers to interview, I remember that Max Weinberg was at the very top. His drumming with Bruce Springsteen personified everything I strove for in my playing: rock-solid tempos, classic fills that paid homage to the greatest jazz and rock drummers, and a booming sound that seemed far too huge to come from his four-piece Ludwig kit. As I began to inquire into his availability, I was surprised when he called me directly rather than having one of his representatives set up the interview. We met in a nondescript motel room in Chicago, where Weinberg had flown to attend a music convention. It was raining, I got lost on my way to the motel, and we spoke late into the night.

—*Andy Doerschuk*

• • •

When did you decide to become a professional drummer?

I guess when I was about eight years old. I started playing when I was six, and when I was eight I had a drum set and I was sort of in a band, a little Dixieland trio. We played for a school assembly, and I got applause. From then on, I was addicted. For me, until I got with Bruce, it was much more about the applause than anything else. Then I realized what hard work it was, and how dedicated you had to be. Thankfully, our audiences have always been pretty good, but you don't want to depend on the audience to get you up. You want to be gotten up through your own devices. You want to capture that moment yourself. For me, drumming was always about working. It wasn't about practicing; it was about making a living.

How much to you practice now?

I go through waves where I don't practice for a long time, and then I'll get into three months of heavy woodshedding. It's difficult to be as dedicated as I'd like to be. But when I'm practicing, I try to get at least two hours a day. And I know what to practice. I don't waste any time; I know right what to go for.

When you practice, do you focus on certain muscles, or do you practice grooves?

I practice technique; I don't practice grooves. I know what you mean: Do I practice, like, beats? No, I never practice beats. What I practice is rudiments, absolutely. The beats come. The beats are like the left side of the brain. The rudiments are what enable you to pull anything off. I work with a metronome. I work on subtle, delicate things, because you lose those subtleties when you play loud rock. When you're playing in stadiums, you have to use the broadest of strokes. But something I don't ever want to lose is the ability to play with subtlety.

Is that why you started taking lessons at one point with the extraordinarily subtle jazz drummer Joe Morello?

All drumming is drumming. I don't think there's any difference between jazz and rock & roll. The object is the same thing: You're a drummer. You're supposed to support the soloist. You're supposed to lend your musical statement to the conversation. And Joe has a method of teaching technique that enables you to speak that language more fluently. Joe's thing is to let the stick do the work; it's just a down motion. Joe is the last descendant of the drumming style laid down by George Lawrence Stone and Billy Gladstone, who were two famous rudimental drummers.

Do you play matched grip?

I play both.

How do you decide whether to use matched grip or traditional grip?

If I have a song where I have to do a double-stroke roll, I'll use traditional grip. When I relax, I use a traditional grip. If I have a blister or a callus on my index finger, I'll turn the stick around. I'm adept at both. I learned to play with traditional grip, and when Ringo came along I got into matched grip. The first drummer in England to play matched grip was a famous jazz drummer in the fifties named Phil Seaman, who was Ginger Baker's hero.

What qualities do you look for in other drummers?

That question brings me back to a concert last summer where I saw Steve Winwood and his band play in New Jersey. I don't know the name of his drummer, but after I saw him play for about three minutes I remember thinking how incredibly commanding the guy's groove was. I listen to a guy's sense of groove. That's what moves me the most—his sense of the beat.

What exactly is a groove?

To my ears, what makes a groove is the amount of controlled relaxation the drummer brings to the music. The great groove drummers of all time—Al Jackson, Bernard Purdie, Russ Kunkel, Jim Keltner—have such facility and finesse; they make it sound easy. I think that's what a groove is. It's that indescribable feeling that turns the corners of your mouth up into a smile when you listen to it. It's what moves you to dance. It's what will draw you into a song. I think that's what drumming is about.

Has your drumming always grooved?

Well, I might not always have grooved, but I was always going toward that thing. In my early career I had a tempo problem, due more to being excited than anything else. I would get wound up and the tempo would accelerate. I solved that shortcoming by using a metronome. In some drummers good time and groove is born, but it wasn't in me. My forte was always playing three-minute songs. I like to play behind singers. My favorite records have always been short pop records where the drums were used as accompaniment.

When you play a song in concert, do you play the same licks you did on the record?

Once I've recorded a song, I'll play it pretty much the same way every time. Same fills, same everything, pretty much.

Is that your decision or an E Street Band decision?

"I play the drums the way Bruce wants to hear them."

It's not really an E Street Band thing. When I saw the Who play in the sixties, there were drum fills I always wanted to hear Keith Moon play, but he never played the same drum fill twice. There's one fill he did in "I Can See for Miles," going to the second verse. Every time that fill comes around, I just have to smile. And I always thought, "Gee, if they ever played that in concert, I'd love him to play that fill in the same spot." But he probably never would. When Kenny Jones played with the Who [after Moon's death] he didn't do any of the same fills, and I was disappointed because those were classic bits in those songs. So my feeling is, once you record a piece of music, when you play it in concert it should represent what you did in the studio as closely as possible.

Was that drum solo section at the end of "Born in the U.S.A." improvised?

A lot of what we did in the studio then was improvised, because we hardly rehearsed. We did that song, if I remember correctly, on a night when we hadn't gotten much done. It was probably around one o'clock in the morning. We were all just hanging around, and Bruce started his chugging rhythm on the guitar. He gave this riff to Roy [Bittan] and Danny [Federici, keyboardists], the "Born in the U.S.A." riff, and I played an appropriate beat, which is what I'm supposed to do. It just fell together. We recorded it once, listened to it, and recorded it again. The second take is the one that's on the record. There's about nine minutes cut out of the end that was us sort of jamming. "Born in the U.S.A." was absolutely effortless to play when we recorded it. It was the most fun I've ever had recording; it was a total throwaway. You can work for days on something and you won't get that kind of performance.

> "The challenge is to do as little as I can rather than as much as I can."

Have you ever given a great performance in the studio but the producer wasn't happy about it?

It depends on who's producing. Bruce produces his own records along with Jon Landau and Charlie Plotkin. So generally, by the time he wants to record something, he knows where he's going with it. That's one of the reasons we don't do that many takes. If I'm working for somebody, I'll keep playing it until they don't want to play it anymore.

You just try to make them happy?

Yeah, that's what the drummer is supposed to do. When you go into the studio working for somebody else, you're in there to play the drums the way *they* want the drums to be heard. That's your job. But if my third take is great and I have the weight in the session to say, "No, I think we should stop," then I'll say that. If I don't, I'll continue playing until the cows come home.

Is there one particular musician in the E Street Band you lock onto to develop a groove?

Bruce. There isn't anybody else but Bruce.

You don't listen to the bass line, for example?

No. I listen to Roy's piano, Bruce's vocals and guitar, and me.

So the bass player, Garry Tallent, follows you?

I wouldn't say he follows me. We've been playing together for so long that Garry knows what I'm going to do. We just play the music. We know how to play Bruce music. Talk to anybody who has been in the band for a long time, and they'll say pretty much the same thing.

Do you give any cues or cutoffs onstage?

No. That's all Bruce. He cues everything. A lot of times he won't cue something because we all feel it. Everything works off Bruce in this band. That's why we're so strong. He's it. If you're not playing off of Bruce, you're not doing your job.

You use a very basic kit.

Yeah, four drums. Ever since I started. Very basic.

How do you feel about drummers who have more than two bass drums?

Billy Cobham knows how to use them. Simon Phillips certainly does. But I find that a lot of heavy metal drummers have eight or nine drums that they *never* use. Tommy Aldridge [of Whitesnake] and Joe Franco [of Twisted Sister] are great drummers who can use all that stuff. But basically, drummers are not hired because they do drum solos. They're hired because they keep good time, they play the beat, they play the song and play the music.

Is it a challenge to do as much as you do on a smaller kit?

The challenge is to do as little as I can rather than as much as I can. If you're in a three-piece heavy metal band, you're going to need more drums. But that's never been my orientation. My favorite drummers have never done that.

Who are your favorite drummers?

If you looked at the top shelf of my record collection, you'd probably see all the Beatles stuff and a lot of the Stones stuff. You'd see Larry Mullen Jr. of U2; I think he's an interesting drummer. I also like Manu Katche. I like what Stewart Copeland did with the Police; he was very innovative, and his playing was exciting. The guy from Big Country [Mark Brzezicki] is a good drummer. Mel Gaynor, who plays with Simple Minds, is a real good drummer. Probably my favorite drummer for a long time has been Steve Jordan. He has a fantastic groove. There doesn't seem to be a lot of styles happening right now, though, which is something that I miss. When I grew up there were so many different styles of drumming. You had Keith Moon, you had Mitch Mitchell, you had Ringo, you had Charlie Watts, you had all different types.

> **"In some drummers good time and groove is born, but it wasn't in me."**

What about Buddy Rich?

Buddy Rich was my all-time favorite drummer. He was the smoothest, most finessed drummer I've ever seen. I loved to watch him play, not just because of his solos, although they were unbelievable. It was because of his subtlety, his command, his touch. When Buddy died, the world really didn't know what it had lost. He was the Fred Astaire of drumming. One guy danced on the floor, the other guy danced on the drums. I heard a guy say, "To really understand what a loss Fred Astaire was, try to imagine who the next Fred Astaire will be." I say the same thing about Buddy Rich.

Your drum sound is easy to identify. How do you feel about people sampling that sound and using it on their records?

It doesn't bother me, because what is a sound? A sound is only a sound. It doesn't sell a record. The playing and the song sell the record. Nobody buys a record because of the drum sound. If you have a great drum sound on a crappy song, it's not going to happen. But you can have a lousy drum sound on a great song, and the record can happen.

Still, you hear TV commercials that obviously try to cop the E Street sound.

Well, when you say "sound," I think "style." I think my style is unique, but I don't think my sound is particularly unique anymore. Ad agencies are notoriously uncreative in their marketing approaches, because they'll take a style like Bruce's, and suddenly you'll hear that sound selling everything from cars to beer. You have a big album by a big artist, and people will co-opt it wherever they can. But I never look at it like they're copping my sound. Everything sounds the same now.

Why don't you consider your own sound unique?

My sound was unique in the seventies, because other than Led Zeppelin we were one of the first bands to go for that big room sound, instead of the "dead" studio sound of the seventies. We did it before Genesis, when we did *Darkness on the Edge of Town* in 1978. But my sound isn't unique now. Everybody's drums sound the same. This preoccupation with sounds is a dismal trend. People didn't think in those terms in the sixties.

> "Nobody buys a record because of the drum sound."

Many of the stylistic differences from those days seem to have melted into broader, more homogenized categories, such as heavy metal.

Well, what is heavy metal? The Who was the first heavy metal band, and then Led Zeppelin. Other than that, what is there? If you listen to Zeppelin, nobody did that better than John Bonham. He was the best heavy drummer. Occasionally I'll turn on MTV and see a heavy metal band that could be interchanged with any one of a hundred other heavy metal acts. I suppose that to a big-band drummer in the sixties all rock & roll sounded the same. But to me it was amazing when the Top Ten could be Jimi Hendrix, the Doors, the Beatles, the Rolling Stones, and the Who. Their music has sustained. So I suggest to young drummers that they go back and study all the great drummers of history. *They'll* give you an education about what you should be doing. I mean, drummers today are not learning how to swing! Everything is so heavily into straight-eighths that they don't know how to move the backbeat around to get different effects. And that's the stuff that you get through study, through listening to a lot of different styles.

How do you feel about drum machines?

I have some interest, but I'm a drummer, not a drum programmer. The reason I got into the drums has absolutely nothing to do with creating rhythms on buttons. I play the drums. I got into drumming because I got a feeling from hitting the drums and bringing a sound out. I mean, the average cat on the block didn't become a drummer because he wanted to push buttons and program a backbeat. He wanted to express something emotional. And I don't think drum machine programming does that.

On the other hand, records that feature drum machine tracks tend to keep much steadier tempo than some of the great records of the past. There were even some time problems on Bruce's first two albums, before you joined the band.

Well, Vinnie Lopez [drummer on the first two E Street Band albums] was a very creative drummer. He did have a time problem, though; he'd speed up and slow down. But at that time, that wasn't really a priority in recording. People didn't focus in on time like they do today. Certainly nobody was recording rock & roll records with metronomes back then. Those albums are just like a rush of energy, and they have their own charm. There's some beautiful stuff that Vinnie played; he got sort of a bad rap as a drummer. At one time he was a hell of a drummer, and then I guess he just lost his focus. After he left the band, David Sancious, a fabulous keyboard player who was Bruce's original pianist, brought in a friend of his, Ernie Carter, who played drums with the band for six or eight months. During that time they recorded "Born to Run," the single. So when Roy and I joined the band, in August of '74, "Born to Run" had already been recorded.

It still sounds like you on drums.

It sounds like Bruce [*laughs*]. See, I play the drums the way Bruce wants to hear them.

ALEX VAN HALEN

Claim to Fame

Interviewed by Andy Doerschuk,
Drums & Drumming, July/August 1988

Back in the late seventies, when most rock bands wore either skinny ties or Mohawks, Van Halen proudly flaunted their Spandex and codpieces while playing a playful brand of hard rock that was considered prehistoric at the time. Little did the music world realize that the L.A. quartet would soon become the catalyst for the resuscitation of metal in the eighties and would continue to lead the charge right up to the present. I spoke to Alex Van Halen in his Hollywood Hills home, just as the band was due to release *OU812,* its second album to feature the windpipe of Sammy Hagar. The drummer was shirtless, and he chainsmoked throughout our conversation, speaking in his unmistakably husky voice that still carried a hint of a Dutch accent, revealing his family heritage. His personality, like his drumming, was explosive, whether laughing at a joke or pointing out a lame question.

—Andy Doerschuk

• • •

Did you ever imagine, when Van Halen was playing in L.A. clubs, that the band would get as big as it did?

Every time that we played, no matter whether it was Gazzarri's or it was a little gig that we put together ourselves just by renting a building and bringing in some lights and sound, we always treated it as if we were playing the Forum. It didn't matter if there were five people or fifty thousand. You can make or break a situation by the way you look at things. At the time we were playing clubs five hours a night, full blast, five to six nights a week, sometimes seven. If we had that wrong attitude of, "Aw, man, we've got to pay more dues—isn't this a shithole," then I think that could have broken the band's spirit. But it never happened. I didn't realize the difference until we played a really small club out in the middle of nowhere, for maybe only ten people in the audience. There was a guy who came by who wanted to be our manager. It was about nine o'clock, first set. Nobody was dancing; people were just sort of watching, milling around. But afterwards the guy said, "Man, I can't believe the kind of energy you guys are puttin' out! It's as if you were playing for fifty thousand people." It had never occurred to us that it should be any different. We always just wanted to play our best and have a great time with it, because after all, the moment it becomes work, then it just isn't happening anymore. That's when the spark isn't there. That's the difference between, say, a technically perfect piece of music that can be made by a machine, as opposed to human beings playing it. So it has a couple of rough edges; it's okay. It doesn't matter. It doesn't need to be perfect.

> "I was soloing through one of Ed's guitar solos, and he looked at me, threw off his guitar, and said, 'We'll continue when you're done. Okay?'"

It does seem that part of Van Halen's appeal is that the band really has fun playing together.

That's what it's all about. No matter what culture, or what city, or what part of the world you go to, music is a very integral part of everyone's lives. There's always a certain type of music that fits a certain kind of mood; it's a basic human thing. You can't help but tap your foot to a song that you like, and as I said before, attitude is definitely a part of it. Once you become deadly serious about your music, you're playing with fire. Don't get me wrong: We don't take our music so lightly that we just go out and screw around. If something isn't totally tight, okay, we'll work on it later and get it a little tighter. But the feel of the music is the most important thing. There are a number of old records where the tempo or tightness is far from perfect, but sometimes you actually want to leave that in.

Tell us about the early days when Van Halen was covering other people's songs.

Well, you had to do everything, because originals were basically a no-no when we were first playing clubs. They wanted people to dance and get off their butts and get thirsty enough to keep buying drinks. So you had to try to satisfy everybody in the audience. Gradually we started putting our own stuff in, and we found that once you get them dancing to a song they know, you just segue into one of your own songs and they'll keep going. It was a good six years of playing clubs before we made the first record, and that was a lot of playing. At the time we were making $25 a gig— enough for sticks, gas, and a couple of six-packs.

It's like, "Hey, it only cost me five bucks to play tonight! Great!"

You've got it. At that point it wouldn't have hurt at all to hire a manager for fifty percent. At the end of the night you'd go, "Here's ten bucks, dude."

I understand that every now and then in those days you'd set your kit on fire during gigs.

Yeah, we used to do it every night. It was great. I think in our earlier days we used to do things that weren't exactly conducive to longevity. It was a very cheap effect, but we couldn't afford much else at the time. We used to put lighter fluid on all the drum heads before the last song. Then the drum roadie would hand me a couple of mallets that were also soaked with lighter fluid and lit. We always had someone standing by with a fire extinguisher, just in case it got out of hand. And one night it did. There was too much lighter fluid, and it was dripping all over me, and I caught on fire. So I started turning sideways while I was playing, yelling to a drum roadie, "Hey, look at my fucking arm!" And the roadie yelled back, "Yeah, man, that looks great!" He thought I was trying to point out how cool it looked. After about 1979 I stopped doing it; it really wasn't worth it anymore.

When Van Halen started getting recognition, a lot of different styles of music were being played in L.A. Did you do gigs with punk or new wave bands at that time?

Yeah, and I think that was a mistake. For instance, we had the Ramones open up for us once. They lasted fifteen seconds; they got beaned. It only makes sense that if someone spends good money to come see you play, they don't want to be uncomfortable. Being searched and having your crotch scratched at the same time isn't exactly the nicest way to start an evening. Then you have to see a band that you don't want to see in the first place. I can sympathize, because we've been at both ends of that. We've opened up for audiences that were just murder, but you keep playing. Those are actually some of the most fun shows, because then you pull out all the stops and go hog wild. I tell you, after a while the audience will catch on and forget that they didn't necessarily come to see you. They like it anyway, so what the hell.

What was your first national tour like?

Crazy. It was like kids being let loose in a candy store. It was everything, and then some, that we always imagined rock & roll to be. We started out on what was supposed to be a three-week tour, and it turned out to be eleven months straight—not a break anywhere. Journey was top bill, then Montrose, and we were the warmup act. We had, like, two feet of space onstage. It was an eight o'clock show, and we started at 7:30—I'm exaggerating, but that's the way it seemed. People were filing in, and we were playing our balls off and wondering what we were doing wrong. But all the years of experience together told us that we obviously weren't in the right situation to begin with. I tell you what, though—it really wasn't that radically different from the days when we were doing the clubs. This was just on a much larger scale, and every night

Alex Van Halen, 1984: The kid in the candy store.

we were in a different city. So you can leave behind the trouble you caused, go to the next town, and start all over again. The thing about that tour is that after being on the road for eleven months promoting the first album, we came back to L.A. and found out it was time for another record. Fortunately, most of the material was already written, so in six days we recorded the second album.

Do you play your parts differently live than in the studio?

I think the whole band plays a little more open live; you take more chances. When you're cutting a track, even though we do record live in the studio, you tend to play a little more conservative. My main hope in the studio is to get everybody grooving with me, so I don't want to spoil a good situation by trying something that just doesn't fit the song and then having to redo it. In a live situation you can throw something in that might be a little out of place. It might make Ed crack a smile and forget what he's playing for a second. So what? It doesn't matter; it's just more unpredictable.

It sounds like you prefer the spontaneity.

Oh, yeah! Because after a hundred shows all the buildings might start to look the same, but you're still playing to a different audience every night. I guess it's a two-way street. You want to give them your best, but at the same time you have to keep it interesting for yourselves.

So you rely on the communication you have with Ed when you play around with the arrangements onstage.

That's the fun thing to do with Ed, because he plays intricately, and he phrases and leaves me room to fuck around. This goes back a long way, since Ed and I have been playing together for so long. When he gives me a little breathing room I take advantage of it, then slip right back in with, maybe, an accent in a hole. That was an old trick that used to fascinate me about Mick Fleetwood. He would be groovin' along, and for no reason on earth he would suddenly do a lick with an accent. For no apparent reason at all! It makes you wonder what's going on in this guy's brain, but I fell in love with it.

That's kind of like Keith Moon's drumming too.

Yeah, except that Moon did stuff like that in every song! Keith Moon definitely had an attitude that I think is not necessarily the epitome of rock & roll, but it had a lot to do with it.

Who were your main influences as a drummer?

When I started learning which was the right stick and which was the left stick, my big influences were Dave Clark and Ringo. But later on I really got into Ginger Baker; I just loved what he did. He never just kept the beat. If you could have isolated his drum parts from the rest of the musicians, they would make music by themselves. He wasn't exactly a very proficient technician; he wouldn't know a ratamacue [drum rudiment] from a Swiss triplet. But he was a natural drummer and still was able to do amazing things. And I can't leave out Buddy Rich. I think a lot of drummers emulated him, both in his attitude and, of course, he had the chops that kicked ass. Then of course there was Louie Bellson, who was more subtle. His was more of a song approach instead of just a driving force. And of course I listened to some of the stuff that Carmine Appice was doing; I really liked his drumming.

Were Baker, Appice, and Bellson your main influences for playing double bass drums?

I think it was a little bit of everybody, because I don't want to lock myself into one specific channel. Obviously jazz sounds different than heavy metal, but there's something to be learned from every drummer.

Describe your favorite live performance.

It was in Chicago around 1980. We had a grand time in the afternoon, we had a grand time before the show, and we were having a really grand time when we hit the stage. Let's put it this way: I did a drum solo during every song. At one point I was soloing through one of Ed's guitar solos, and he looked at me, threw off his guitar, and said, "We'll continue when you're done. Okay?"

"The feel of the music is the most important thing. There are a number of old records where the tempo is far from perfect, but sometimes you want to leave that in."

So did you just keep on soloing?

Oh, yeah; I was on a roll that day [*laughs*]. It was also the last time I did something like that. But ours are still some of the most unpredictable shows in the world, both for the audience and us.

How about your favorite recording with the band?

The stuff in "Hot for Teacher" [from *1984*]; there was some really quick shuffle stuff. That comes pretty easy to me. I don't know; I like all the records I've played on. I like it when we use wacko sounds, like on "Inside" [from *5150*]. The drum sound was kind of interesting, and the song totally doesn't make sense. It was just something we wanted to try; there were no rules.

> "I caught on fire. So I started yelling to a drum roadie, 'Hey, look at my fucking arm!' And he yelled back, 'Yeah, man, that looks great!'"

Was the opening solo in "Hot for Teacher" worked out in advance?

No. Ed just said, "You've got sixteen bars; just go ahead and set it up."

On "Hot for Teacher" you're definitely using two bass drums, but on "Inside" it sounds like you're using only one. How do you decide which approach to follow?

My feet were never really that quick. I could never get really fast triplets going, like what [John] Bonham used to do. It's just not inherent in my body. So I figured, why not use both feet? Now I can do fast triplets; it's a cinch. I just play the backbeats on the snare and the other two notes with my feet. I like to learn and pick up from everybody—which reminds me of something that comes from left field. Mike Tyson, the boxer, said that ten percent of boxing is physical and ninety percent is in your mind. And this can apply to drumming. Don't limit yourself. Nobody says that you have to play drums a certain way, unless you believe it. If you have total independence, which only can come through practice, then you can make your feet do anything you want, while your hands are doing something else. It takes time to get to that point. I used to watch Steve Smith play, and it used to drive me nuts because he's ambidextrous. Sometimes he rides with his right hand on the cymbal, and then he'll switch to his left. It used to drive me up the wall when I was trying to learn a pattern he was playing, because I'm not ambidextrous. I've just never practiced playing that way. I'd rather spend my time doing other things that are more musical.

It does look cool, though, when drummers switch between right- and left-handed styles.

Yeah, but only to other drummers. You know, on a broader philosophical side, it really comes down to whatever makes you happy. There have been a number of times when I've played something that I really felt kicked ass. Then someone will say, "What part are you talking about? I didn't hear anything." Then I'll do some simple thing and they'll say, "Yeah, I loved that!" I'll just wonder to myself, What the hell was that? But the young, up-and-coming drummers out there should know that they should just play to make themselves happy. If you're waiting around for someone to applaud at your intricate drumming, and they don't, you might miss a beat while you're busy getting pissed off about it.

Your tempos on record are very solid. Do you ever record with a click track?

No. From the beginning, with the first record, Ted Templeman [Van Halen's producer up to *1984*] insisted on no click tracks. He said, "We're doing this like human beings." There were times when I'd want to use a click track, but it just wasn't happening. It's funny—I always thought my meter was a little wacko, because I do tend to flow with whatever's going on. But I think you can tell when a drummer is playing to a click track. It makes an added complication because sometimes the guitarist might get ahead of the drummer, and everybody gets off. I don't care how good a drummer is— no human can be perfect.

So a click track can be inhibiting in the studio.

Some people get used to it. Thumbs up to them. But, at least with Van Halen, we'd rather get the four of us in a studio together and make something out of it, instead of doing one track over and over until it's perfect and then layering everybody's part over it.

What's it like to play in a band with your brother for so many years?

Ed and I, especially because we're so close, are probably the ones who fought the most. We'd duke it out once in a while. No harm done, just like typical brothers. But yeah, Ed and I were always together. We'd go through different bands, different phases.

It seems like you've been able to withstand pretty major changes, like David Lee Roth's departure.

I don't want to get my ass in a sling by starting a bullshit thing all over again. But I can say that it wasn't as if we were in the market for a new lead singer. We really just wanted to keep the band together. The band is like a marriage. It's not a situation where four or five people get together and say, "Let's write some hit tunes, make a lot of money, and go home." That's not the way it works with us, and that's what fell apart with the previous situation. It's a hard situation in that if I don't answer the questions, then somebody else will do it for me. The end result is that I really don't care. There were many years that were great together, and that's it—case closed.

VINNIE COLAIUTA

Personal Best

Interviewed by Greg Rule,
Drums & Drumming, January 1991

After establishing his seemingly unpronounceable name among drumming fanatics by playing with Frank Zappa and Joni Mitchell during the late seventies and early eighties, Vinnie Colaiuta turned into a session in Los Angeles in 1983. As the gigs poured in, Colaiuta revealed his incredible depth, drumming with equal finesse for pop and jazz artists and anything else that came his way. While his reputation remained powerful among hardcore drummers, his public profile decreased. Finally, in 1990, the band bug once again bit Colaiuta as he agreed to become the full-time drummer for Sting. It was the perfect vehicle for his various percussive talents—and big news in the drumming world at the time. *Drums & Drumming* interviewed the high-strung drummer just as he began his first tour with Sting.

—*Andy Doerschuk*

• • •

How did you get started as a drummer?

I always reacted to music, and I always had some sort of attraction or disposition toward music. I did the typical thing a kid does, setting up pots and pans on the sofa like a drum set. When I got my first kit [at age seven], without having any lessons or anything I could just sit down behind it and play. I never had a problem knowing what to do with my feet or hands. I guess that's just part of the gift that the Lord gave me.

When did you begin taking lessons?

When I was fourteen. I went to the junior high band director, and he gave me a book that taught me the basics of how to hold the sticks and how to read. I took to it like a fish to water. There was no turning back, ever. I just kept pushing ahead at my own pace. I think my teachers picked up on the fact that I was a fast learner and that I seemed to have an accelerated growth potential. I always showed an aptitude and interest in what I was doing.

Your strongest early influence was Tony Williams. How did you get into his music?

I was in a stage band competition, and this other drummer came up to me and asked, "Who's your favorite drummer?" I said, "Buddy Rich." So I asked him who his favorite drummer was, and he said, "Tony Williams." I was like, "Who?" So he told me to go buy the record *Ego*. When I first listened to it, it was so alien to anything I'd ever heard before. About two years later I put it back on the turntable, and it was like I'd just opened the lid to the Ark of the Covenant or something. It was as if the sky had opened in my head. I went out and bought every Tony Williams record that I could get my hands on. From that point I realized that Tony was the genius of the drums. I realized what a force he was and how powerful and fruitful his musical statement was. It changed my life; it made a profound impact.

Eventually you wound up studying at Berklee.

Berklee was a turning point for me conceptually, because I started listening to different kinds of music. Fusion was at its heyday, and I was really getting into Miles, McCoy Tyner, and Alphonse Mouzon. At that time, Alphonse was way left; conceptually, he was so far advanced. It really shifted my head and made me realize that because of my rudimental background I almost had to empty my mind in order to grasp the concept. I really loved what I was hearing, and I wanted to absorb and be able to assimilate that style. The exciting part of all this for me was that it was all so new: Mahavishnu, Cobham, Gadd, Tony, all of those guys were breaking ground. I was just very happy to be fed with so much of the muse, from so many directions and personalities. I went through periods where I tried to imitate Tony and Billy [Cobham], but I eventually realized how dangerous it was. I began to ask myself, "What am I saying?" I wasn't saying anything. It had been said before and had a reason for being said, but I didn't have a reason. I wasn't making a statement; I was just repeating it, like a parrot. By imitating and copying someone else, a person becomes a parrot. I saw the trap and I knew, as great as those guys were and still are, that I had to find my own voice.

When did you notice that you were moving beyond imitation and starting to develop your own sound?

I don't think there was a particular day when I woke up and said, "I am now me." Over the past few years I've started to see it, but it's so hard to pinpoint something like that. Evolution never stops. Some people define identity based on comparison, but that whole "better" or "worse" thing isn't what it's all about. It's a matter of the acquired skills that you think are necessary to express the truth within yourself. Whether or not a guy can play by someone else's measured standards is a thing created in the minds of people who do it to make themselves feel comfortable or justified. That's why the whole idea of drum competitions and drum battles is complete bullshit to me. People will say, "You're wrong, Vinnie, because it drives kids to excel." And, yeah, if it's healthy competition. There's a fine line where healthy competition becomes unhealthy. Where someone who's so enamored with himself discards the validity of others and, in turn, influences other people to discard the validity of other things—I'm sorry, I can't hang with that. There are plenty of other ways to make someone excel, by encouraging them to be the best at what they can be, not to try to be better or faster than some other guy. You can scar people with that. You're dealing with psyche, the human spirit, and you can't impose these stupid kinds of guidelines. It's so typical of the American way of thinking—bigger is better—and I, for one, don't buy into it.

> "I went through periods where I tried to imitate Tony [Williams] and Billy [Cobham], but I eventually realized how dangerous it was."

Well, if you don't develop an individual identity through competition, how do you do it?

I don't know if your identity is something you arrive at consciously. I keep referring to emptying your cup. I believe that emptying your cup is what gives you your identity. Some people do it in a conscious way: They look for a trademark or a gimmick or something that will set them apart, and sometimes it does that. But you know, the only thing that is constant is change. Your personality, if you don't filter it with anything, will come through you via what you are. Maybe there will come a day where you'll want to stop changing, and that's what your identity will be. Or you'll continue to change, and that's what your identity will be. That's how I see my identity.

We've talked about drummers who have influenced you. What about teachers?

Gary Chaffee [at Berklee] was a fantastic teacher, the greatest. At the time I was there, Gary's teaching method was all loose-leaf. He was still writing it as he went along. But aside from the information I was getting from him and his approach to that information, I was also getting conceptual feedback, which was so important.

You even took lessons after establishing yourself as a headliner in the drum world. Who did you study with?

I went to several people: Dick Wilson, Joe Morello, and I hung out with Jim Chapin a lot. I focused on complete body movement rather than zeroing in on snare drum technique or whatever. I spent a lot of practice time thinking about the way my arms and legs moved, trying to make sure I wasn't expending unnecessary energy or inhibiting my speed and comfort. I gained a lot of insight from that experience.

Did you make any adjustments to your stick technique?

I've experimented with matched grip a time or two, but I've pretty much remained a traditional-grip player. I try to be conscious of several things when I play. One is trying to keep my arms in a perfectly straight line, from elbow to palm. My right hand is pretty much palm downward, or half turned over with a gap in between the thumb and the first finger. I try to keep the fulcrum between the thumb and the first joint of my index finger, and I cup my fingers around the stick. Sometimes, for finger execution, I might twist my left wrist, or turn it over to create a leverage, but usually I try to keep my hand in the same position. When I play a fill around the toms, that's when I'll shift from finger technique to my wrists and arms.

> "The whole idea of drum competitions and drum battles is complete bullshit."

Should matched-grip players experiment with traditional grip?

Yeah, I think it's a great idea because, psychologically and physically, it affects the way you approach things. I think traditional grip has a lot to offer, not just because of tradition, but because of its physical and psychological uniqueness. Those three factors work together. You just do different things because it's a completely different motion.

Is stick slippage a problem for you?

I only have problems when I play an extended drum solo under bright stage lights. If I start sweating, I start choking up on the sticks, which inhibits my speed and cleanliness. When that happens my sticks start sliding up into the second joint, which I usually don't allow them to do. If you play in air-conditioned studios all the time, it's never a problem. But I'm one of these guys that starts sweating easily. I mean, I bend over to tie my shoes and I break into a sweat. I've tried wearing gloves, but now, if I do anything, I'll just sand the ends of the sticks.

Can you describe your foot technique?

I've had a lot of schooling, but I also, in some ways, have a "street" approach—a natural, organic approach. I studied a lot of hand technique, but I never went to a guy and studied foot technique. So I've always played—and I think it's considered incorrect by a lot of people—with the heel up off the pedal, and I bury the beater, so to speak. The only way I've modified it over the years is by keeping my heel up when I play loud and putting my heel down when I play soft, concentrating on lifting the beater off the head in that situation. Another important aspect of bass drum technique has to do with how you sit. I think that if you sit at a certain height, where your back is real comfortable and your thighs are parallel to the ground, then you won't use the upper part of your leg to throw weight around, because that wastes energy. What I tend to do is bounce off my calf muscle—the lower leg—just like I bounce on a hi-hat pedal. If I have to throw weight, it comes more from the hip and upper body via the calf, not from the upper leg. Lifting the leg wastes energy.

Although you made your name through working with Frank Zappa, you've since built a strong reputation as a session drummer. What was it like to move from working steadily with a band to taking studio calls?

Some people say that I'm a prostitute. But no, I'm a hired guy, I'm a freelance session player, and this is how I earn my living. My whole thing is based on whether I feel the artist is on the level, and if the money thing is straight. Most of my calls are record dates, jingles, television or motion pictures, or people I already know. If I get called by a new person, and I don't know what the music is like, I try to get a feel for the gig and whether they're on the level. If it's okay, then they tell me how long it's going to be, and I check my availability and I tell them my price.

What do you do if you're asked to play an embarrassing or inappropriate drum part, and you know your name is going to be on the credits?

> "I did gigs where I had to play so hard that I bled on my drums."

Usually, I play the part that I think is right for the song, based on my developed musical instincts. But the producer might say, "No, play this," and I may know in my mind that it's not happening. But I can't lose sight of the fact that, as a session drummer, I'm hired to do what I'm supposed to do. So I'll play what they want me to play and hope they can hear that it's not working. When I suggest a change to someone, I can't be wishy-washy about it. I have to say, "I don't think this part is working, and here are the reasons why." Another thing to realize is that it's not just my name on the credits; it's the producer's name also. He or she has to assume a share of responsibility for the outcome.

What happens when some producer asks you to play a song in the style of another drummer? How often does that happen?

Not much any more. Once in a very great while. When that happens, I'll just play what I think they want to hear. I mean, if it's a thing where they want me to sound exactly like that guy, then I'll say, "Call him." If they use it to try to give me a general idea, like, "We want a groove kind of like '50 Ways to Leave Your Lover,'" then that's cool. But most people call me because they want me to play like me.

What have you learned about the business aspect of music?

Well, that's a whole other issue. First of all, it's a cutthroat business. Some people are real political to try to get their way, and they step on other people in the process. It's important to not be blind to the business aspect. Most musicians and creative people get bored with that type of thing fairly easily—I know I do. But I try to be aware of what I'm getting into and know up front how I'll be handling a situation financially.

I have to know whether I should accept payment by the song or by the hour. I can get ripped off if I make the wrong decision. If I choose to get paid by the song and the session takes ten hours, then I get ripped off. You have to know the business aspect of things and the psychology of how to read people.

Do you manage yourself?

Yes.

Would you recommend self-management to other musicians?

Sure, unless you have delusions of being some star and you want to pay a manager a certain percentage. I mean, you're going to get a call from a service, or producer, or contractor, and then you book yourself on a date. What do you want a manager to do? He's not going to go out and find you more work or anything—at least not in a session situation. In this business, it's word-of-mouth and contractors. It's a lot of work for me to do it myself, but I feel that I have to deal with these people personally to find out what I'm in for.

Are you pleased with the way your career has gone?

Yeah, sure. But I need a good balance. I like to go out and play live when I can, plus do good sessions. People might look at that and say, "You want everything, Vinnie." But no, it's not that. I think that when you reach a certain echelon, it's just a matter of wanting to be happy at what you're doing. Lately I've been able to do some really great projects, so yeah, I'm pretty happy at this point.

Anything you would do differently if given the chance?

I probably would have tried to be more in control of things earlier on. I did gigs where I had to play so hard that I bled on my drums. Sometimes people think that they have to do something that they really don't have to do, and I should have exercised more control over that type of thing. But other than that, I'm very satisfied.

What about the future?

I want to play the drums as long as I have a willingness to play the drums, and as long as I'm physically able to play the drums to a standard that I think is acceptable. As long as I'm able to meet those objectives, then that's how long I'll be behind a drum set.

LARS ULRICH

Blood, Sweat & Metal

Interviewed by John Olson,
Drums & Drumming, December 1989/January 1990

By the time *Drums & Drumming* published the following interview with Metallica's Lars Ulrich, the drummer had ascended to the top of the metal drumming hierarchy. While his playing possessed a raw appeal and infectious energy, he didn't earn his status by being a technical virtuoso. In fact, Ulrich has always downplayed his drumming abilities, choosing instead to emphasize his role as a member of a hard-working team. But as Metallica's founder and spokesman, Ulrich helped strip the glam from eighties metal by adding several layers of sweat and blood, and in the process became one of the most influential drummers of the day. Our interview followed the release of Metallica's adventurous album *And Justice for All*, which reached the Top Ten without the support of a hit single or MTV coverage. As usual, Ulrich was outspoken and articulate in what became his first cover story with a drumming magazine.

—Andy Doerschuk

•   •   •

You have an unusually high profile in Metallica. Unlike many drummers, you contribute significantly to the band's songwriting, and you also act often as its spokesman. Is that because you were a co-founder of the group?

Not necessarily. It has more to do with my personality; I just like to get involved. I don't think it should have anything to do with whether you're a drummer or a singer or a keyboard player, or whatever. I play drums because I like to play drums. But that shouldn't mean I can't be involved in anything else that goes on. Why is the singer the only one that does interviews if everyone else has something to say? James [Hetfield, guitarist] keeps more of a low profile; he doesn't like to do a lot of interviews. I actually have a lot of fun sitting and talking Metallica with people in interviews. I guess James and I have a setup that works well because of the way we write and arrange together.

Does your role in writing material center on what happens in the rhythm part?

It varies. I don't think you can pinpoint it and say, "This is it, period." James obviously comes up with the main part of the basic riffs, although if I hear some riffs in my head I'll hum or sing them to him, and he picks them up on guitar. My main thing is arranging what form or shape the song will take. Some people call it arranging; I prefer to call it building a song. What do we need to do for middle parts and bridges? What kind of feel should the choruses have? Where should we change tempos? How does the song progress? James and I aren't limited to just our own things. Our whole approach is "open season."

Musically, too, you seem to avoid the typical "drummer in the background" syndrome.

I've always wanted the drums to play a larger role in the overall sound than just some sort of background timekeeper. I'm so tired and bored with the stereotypical way that heavy metal drums just hang out in the background and count to four. If you can use guitars and vocals to color the music, why can't you use the drums to color the music too? The basic skeleton of the Metallica sound is the rhythm guitar and the drums.

Do you have a particular approach to laying down the drum track?

When I record in the studio, I do it in a very different way, probably, from other people. We basically *build* a drum track, instead of going out and knocking it straight through. We never record more than one person at a time. A lot of people find that hard to believe because it ends up sounding so live. When I play a drum track I use every ounce of energy that I have in my body. I can put out a lot more for two minutes than I could if I had to pace myself over an eight-minute song. So we record the song in pieces. We start at the beginning, and when things get off from the click track, we stop and retune the snare drum. What happens is that I end up hitting so hard that the snare drum will need tuning after every three takes. I sometimes go through four or five snare skins in one song. It's kind of a bizarre way of recording, but I'm really comfortable with it.

It seems like a tedious way to record.

I'd say on some of the longer songs it might take two days to do a drum track. What's really annoying is when I get into a rhythm and it's really cooking, then I'll have to stop for 45 minutes while they change heads and match up the sound. By that time I sometimes get cold and lose the vibe. Sometimes it takes another hour to get back into it. It's a very time-consuming way of recording, but at the end of the day it works best for me. And if you've noticed, the stuff is very, very tight.

It sounds like you often have the kick and snare hitting together with a choked cymbal sound. Are you grabbing that cymbal with one hand?

Live, I do, yeah.

Is that an overdub in the studio?

Well, there are occasional places where, because of the attention to detail that I demand in the studio—I'll say this under complete pressure here—that Flemming [Larsen, Ulrich's drum tech] actually puts on these dishwashing gloves and catches the occasional cymbal [*laughs*]. He does it when it makes sense for the tightness and the continuation of what we're doing. But live, obviously, I do all that myself.

It gives it more punch when you have all three things happening at once.

I hardly ever hit my kick and snare at the same time, but as you noticed, I like to hit snare with cymbals a lot. I don't know who decided that you're supposed to hit cymbals with a kick drum. I think that throwing cymbals in on the snare drum is one of the most effective accents.

"I'm so bored with the stereotypical way that heavy metal drums just hang out in the background and count to four."

What tuning techniques do you use?

It depends. There are always two distinct situations: There's the studio, and then there's live. In the studio, I'll have to say that I'm a perfectionist. I pay attention to details that most other people would laugh at. But when you're playing in a 20,000-seat arena, it just doesn't matter that much. Flemming does all the tuning because he's very patient and can sit with a snare drum for an hour. If I sit tuning a snare drum for an hour, I'll be pulling my hair out! We have a good setup in the studio. Flemming's always there. I can go lose my head in something else, so I don't get too burned out while he does the tuning. We don't do anything secret or elaborate.

What about muffling?

We sometimes muffle. If there are specific parts of songs where we're not using the toms, I'll take them off the kit or cover them completely with a towel to avoid any ringing. For the snare drum in the studio, we duct-tape a piece of 15"x15" felt cloth across the top portion of the drum, letting the cloth hang over the side. Usually on the toms we'll take a piece of duct tape, fold some cloth inside it, and tape it on.

Your style of playing must demand a great deal of energy. What are your tips for staying in shape?

Lars Ulrich, 1989: A larger role in the overall sound.

Well, one thing's called "touring." That's the main tip. Again, there's two distinctly different answers: on the road, and off the road. We're at our 240th show [of the band's tour at time of interview], and we play about two hours and ten minutes, on average, each night. So without trying to make it sound too easy, I'll have to say that the staying-in-shape part of it is basically on autopilot at the moment. When you're on the road this long, you find a balancing point: You know how far you can push yourself and still go on and do the best show you can. We all know our limits on the social side out here. A few years ago we didn't know where to stop and still be able to go up and play. Nowadays, we're a headliner doing arenas, so obviously we don't want the show to suffer one percent.

How much do you guys imbibe when you're touring?

I basically don't drink any hard liquor anymore; I just drink beers now. I think hard liquor slows you down a lot more. Also, I like to do some warmups before we go onstage. Earlier in the tour I used to warm up for fifteen or twenty minutes, running in place. Now my body is so used to this kind of thing that I warm up for about five minutes. Our tour manager massages my right arm with Ben-Gay for about five minutes, and that warms it up nicely. My right arm is usually the main thing, because we start with a song that is pretty fast on the hi-hat, so playing it cold really wouldn't work too well. Ever since he started doing that about six months ago, I've found that I don't need to do nearly as much warming up or stretching as I used to.

What about when you're off the road?

That's obviously a different situation, and one that I don't look forward to with great enthusiasm when this tour is over. You can get out of shape and pork up very quickly. I usually run, which I like for various reasons. It keeps the whole breathing apparatus going, which is important for playing drums, so you learn how to pace yourself. I especially like running after writing songs all day, because it's an hour or forty-five minutes a day when I can concentrate on whatever I want to do. It's almost a meditation kind of thing, where I can focus on what can be better about songs or whatever. I think there are a lot of benefits to it, other than just running up and down the block and sweating. I'm *not* running at the moment: What we do onstage in a week basically takes care of staying in shape out there.

Since you're nearly always playing both of your bass drums, how do you keep balanced on the stool?

I know other people have probably known this for hundreds of years, but I've just realized that balance has so much to do with solid timekeeping. Every time I lose my balance, I get off. So I've started concentrating on finding a center point somewhere in my body, and using that as the middle part of the scale. I always rest my left foot, which is my second kick drum, on the drum pedal itself while keeping time with my heel. I actually only go to my hi-hat pedal when I need to, which is only on one or two songs. I always have the hi-hats resting loosely on top of each other, so I can pick them up when it calls for some hi-hat action with the sticks. I play a lot of triplets with my feet, basically on the slower stuff. I always do the triplet with the *one* beat on the second kick drum, so that's why I keep my foot over there.

> "I'd rather hear drumming that complements the song instead of some guy doing 29 fills just to get off on it."

Who are some of your favorite drummers?

It's very seldom that I sit down and listen to a "Joe Superstar" progressive drummer. I think one of my favorite drummers now is Phil Rudd, the guy that used to play in AC/DC. The groove that he set in those songs is absolutely incredible. He never hit the toms or anything, but where that groove was set up is something that I've been getting into a lot. The first drummer in Iron Maiden, Clive Burr, had a really good sense of playing the right part in the song. I'd rather hear drumming that complements the song instead of some guy sitting down and doing 29 good drum fills just to get off on it.

Which songs best represent your playing?

The one that springs to mind first would probably be "… And Justice for All," because I think that's most representative of what we're talking about. It's a good example of something that's really sideways and different from the *one-two-three-four* thing, but at the same time, it grooves. Whatever situation you can set up, if it grooves it doesn't matter if you count to four or if it's 29 over 7.

What song do you most enjoy playing live with Metallica?

That varies all the time. I really like to play a song called "For Whom the Bell Tolls," which is from the album *Ride the Lightning*. I think "Harvester of Sorrow" has a really good groove in it. I try to put the snare drum a little further back on the beat on that one than I did on the album, which sets up a really nice, bouncy kind of groove. I like to play "One" and "Welcome Home (Sanitarium)." I basically like them all—otherwise we wouldn't have written them! We pride ourselves in saying that we never write a filler song. We never let an album be carried by three or four songs and then have five crap filler songs. I'll stand behind every song we've ever written. One thing I've always imagined, but it would never be possible, would be to record a studio album *after* we've played the songs for a year on the road. It would be incredible! I hate when you come up with a great idea for a fill in a song a month after you've recorded it.

> "What we do onstage in a week basically takes care of staying in shape."

As Metallica's popularity endures, do you find yourself being careful about the effect you have on your large following?

I think the minute you start thinking about that stuff, you've lost it; you start chasing yourself around in circles. Part of what has made Metallica successful is that we look very much inward, making sure that we feel comfortable and are happy with what we're doing. As arrogant as this might sound, we are basically doing this for ourselves. Some bands, more power to 'em, say, "We're doing this for the people," which is fine, but it has to start from within first. We don't depend so much on media like radio and video. We basically tour a lot and build a solid fan base of people who respect what we do. The best thing to do is not worry about how people will react to what you're doing—just do what comes naturally.

If you weren't in Metallica, would you still be playing drums?

That's a really good question. I think the answer might surprise people: If I weren't in Metallica, I'm not sure I would be playing drums. It's hard for me to picture myself in any type of musical situation other than Metallica. Whenever Metallica ends, be it five, ten, or fifteen years—knock on wood—I'll probably end up doing something completely different in the music business. I'm not one of those guys that has a mental breakdown if I go a week without sitting behind a drum kit. I don't live drums eighteen hours out of every day. Metallica is the only band I've ever been in, and I kind of foresee it staying that way until whatever time I decide to pack it in. What interests me is being in a band and working on everything that goes with that. I can bash on my drums for an hour or so by myself, but if James isn't there with that rhythm guitar to kick me in the ass, I get really bored and go back in the house [*laughs*]. What got me going in the beginning still holds up ten years later. I've just always wanted to be in a group with other musicians.

Photo Credits

Jay Blakesberg 6, 14, 150, 183, 215
Steve Jennings 246
Veryl Oakland 109, 157, 232
Ken Settle 39, 60, 64, 81, 94, 138, 168, 189,
Neil Zlozower 54, 88, 260, 273

INDEX

Buchanan, Roy, 162
Buddy Rich's sextet, 196–197
Bullock, Hiram, 209
Burbridge, Oteil, 217, 219
Burr, Clive, 274
Burrell, Kenny, 27
Burton, Gary, 177
Byrd, Billy, 65
Byrne, David, 120, 131, 132

C
Cage, John, 83, 87, 118, 125
Callender, Red, 163
Cameo, 58
Campbell, Glen, 197
Campbell, Joseph, 103
Capps, Al, 164
Caravanserai, 29
Cardona, Milton, 179
Carlos, Wendy, 83, 113–119
Carmichael, Hoagy, 97
Carpenter, Karen, 164–165
Carpenter, Richard, 164–165
Carpenters, The, 165
Cars, The, 148
Carter, Elliott, 128, 183
Carter, Ernie, 256
Carter, Ron, 199, 204, 208
Casady, Jack, 198, 199
Catlett, Big Sid, 225
CBGB, 65
Chaffee, Gary, 266
Chambers, Paul, 208, 211
Chapin, Jim, 266
Charles, Ray, 20, 169
Chess, Leonard, 7, 8
Chicago blues music, 19
child prodigy, 87
Chopin, Frédéric, 114, 137
Chord Chemistry (Greene), 61
Chowning, John, 183
Christian, Charlie, 4, 5, 61, 65
Chronic, The, 77
Circle Star Theater, 3, 18

Circus (magazine), 55, 83
Cissy Strut, 240
CK. See Keyboard
Clapton, Eric, 26, 28, 29, 51–52, 55, 59, 102, 137, 174, 175, 241, 243
Clark, Dave, 261
Clark, Petula, 95
Clarke, Kenny, 235
Clarke, Stanley, 158, 194, 195, 208
Clash, The, 142, 149
classical music, 86, 96–97, 182
classical rock music, 97
Clayton, Adam, 74
Cliftons, The, 169
Clinton, George, 189, 190
Closer, Charlie, 150
Cobham, Billy, 58, 239, 254, 265, 266
Cochran, Eddie, 64, 65
Cocker, Joe, 170
Colaiuta, Vinnie, 264–269
Cole, Natalie, 159
Coleman, Ornette, 58, 59, 199
Collins, Patti "Sweet Lipps," 187
Collins, Phelps, 188–189
Collins, Phil, 237–243
Collins, William "Bootsy," 187–193, 189p
Coltrane, Alice, 29
Coltrane, John, 27, 28, 29, 30, 58, 59, 62, 175, 195, 199, 211, 230, 235, 238
Colvin, Shawn, 43
composing, 110, 136–137, 182–183, 212
   in jazz music, 231
computers, 33, 34, 117, 148, 193, 203, 227–228
consciousness, 100–101
consumerism, 103
contemporary music, 87, 233, 235
Cooder, Ry, 11, 124
Cooke, Sam, 169
Copeland, Stewart, 254

Serious Players.

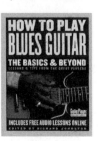

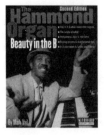

PLAYING FROM THE HEAR

"A love-fest of ideas, attitudes, fears, inspiration, perspiration, insanity, brilliance, dumb luck, and everything else that can drop-kick a creative muse into overdrive….The next time you hear a great song on the radio, you'll have a better understanding of how that montage of sound melody, and passion came to be."

—**MICHAEL MOLENDA**, EDITOR IN CHIEF, *GUITAR PLAYER*; EDITORIAL DIRECTOR, MUSIC PLAYER GROUP

Through the eyes and ears of top music writers, *Playing from the Heart* brings you close some of the best players in popular music. Drawn from the rich archives of *Guitar Player,* *Player, Keyboard,* and *Drums & Drumming,* these classic interviews and photos reveal the s artistry, and personality of world-class musicians in rock, blues, jazz, and more.

Provocative, often controversial, and always insightful, these interviews get to the heart of e player's creative process: their musical ideas and innovations, playing styles and techniq equipment, influences, and more. Plus you'll learn the "backstory" of each interview, direct f the writers and editors.

THE INSIDE TRACK ON 43 TOP ARTISTS, INCLUDING

GUITARISTS	BASSISTS	KEYBOARDISTS	DRUMME
Chuck Berry	Jack Bruce	Chick Corea	Ginger Ba
The Edge	Bootsy Collins	Keith Emerson	Phil Colli
Tom Morello	Phil Lesh	Billy Joel	Max Roa
Bonnie Raitt	Marcus Miller	Trent Reznor	Lars Ulri

Editor **Robert L. Doerschuk**, winner of two ASCAP Deems Taylor Awards for excellence in music journalism, has held editorial positions with *Keyboard* magazine, Sonicnet, www.allmusic.com, and Harmony Central, and is former editor in chief of *Musician* magazine. Author of *88: The Giants of Jazz Piano* and a respected jazz pianist, Doerschuk has sat in and jammed with such major artists as Wynton Marsalis, B.B. King, Prince, Stevie Ray Vaughan, Jerry Garcia, and many others.

AN IMPRINT OF
THE MUSIC PLAYER NETW

Backbeat Books

GuitarPlayer   **BASS PLAYER**   **KEYBOARD**

$19.95   ISBN 0-87930-70

5 1 9 9

9 780879 307042

www.backbeatbooks.c